SPORTS SKILLS

SPORTS SKILLS

Amitabh Suri

CRESCENT
PUBLISHING CORPORATION

[The responsibility for the facts stated, conclusions reached and plagiarism, if any, in this book is entirely that of the Author. And the Publisher bears no responsibility for them, whatsoever.]

Sports Skills

First Published : 2009

ISBN 978-81-8342-106-5

Published by :

CRESCENT PUBLISHING CORPORATION
4831/24, Prahlad Street,
Ansari Road, Darya Ganj,
New Delhi - 110002
Ph. : 23272541, 23257835
Fax : 91- 011- 23257835
e-mail : campusbooks@hotmail.com

Printed at :
Roshan Offset Printers
Delhi

Preface

Defining sports skills is a difficult matter, as it cannot be compartmentalised within certain words. The truth is that skills are very akin to talent, often an endowed trait, refined by practice, and which often wanders into the discussion of nature v/s nurture. However, it cannot be denied that skills are crucial to the average sportsperson, without which nothing can be hoped to be achieved, and the development of which is central to the way an athlete performs. Skill development is a lengthy, disciplined process, which when taken in the context of sports, exacts innate talent controlled training and extreme dedication.

This book in the encyclopaedia of sports concentrates its focus on providing a comprehensive and informative manual on sports skills. Beginning with an elaborate discussion of what entail sporting skills, it makes a conscientious effort to delineates the practices which can be incorporated within the training environment by both trainers and athletes to develop skills which not only provide the basics for playing a sports, but are also crucial for development of technique and style. It evaluates skill development in all its dimensions, making a technological as well as manual assessment of the process, apart from taking into account current trends and practices in the field.

It is hoped that the erudition and insight of the book serves well for the readers.

Amitabh Suri

Contents

Preface v
1. Sports Skill Teaching 1
2. Physical Performance 39
3. Exercise Domain 93
4. Sports Fitness 127
5. Coaching 160
6. Psychological Well-being 176
7. Short-term Performance 188
8. Skills for Health 227
9. Sports Dieting 261
10. Sports Technologies 285
Bibliography 299
Index 301

1

Sports Skill Teaching

Running is the first exercise of an athlete's routine. Athletes begin warming the muscles by running slowly for three to five minutes. This circulates the blood through all the muscles, thus providing them greater flexibility for stretching. The run starts out slowly, and then gradually increases in speed to its completion; however, the athletes never reach even 50 percent of their maximum effort by the end of the run. Remember, the sole objective of this phase of the warm-up is to circulate the blood and warm the muscles in preparation for more strenuous activity.

Stretching is one of the most critical parts of the warm-up and an athlete's performance. A more flexible muscle is a stronger and healthier muscle. A stronger and healthier muscle responds better to exercise and activities and helps prevent athlete injury. Please refer to Stretching information within this section for more in depth information.

Although it is important to warm up all muscles, the most important muscles in football are groin, hamstring, thigh, calf and achilles. Players are encouraged to take their time and ease into stretches. Sharp, sudden movements can cause damage and injury to athletes. It is also important to maintain steady breathing while stretching-breath in through the nose and exhale through the mouth.

Drills are progressions of learning that start at a low ability level, advance to an intermediate level and, finally, reach a high ability level. Encourage each athlete to advance to their highest possible level. Kinesthetic movements are reinforced through repetitions of a small segment of the skill to be performed. Many times, the actions are exaggerated in order to strengthen the muscles that perform the skill. Each coaching session should take the athlete through the entire progression so that he/she is exposed to the total of all of the skills that make up an event.

The cool-down is as important as the warm-up; however, it is often ignored. Abruptly stopping an activity may cause pooling of the blood and slow the removal of waste products in the athlete's body. It may also cause cramps, soreness and other problems for Special Olympics athletes. The cool-down gradually reduces the body temperature and heart rate and speeds the recovery process before the next training session or competitive experience. The cool-down is also a good time for the coach and athlete to talk about the session or competition.

A thorough cool-down also disperses most of the lactic acid that accumulates in the muscles during a hard workout. Not cooling down properly after intense exercise leads to stiff and painfully sore muscles the next day. The warming up and cooling down process is of paramount importance to the well-being of the player's safety, and role of the coach is to make sure that the player has adequately followed his instructions.

STRETCHING

Flexibility is a major element in an athlete's optimal

performance in both training and competeing. Flexibility is achieved through stretching, a critical component in warming up. Stretching follows an easy aerobic jog at the start of a training session or competition.

Begin with an easy stretch to the point of tension, and hold this position for 15-30 seconds until the pull lessens. When the tension eases, slowly move further into the stretch until tension is again felt. Hold this new position for an additional 15 seconds. Each stretch should be repeated four to five times on each side of the body.

It is also important to continue to breathe while stretching. As you lean into the stretch, exhale. Once the stretching point is reached, keep inhaling and exhaling while holding the stretch. Stretching should be a part of everyone's daily life. Regular, consistent, daily stretching has been demonstrated to have the following effects:

- Increases the length of the muscle-tendon unit
- Increases joint range of motion
- Reduces muscle tension
- Develops body awareness
- Promotes increased circulation
- Makes you feel good

Some athletes, like those with Down syndrome, may have low muscle tone that makes them appear more flexible. Be careful not to allow these athletes to stretch beyond a normal, safe range. Several stretches are dangerous to perform for all athletes and should never be part of a safe stretching programme. These unsafe stretches include the following:

- Neck Backward Bending
- Trunk Backward Bending
- Spinal Roll

Calf stretch

Stretching is effective only if the stretch is performed accurately. Athletes need to focus on correct body positioning and alignment: take the calf stretch, for example. Many athletes do not keep the feet forward in the direction that they are moving.

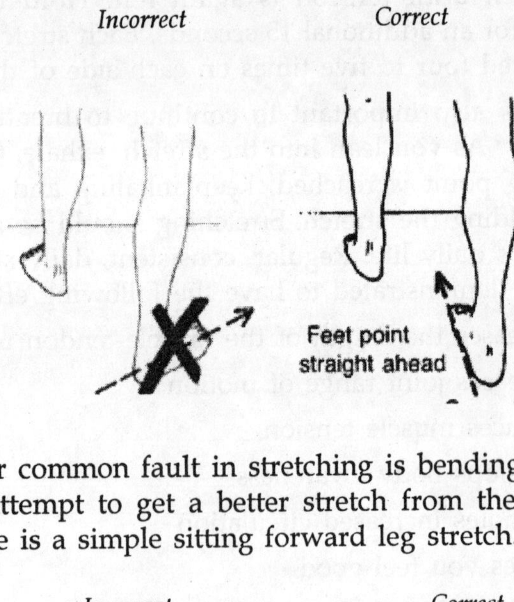

Another common fault in stretching is bending the back in an attempt to get a better stretch from the hips. An example is a simple sitting forward leg stretch.

As you can imagine, there are a host of stretches and variations to them to achieve your goals. However, we will focus on some basic stretches, highlighting major muscle groups. Along the way, we will also point out some common faults, illustrate corrections and identify stretches that are more event specific. In addition, we will also have some reminders to keep breathing while stretching. We will start at the top of the body and work down to the legs and feet.

Coaching tips

- Try to have a low player/coach ratio.
- It is important that coaches and assistants make sure that stretches are being done effectively and are not harmful to the athlete. To do this may require direct, individual physical assistance, particularly with lower-ability players.
- Some stretches require a good sense of balance. If balance is a problem, use stretches that can be done while in a sitting or prone position.
- Coaches should attend to athletes doing the exercises improperly, as well as provide personal attention and reinforcement to those doing them effectively.
- Use stretching as a "teachable moment" with athletes. Explain the importance of each stretching exercise and which muscle group is being stretched. Later, ask the athletes why each stretching exercise is important.

Plyometrics in Football Training

You do not need to schedule specific workouts emphasising plyometric training. For football players, plyometric drills can be incorporated after the warm-up and preceding the main body of training. These drills should emphasise a full and smooth range of motion more than eccentric overload and use the pre-stretch of the muscle to facilitate rapid movement, mechanical efficiency and coordination.

As with other types of training, plyometric exercises are performed in intervals over the course of the season. Volume and intensity will vary over the course of the season. In general, the volume of plyometric exercises for football players will be low to moderate. The intensity also will be low to moderate. Begin each season with a gentle introduction to plyometric training using simple rhythm drills. As your athletes become accustomed to the exercises and their fitness grows, gradually increate volume and intensity.

Once athletes have learned basic rhythm skills, slowly introduce power exercises. Football players will employ a small volume of power drills combined with rhythm exercises. As the competition phase of the season begins, plyometric work stresses rhythm and speed development. Once the peak competition phase starts, reduce plyometric training to one light session per week, though your athlete can continue to include plyometric drills in the warm-up. Stop any strenuous plyometric training 7-10 days before playoffs begin.

Rhythm Drills

Rhythm drills are a good method to help players develop strength through plyometrics. These drills usually follow stretching and flexibility exercises, and are done in conjunction with strength exercises, such as sit-ups and lunges. In addition, rhythm drills help players enhance both overall fitness and specific muscle development.

Types of rhythm drills

– Skipping - Easy
– Skipping - High
– Skipping Kicks
– Butt Kicks
– High Knees

Butt kicks

Butt kicks are a universal drill throughout sport. They are a great drill used in football training to help athletes develop those fast twitch muscles needed for the constant starting, stopping, pivoting and turning required in football. While doing butt kicks, the back is straight with a slight forward body lean.

The body lean is natural as the player would assume while running. Remember, arms are legs higher up. Encourage your athletes to keep pumping and driving them throughout the drill. Emphasise quickness in bringing the heels to the buttocks, not in moving up the football field. You can even have your athletes practice the drill while stationary and add movement once they have mastered it to the best of their ability.

Football requires running for extended periods of time; therefore, your players must be able to produce energy aerobically. Aerobic fitness is important for three primary reasons. Although football players, need to be aerobically fit, they do not need to be distance runners. Be balanced in your approach to fitness. Set standards, yet do not place fitness ahead of the ultimate goal of developing good football players and a good football team. A fit, skilled team is much more powerful than a fit, unskilled team. Following are benefits of aerobic fitness.

- Creates good cardiovascular capacity and strengthens muscles and tendons.
- Allows players to run at a steady pace without incurring oxygen debt, getting really tired and unable to recover.
- Allows your players to recover quickly from short sprints, making them more effective in the game.

Aerobic fitness is best developed during preseason training. However, if your schedule cannot be extended to include fitness in the preseason, you can integrate fitness exercises and activities into your weekly training sessions. This can be achieved through steady pace runs, ball skill drills or fitness circuits. For more information on general fitness, please refer to the Athlete Nutrition, Safety and Fitness section in the general coaching section.

Steady Pace Runs

These runs are slow, continuous long-distance running. These runs can last for 20-30 minutes. You can add variety to these runs by having your players run with the ball through cones, around benches or defenders.

Anaerobic Fitness

Football demands both aerobic and anaerobic capacity. During games, football players must be able to sprint hard, recover quickly and then sprint hard again. Anaerobic training starts once your athletes have developed basic aerobic fitness, because recovery capacity is developed by increasing aerobic fitness. In football, the demand for anaerobic speed is relatively short. The important point here is the ability of the player to recover quickly from multiple speed bursts.

Fartlek Runs

Fartleks, also known as speed play, is another effective tool for football training because it can closely resemble the type of running during the course of a game - varied pace. Fartleks are easy to integrate in a workout. Players can jog one side of the field, sprint the other side. You can increase intensity and variety by jogging two sides and running one side or running two sides and jogging one side, etc. You can mix the jog-sprint sides according to the fitness and ability level of your players.

Shuttle Runs

Shuttle runs are a staple in football training. Essentially, shuttle runs are repetition or interval runs that involve numerous changes of direction. You can change the following sample shuttle run to meet the needs of your players. Just remember to keep the basics in mind when developing the run - athlete ability and fitness level.

1. Runs 5 yards and back
2. Runs 10 yards and back
3. Runs 15 yards and back
4. Runs 20 yards and back
5. Runs 25 yards and back
6. Repeat 3-4 times

Strength Training

Strength training is important for football players. The basic elements of speed, mobility and endurance are all functions of muscular strength. According to the President's Council on Physical Fitness and Sports, improvements in absolute muscular endurance, motor ability and athletic abilities are directly associated with an individual's muscular strength.

Strength training for football usually has two purposes.

1. Improving overall strength
2. Developing muscle balance and preventing athlete injury.

Football running requires significant anaerobic energy which is directly related to muscle strength. Therefore, a muscle with greater strength can respond better to race challenges without incurring extreme fatigue and requiring a longer recovery period. Basically, strength training improves an athlete's ability to run fast and produce anaerobic energy. Football players need to be able to run fast, sometimes very fast.

The following basic strength training routine can be accomplished outside of the weight room and easily incorporated into an athlete's home training programme.

Sample Strength Training Routine

1. Light running to warm up
2. Push-ups
3. Lunges
4. Sit-ups - Crunches
5. Medicine-Ball Throws (please refer to Nutrition, Safety and Fitness section for medicine-ball throw exercises)
   - Overhead Toss
   - Forward Toss
   - Side Toss
   - Straight Arm Forward Toss to Partner

CONTROL-RECEIVING

The aim of the game is simple: score goals. To score goals, your players need to develop both good shooting technique and a positive attitude toward taking shots whenever they have a good opportunity. Players enable themselves and develop good shooting technique and positive attitude by developing good control-receiving skills.

The beginner player usually reacts to a ball by kicking it rather than trying to control it. If the player does attempt to control the ball, it tends to bounce off the foot or the leg and is usually recovered by another player. The intermediate player has the ability to get behind the flight of most balls that come within playing distance. The player successfully brings a rolling ball under control using the inside of the foot and makes a good attempt at controlling air balls using the chest. While control is good, the player will often lose composure and the ball when pressured by opponents.

Teaching Control-receiving

In football, the first touch is the most important. The easiest way to receive a ball is with the inside of the foot. The player stands in a relaxed position with their eyes focused on the ball and adjusts their position to remain in the flight of the ball. The nonkicking foot is slightly in front of the other foot. The kicking foot meets the ball and is then immediately withdrawn on the moment of impact. This will generally push the ball away from the player's body.

1. Use the inside of the foot to bring a ground ball under control. All the body weight should be on the supporting leg with the receiving foot raised slightly off the ground.
2. Relax and cushion the ball rather than offer resistance against the ball. The aim is to absorb any pace by meeting the ball with a cushioned touch. The ball is given as large an area to land. The chest, head, thigh or foot is withdrawn as contact is made.

Teaching Cushioning the Ball

1. Player must stand lightly as the ball approaches.
2. Position him/herself in the ball's line of travel.
3. Assess their options, then decide which part of the body they want to control the ball with.
4. Look directly at the ball.
5. Position their nonkicking foot ahead of the ball.

6. Use arms for balance.
7. Bring the striking foot back at the moment of impact.

Receiving a pass using inside of foot

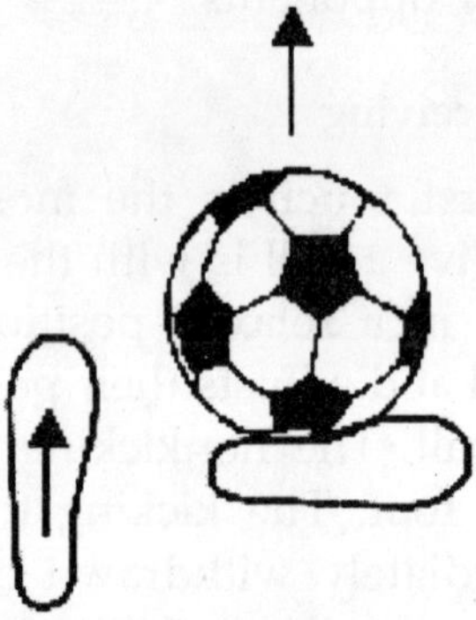

1. Receive the ball even with the toes of the plant foot or a little in front.
2. Stiffen or relax the receiving foot so the ball stops about one step away, enabling the athlete to quickly take one step and strike it. It is this step that gives power to the pass.
3. Be sure the receiving foot is 4-5 inches off the ground. If the receiving foot is too low, the ball will pop up and contact the ball on the back part of foot - under the anklebone, not near the toes. Pull the toes up so the foot is parallel with the ground, not pointing downward. If a player cannot remember to raise their foot, have them practice by raising their foot higher than the ball and then bring the foot down in front of the ball to stop it. This will help them to remember.
4. If you want the ball to go to the left or right, instead of straight in front, the athlete must angle their foot

and contact the ball more in front or behind, depending on whether they want the ball to go left or right.

There are three important points for good ball control.

1. The first touch protects the ball from challenging players and does not give them a chance to regain possession.
2. Play the ball into available space to allow for the next touch.
3. Allow the game movement to start or continue by gaining or keeping momentum.

A poor first touch will risk taking the momentum out of play and increase the possibility of losing possession. Some players make the mistake of killing the ball dead and not concentrating on getting it out of their feet. The first touch is meant to ensure that a time wasting second touch is not needed to get the ball out and ready for the next action. The general technique for controlling the ball requires several simple skills which can be acquired through correct training practices.

The first key element in ball control is to place the controlling surface into the ball's line of flight. The body weight is well distributed, so it is possible to move forward, backward or sideways. Keep the head steady and watch the ball carefully to judge its flight and speed. It is difficult to keep one's eyes permanently on the ball. Better players are able to take a quick glance to know what is happening around them before contact is made.

The second step is making an early judgment in choosing the right technique and body surface to control.

– Wedge control involves a more rigid surface where the player attempts to force the ball downwards or into space so they can move onto it.

– A cushioned control involves taking the sting out of the ball. This involves pulling the surface back, just when the ball makes contact. The body becomes elastic so that the ball simply drops at the players feet. This particular technique is very useful when closely marked; for example, a forward receiving the ball on the chest with his back to goal.

Control also requires good mental abilities, such as confidence and total concentration. A composed player is one who is calm, relaxed and unhurried in his movements. Confidence plays a big part in this as athletes who know what they can do and are confident in their ability are more likely to show great technique and succeed. Those who do not have confidence will be indecisive and their technique hurried.

When training, players can exaggerate the movements to get the feel of the right technique. Younger players can learn from the coach, who can demonstrate the technique, break it down and practice the individual elements and, eventually, practice the whole technique. Once the basic techniques have been mastered, the coach moves on to more advanced techniques and skills. These techniques and skills concentrate on improving control in pressure situations (for example, defenders coming from the side, front, back), control while moving at pace, control which involves an immediate layoff and controlling the ball for a teammate. The ball is received constantly from all angles, speeds, heights and surfaces.

Some common problems when controlling the ball are described below, along with a training method than can be used to improve technique.

Problem No. 1 - Ball path has been misread and the player has missed the pass

Repeated practice using passes from different distances with varying intensity. The coach must encourage player to keep their eyes on the ball at all times and get their body in line.

Problem No. 2 - Player is indecisive when choosing controlling body surface

Player shouts the type of body surface they will use. The server provides the pass and vice versa until the player gets the right feeling for the choice of technique.

Problem No. 3 - The player does not get the ball out of their feet and needs a second touch.

Encourage the player to relax and exaggerate the movement. Repeated practice using passes from different distances with varying intensity.

Problem No. 4 - The ball bounces off the player and control is lost.

Encourage the player to exaggerate the movement, especially the relaxation phase, first without the ball and then using gentle service, eventually building up service difficulty. Try using smaller or lighter balls. The excellent ball control is an essential part of successful football. Like all other techniques, practice makes perfect, and it is hoped that the above not only encourages coaching and learning but also provides information on how to analyse and improve ball control technique.

Control-Receiving Drills

Lower ability - control and shoot

Purpose of the drill

- Quick control
- Teach players to think game-like situations.
- Increase individual skill and confidence.

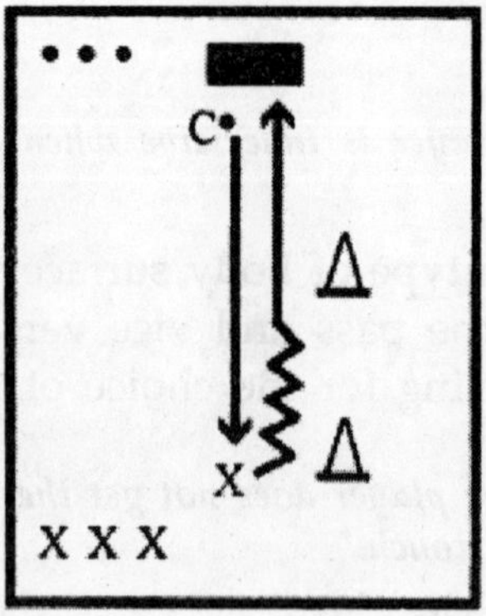

Points of emphasis: 1.First-touch control 2. Think quickly and react. When to use: Teaching positional play and also teaching players to react quickly in game-like situations.

Steps

1. One coach per four players.
2. Set up a 4-yard-by-2-yard goal.
3. Place a starting cone 12 yards out and a shooting cone 6-8 yards out.
4. Coach rolls the ball out slowly to player who must control it then dribble and shoot within three seconds. Score one point per successful control/shot.
5. Same player repeats three times then goes to back of line.
6. With more mobile players, roll the ball slightly to one side, and make the player move to get behind the ball, control it and shoot.

Intermediate Ability - Control and Shoot (with chasers)

– Develop quick thinking in players.
– Develop good player reaction under pressure.

Steps

1. Divide players into three teams: shooting team, defending team and goalkeeping team.
2. Set up a 4-yard-by-2-yard goal, shooting cone at 15 yards and a defender's cone at 20 yards.
3. Coach stands to the side of the goal and rolls out a ball to the shooter.
4. Shooter controls the ball, then dribbles and shoots.
5. As the shooter receives the ball, the defender is released and tries to chase and tackle the shooter.
6. Shooter can shoot at any time. Goalkeepers must remain within 1 yard of the goal line.
7. Players return to their group after the shot.
8. Rotate groups after five minutes.

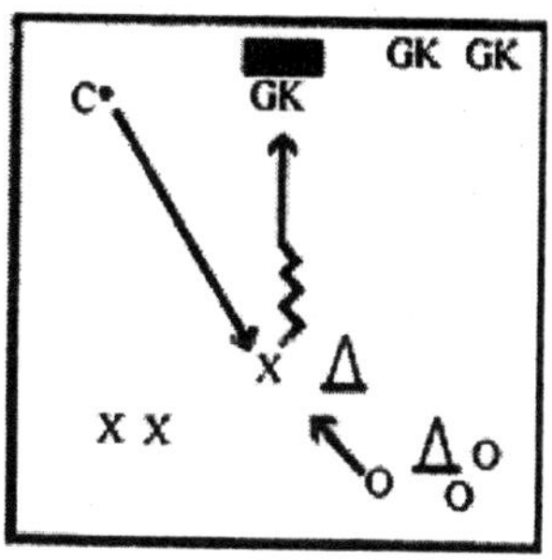

Points of emphasis: Allow players to express themselves. When to use: Good when preparing players for games and increases the chances of them thinking correctly when under pressure.

Coaches' tips for control-receiving

1. Help lower ability players move into position and get behind the flight of the ball. Use gentle physical prompting when necessary.

2. Many players are too excited and caught up in the game to relax when the ball arrives.
3. Coaching a player to slow down, relax and concentrate is as important as coaching the correct receiving technique.
4. Have players receive the ball with different parts of their body - thigh, knee and chest.
5. Players can work with a partner and toss the ball to each other. Let the ball hit the different parts of their body and drop to their feet.
6. Emphasise the importance of the first touch.

Tips for competition

1. Give positive reinforcement to players that control the ball.
2. Play a make-shift game, allowing players only two touches.
3. Begin by giving players room to control the ball and then increase pressure from opponents.

Dribbling

Dribbling is the skill of running with the ball at your feet. The player is speeding forward through open space, maneuvering out of tight situations and feinting to beat opponents. It is perhaps the most expressive and exciting part of the game.

The beginner player typically kicks the ball some yards away and runs after it, rather than keeping it close and under control. Dribbling under control tends to be difficult because the player dribbles with the toe. These players can change direction slowly but will often lose the ball when pressured by an opponent.

The intermediate player can move the ball forward with the toe pointed down, keeping the ball close and under control. The player can change direction, using the inside or outside of the foot to beat opponents, but may have difficulty executing fakes to beat opponents.

Teaching Dribbling

When dribbling, the most important aspects are balance and coordination. To be able to go around a player, the body must be flexible enough to change direction by shifting weight quickly, while still maintaining balance and the ability to think quickly. When asking a player to jog round the field to warm up, it is better to do this with a ball at his/her feet to help increase confidence in ball control when running.

A lot of skill in dribbling develops from players' confidence, therefore it is important to praise and motivate at training. Dribbling essentials are close control, changing direction or pace, and disguise. Players are not robots; always encourage them to express themselves.

1. To help develop touch and control of the ball, the player dribbles forward using the top of the foot along the outside of the laces.
2. Point the toe down toward the ground.
3. Keep the ball close, within one yard from the body.

Dribbling Drills

Lower ability - Dribble in the square

Purpose of the Drill

– Player awareness.
– Confidence in holding ball in tight situations.

Steps

1. Designate a 15-yard-by-15-yard square.
2. Every player has a football.
3. Players dribble around inside of the square, avoiding collisions with other players.
4. Encourage the use of both feet.
5. Encourage changing direction while looking up.
6. Introduce different dribbling techniques.
7. Coach can play as a chaser. Players must try to avoid being kicked out of the square.
8. Play for 30 seconds.
9. Award one point for keeping the ball safe.

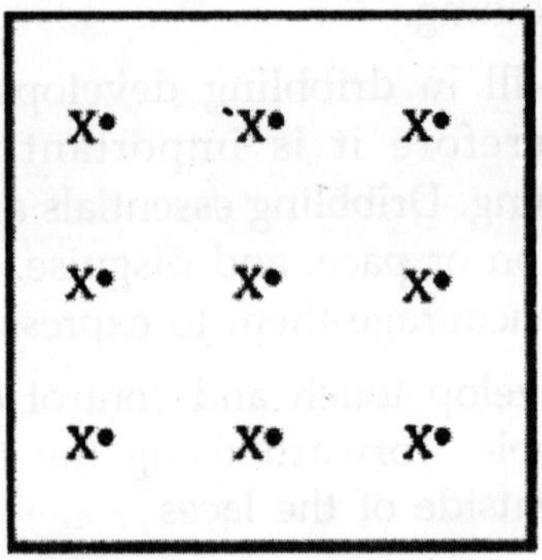

Points of Emphasis: Be aware of surroundings
When to Use: As a fun exercise while still teaching techniques.

Cone drills

– Encourage players to keep close control without the pressure of an opponent.

Steps

1. Set up seven cones in a straight line.
2. Place a gate, using cones at either side.

3. Demonstrate first without ball, then with ball.
4. Have players weave through cones slowly without the ball, then with the ball.
5. Correct players who lose control or weave too wide.
6. Encourage players to use both feet.

Purpose of the drill

– Player under pressure in confined space.
– Player must learn to think quickly.

Steps

1. Play on a minifield of 20 yards by 15 yards with 4-yard-wide goals.
2. Form two teams of three players. One is a goalkeeper.

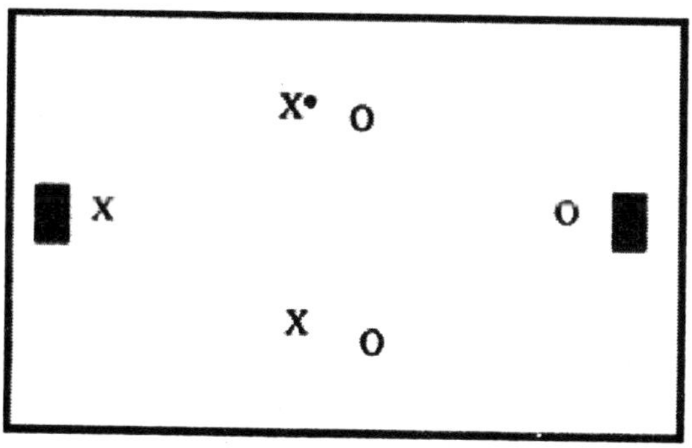

Points of emphasis: Learn the ability to think and react quickly under pressure. When to Use: Players who are beginning to express themselves on the field.

3. Play a regular game, except that when a player gets possession of the ball, the player must immediately dribble against an opponent and try to get past the player.

4. A player cannot pass the ball until this is done.
5. Award one point for successfully dribbling past an opponent and three points for each goal scored.

Coaches' tips for dribbling

1. For lower energy players who will not dribble very much, it is important for the coach or an assistant to work individually with them, and use gentle physical prompting (e.g., hand on the middle of the back) to create some forward motion.
2. For higher energy players who dribble out of control and kick the ball 10 yards or more ahead, start by walking with the player and concentrate on dribbling under control before speeding up.
3. For players that have mastered dribbling, have them dribble with their head up, viewing the field of play.
4. Have players dribble, using imaginary players.
5. Start by instructing the player on how you want them to go around the opponent, then allow them to express themselves.
6. Encourage the use of individual tricks, as in dummies and stopovers, turns and dragging the ball back. This will keep the player interested and also increase their confidence.

Tips for competition

1. Encourage players to dribble and try to make a move to beat an opponent. The only way to improve your moves is to use them.
2. Play game-like situations and give the player the option to dribble or pass.
3. Encourage players to dribble to create space.

4. Players need to be aware of teammates' positions before dribbling.

Shooting

The aim of the game is simple: score goals. To score goals, your players need to develop both good shooting technique and a positive attitude toward taking shots whenever they have a good opportunity. If you do not shoot, you will not score.

The beginner player is able to kick in the general direction of the goal, but without any consistency or power. They usually kick the ball with the toe or, awkwardly, with the inside of the foot. The player may slow down or stop before attempting to shoot and finds it very difficult to shoot a ball that is rolling across the body.

The intermediate player has a positive attitude toward taking shots and is able to shoot with a reasonable degree of accuracy. This player is able to shoot with the top of the foot (instep) to generate power. The player will occasionally connect successfully with a rolling ball but has learned to increase success by controlling the ball before shooting. The player is still likely to lose composure and effectiveness under pressure and has not mastered the advanced skill of volleying the ball out of the air.

Teaching Shooting

1. When shooting, approach the ball slightly from the side, not straight on. This allows the foot to make a more natural and effective strike on the ball.
2. Place the nonkicking foot at the side of the ball.
3. Swing the kicking foot backward with a bent knee.
4. Keep your eye on the ball and head still.

5. Swing the kicking foot forward with knee pointing down.
6. Kicking foot follows the ball as the knee straightens.

Shooting Drills

Lower ability shooting

– Shoot the ball as far as possible, using the correct technique.

Steps

1. Set up cones at 1-, 2-, 3- and 4-meter intervals. Cone distance can vary, depending on athlete ability level.
2. Line up and shoot the ball as far as possible.
3. Record distance.

Lower ability shooting accuracy

– Accurately shoot through two cones, using correct shooting techniques.

Steps

1. Set up two cones 2 meters apart at a distance of 5 meters.
2. Player shoots through cones (goals).
3. Five shots per player.
4. Record goals accurately scored, using correct technique.

Lower Ability - Shoot Out!

– Allows players to shoot in game-like situations.
– Allows players to position themselves before shooting.

Steps

1. Use a regular goal or maker cones.
2. Place a starting cone 15-20 meters from the goal.
3. Three players on the shooting team; three players on the goalkeeping team.
4. Shooter has three seconds to dribble and shoot.
5. Coach counts down, 3-2-1-shoot.
6. Goalkeepers rotate after each shot.
7. Five shots each, then change teams.

Intermediate Ability

- Players gain confidence in going past a defender before shooting.
- Encourage game-like situations that players can relate to during a game.

Steps

1. Designate a 20-meter-by-20-meter square with goals at opposite ends.
2. Form two teams of three players.

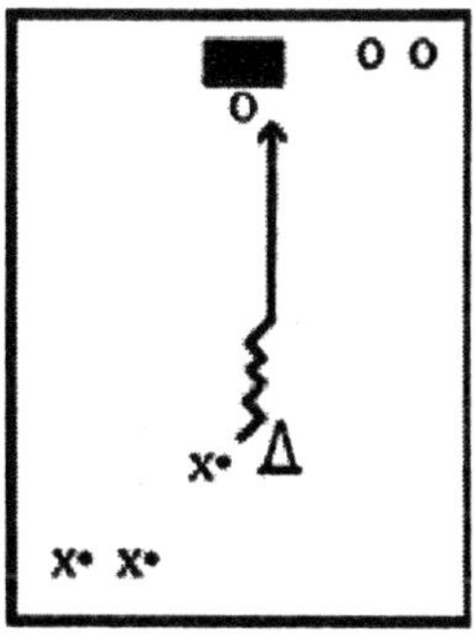

Points of Emphasis: When the player gets past the defender, they must position themselves correctly before shooting. When to Use: At any training session to perfect forward play or defense.

3. Number equally matched players, 1-2-3.
4. Play No. 1 from each team on the field with No. 2 in goal and No. 3 behind the goal as a chaser.
5. Play one vs. one for one minute.
6. Coach rolls in spare balls when needed.
7. One point for each shot on target and three points per goal.
8. Rotate players.
9. Keep the team score.

Coaches' Tips for Shooting

1. As a general rule, teach players to control the ball before trying to shoot. Shooting a rolling ball is a difficult skill, and only the most advanced Special Olympics players will accomplish it successfully.
2. Encourage players to shoot toward the corners of the goal, not to the middle of the goal.

TACKLING

Tackling refers to the skill of using your feet to take the ball away from an opponent. A truly successful team must be built on sound defensive abilities. As such, the ability to track, close down and tackle an opponent is a key to success for any team.

Whatever the position or role of a player on the pitch, the ability to tackle and win possession of the ball is vital. Defending is one of the least glamorous jobs on the pitch. However, any football purist will appreciate a perfectly timed tackle as much as any other game technique.

As with all other football techniques, mental aspects play an important role in successful tackling. A player must be 100 percent committed and determined to win the ball, while always keeping a cool head. A player should never deliberately try to hurt an opponent. Halfhearted challenges will not only lead to failure to win possession but also increase the risk of injury. Similarly, high levels of concentration and composure are needed as well as strength for good tackling. Good technique can help compensate for players who are weaker in other areas. A player must be able to anticipate the attacker's actions and recognise the right moment to tackle. A player must also know which tackling technique to choose, depending on the position and movement of the attacker. This will be developed through practice and game situations.

The beginner player will usually chase the ball or an approaching opponent and make some kind of effort to kick the ball away. The player is either tentative and may fear making tackles or is somewhat out of control and makes contact with just about everything, except the ball.

The intermediate player can successfully focus, track and close down on opponents dribbling the ball. The player has the coordination to make good, strong contact on the ball, using the inside of the foot. However, this player will often fall for fakes from the attacking player.

Types of Tackles

1. Front Block Tackle
2. Side Block Tackle
3. Ground Block Tackle
4. Sliding Tackle

To win ball possession, all players, including forwards, need to be able to correctly execute these different tackling techniques. Players who do not tackle correctly will give away free kicks, increase their chances of getting hurt and generally improve their opponents attacking chances.

When a defender meets an attacker head-on and with his body square to the ball, a player makes forceful contact with the inside of his boot, often at the same time as his opponent. The defender needs a sound base where his weight is transferred over and through the ball. The supporting foot must be next to the ball. The upper body must lean into the tackle, and the whole body works through the action. Steady and even pressure is applied, using the tensed-up leg muscles.

Coaching tips

- Keep eye on ball.
- Upper body weight forward.
- Coordinate body movement.
- Apply maximum force, aiming to block the ball, rather than kick it.

Use this tackle when an attacker has partially gone past a defender or when the defender tries to close down an attempted angled pass. This technique requires good balance, due to the block being made with an outstretched leg. The outstretched leg needs to be tensed to make strong contact with the ball. A stable base is required to quickly carry out the action. Finally, the overall timing is very important.

Coaching tips

- Keep eye on ball.
- Teach athletes to not sell themselves as the attacker. Feint to shoot or pass.
- Try to touch shoulder to shoulder before tackling, as this can help reduce the risk of tackling too far away and letting the ball pass by the players leg.

Ground Block Tackle

If the attacker is in space and the block or side tackle cannot be used, the ground tackle is a useful technique. The defender "throws" him/herself into the ball to stop the attacker from going past. However, the defender stays on their feet as long as possible. The player accelerates into the action by dropping their hips, allowing the body to go quickly to the ground. Their contact leg is slightly flexed and as tense as possible and body weight is as far forward as possible to provide an overall firm contact. The heel of the contact leg can be anchored or pressed on the pitch to increase rigidity.

Coaching tips

- Keep eye on ball.
- Be patient.
- Use this tackle only as a last resort once the action is executed, and the defender is momentarily out of the game.
- Aim to execute the tackle and get back on your feet as quickly as possible.

Sliding Tackle

This is probably the most exciting tackle. The defender uses this particular technique as a last resort to prevent the attacker from getting past him. To execute this action, the defender slides on the ground into the ball and plays it, using his outside leg. This action is particularly useful if the ball is next to the touchline where it can be played out into touch. The slide tackle can also be used as a means of winning the ball and turning defense into attack. The defender slides in a low sideways position and brings the tackling leg backward and swings it at the ball. The player attempts to trap the ball to gain possession, however, if the situation is dangerous, they player may want to try and play the ball directly into touch.

Coaching Tips

- To develop and improve tackling technique, the coach will have to design simple practices which involve repeated one-on-one situations where a defender is encouraged to utilise a wide range of tackling techniques as mentioned above.
- The coach must also be prepared to personally demonstrate tackling technique where necessary.

Tackling Drills

Lower Ability—Tackle the Coach

- Encourage players to commit themselves to the tackle.

Steps

1. Designate a 15-yard-by-15-yard square.
2. Each coach has a soccer ball.
3. Players try to pursue and tackle coaches. Coaches can call out the name of specific players, who then try to tackle.
4. One point can be given for simply making any kind of foot contact with the coach's ball, or, for a higher ability group, the ball must be cleared out of the square to score a point.

Coaching Tips

- Do not tackle unless you are sure you will win the ball.
- This can be used as a fun exercise.

– Creates interest because players always like to beat the coach.

Intermediate Ability

Purpose of the drill

– Assists timing of tackles.
– Increases friendly competition between players.

Steps

1. Designate a 10-yard-by-15-yard square.
2. Form groups of three; each group with one ball. One group plays, while other groups rest.
3. Two players stand at one end with the ball. The third player stands at the other end.
4. Player No. 1 dribbles and tries to get past No. 2 and over the end line. Player No. 2 must try to tackle and either regain possession of the ball or force it out of the square. If No. 2 successfully wins the ball, he/she dribbles against player No. 3. If No. 2 is beaten to the end line by dribbler No. 1, No. 1 turns around and dribbles against player No. 3.
5. Award one point per successful tackle.

Coaches' tips for tackling

1. Beginner players often rush in too fast and get wrong-footed by a simple move by the opponent. As these players run to an opponent, cue them to "slow down" and "concentrate on the ball."
2. Higher ability players can learn to slide tackle. These tackles are always made from the side of the dribbler with all the contact being on the ball. Slide tackles are very useful if a player has been beaten and is pursuing an opponent. This technique, however, can

be dangerous if not done correctly. Use an experienced player to teach this to a higher ability player.

3. Organise players in pairs with a ball. Have them kick the ball at the same time. This can result in a "boom" from the ball, getting them used to 50/50 balls and preparing them for tackling.
4. Encourage players to run through tackles. This is done by keeping the legs moving when in close contact or in a 50/50 ball situation.
5. Encourage players to jockey until the time is right to tackle.

Tips for competition

1. Do not play your defenders too far back. Have them play close to the opposing players with no more than a 5-yard cushion.
2. Only tackle when you think you will win the ball.
3. Only commit to the tackle when you are in the right position.

Goalkeeping

Goalkeeping is the skill of protecting your goal from the shots of opponents. It is perhaps the most important position on the field; however, it is often the position most neglected by coaches. A sound, confident goalkeeper does more than just stop shots. The goalkeeper is the source of confidence for the entire team. Goalkeeping is not a position for everyone and takes good concentration and confidence. Make sure that your goalkeeper wants to play in goal and has the strength of character to be successful. Goalkeeping entails some additional safety hazards. It is important that coaches select players who can learn to play this position safely.

Except in small-sided play, each team must have a designated goalkeeper. The goalkeeper is the only player on the field who can legally use their hands, and then only inside the penalty box. Once the goalkeeper picks up the ball they have six seconds to punt it or release it. The goalkeeper is allowed to pick up the ball, run with it and then punt it, throw it or drop it and dribble or kick it. However, they cannot touch it with their hands outside the penalty box. Once the goalkeeper drops the ball, they cannot touch it again with their hands until an opponent has touched it.

The goalkeeper has special protections inside the penalty box. The ball may not be kicked if the goalkeeper is touching it with their hand or arm. The referee will call a foul if the goalkeeper is endangered. The goalkeeper must wear a shirt or jersey that is recognisably different from all other players. Goalkeepers often wear special jerseys with padded elbows. In hot weather, do not put a goalkeeper jersey on a player. They can get overheated and become sick. Instead, have them wear a different colored shirt (one shirt only) or a mesh training vest over their shirt.

If the goalkeeper has a strong leg, let them take goal kicks. Encourage the player to play aggressively: push up on the attack and come out to the edge of the penalty box or beyond to play like a second sweeper. If the goalkeeper picks up the ball and no opponents are close, encourage him to drop the ball, dribble it out and kick it. Once the goalkeeper drops the ball or is out of the penalty box, the goalkeeper can play like a field player. However, the goalkeeper cannot touch the ball with his hands. Encourage the goalkeeper to play aggressively and take chances; everyone will have much more fun if you do, and more athletes will want to play goal.

Goalkeepers tend to get blamed for goals when, most of the time, it is not their fault. If the other defenders are doing a great job, there will not be any shots on goal. Tell your goalkeeper before the game that the other team is expected to score goals, and that it is not the goalkeeper's fault if they score. Do not let anyone else, players or parents, blame the goalkeeper. In fact, after the game, have the rest of the team thank the goalkeeper, even if they did make mistakes.

Encourage everyone who wants to try playing goalkeeper. You will be surprised who is good, and you really cannot predict until they actually play the position. At the very least, it will give all the players respect for how tough the position is, and they will be less likely to blame the goalkeeper when goals are scored. However, do not make an athlete play goalkeeper if they do not want to play that position.

A goalkeeper needs different skills from other players. The goalkeeper needs speed off the mark, the courage to dive on the ball and the ability to throw and catch accurately. The beginner goalkeeper is effective only if the ball is played directly at them. This player often reacts to ground balls by kicking them away rather than using their hands. The player has limited ability to time an effective dive for shots going into the corners of the goal. Throwing the ball out to teammates may be inaccurate.

The intermediate goalkeeper has a good awareness of the goal and of basic goalkeeping techniques and responsibilities. The player shows good lateral motion to get in a good position to take a shot, and will usually attempt to get their hands to the ball. The player attempts to dive for ground shots, although these dives may be slow. This level of goalkeeper will generally not be able to drive for shots in the air or attack crosses in the air.

The intermediate goalkeeper is typically able to distribute the ball accurately to teammates.

Teaching Handling Balls

1. Goalkeeping consists of occasional flurries of action and a lot of standing and waiting. Maintaining concentration when the ball is away from the goal is critical.
2. As the ball approaches, the goalkeeper is in the ready position with their hands up, about waist height.

If the ball is rolling along the ground, the goalkeeper must get behind the line of the ball and either scoop the ball up with the legs straight and together or go down on one knee and scoop the ball up. For a ball coming in the air, a goalkeeper secures the ball with both hands. The two hands need to work together as one unit.

It is important to learn how to dive safely, without jarring the body. By lowering the center of gravity before diving, the impact on the ground will be less and the speed to the ball increased.

Teaching Distributing the Ball

1. When throwing the ball out (required in 5-a-side), goalkeepers need to look wide to the wings (near the sidelines), not up the middle. Other players should get wide quickly and be open to receive the throw.
2. The throw can be underhand (like bowling), overhand (one-handed, like baseball), or a two-handed throw-in style. Goalkeepers need to try to distribute the ball quickly before the opponents have a chance to regroup.
3. In 11-a-side, a goalkeeper can punt the ball after gaining possession. This is usually the most effective

way for a Special Olympics goalkeeper to distribute the ball.

Goalkeeping Drills

Lower ability

- Teach players correct techniques.
- Build confidence.

Steps

1. Set up a triangle using large cones or flags, 4 yards per side.
2. Position a goalkeeper on each side of the triangle. Coach stands in the middle with several balls.
3. Go around the group working on basic goalkeeping fundamentals.
4. Goalkeepers throw ball back to the coach.
5. Do the same, but throw the ball randomly to keep goalkeepers thinking and mentally alert.

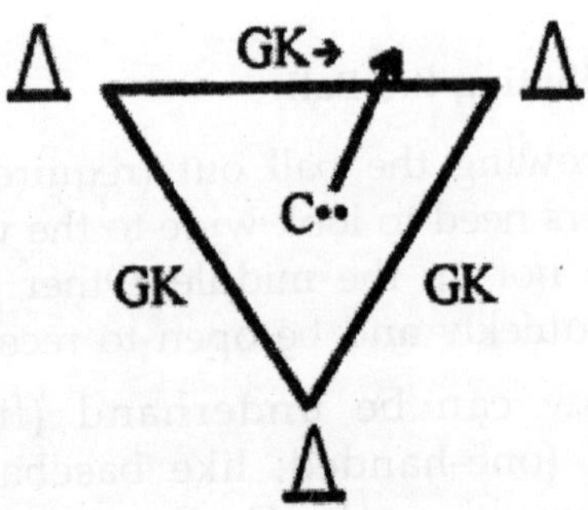

Coaching tips

- Ensure correct techniques are used.

– Use with lower level players or at the beginning of training so that players master the correct basics.

Intermediate Ability - Goalie in the Middle

– Increase player's ability to think quickly.

– Increase player's agility when making saves.

Steps

1. Mark out a central goal, 4 yards by 2 yards by 2 yards (or full-size goal for 11-a-side players), with flags or cones.
2. Goalkeeper stands in the middle.
3. Goalkeeper receives different kinds of shots (easy at first, then build up to hard shots).
4. Goalkeeper takes a ball from one side, then quickly turns around and takes a shot from the other side.
5. Count number of saves made before a goal is scored.

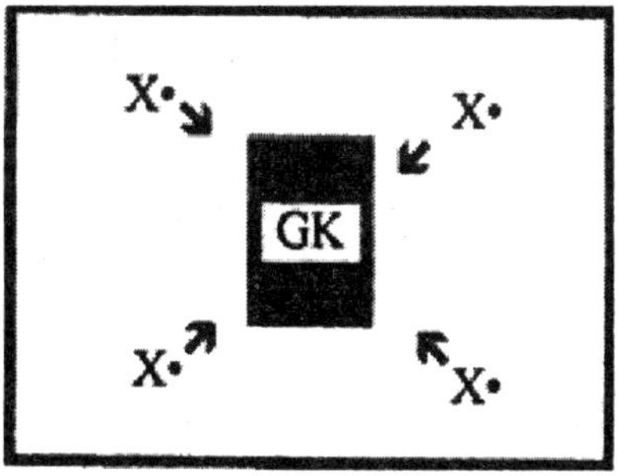

Coaching tips

– Keep goalkeeper interested.

– Vary shots.

– Use one-on-one coaching while the rest of the team is learning specific skills.

Coaches' tips for goalkeeping

1. A lower ability goalkeeper should be taught to stay close to the goal at all times and not wander out. Remind the goalkeeper to glance over their shoulder when the ball is away from the goal and to maintain position in the center of the goal. As a guideline, a goalkeeper should not go out to either side further than the goal post.
2. Teach all of the players not to blame a goalkeeper when the other team scores. Have a defender get the ball out of the net as quickly as possible to restart the game.
3. Teach other players to be supportive. If you have a higher ability player who wants to learn to be a goalkeeper, it would be helpful to find a goalkeeper coach.
4. The goalkeeper needs to be able to communicate to their field players. This is very important when the goalkeeper is going for the ball at the same time as the defender. The goalkeeper is responsible for calling the other players off of the ball.
5. Always kick to a player on the wing, and not up the middle.
6. Be aware of positions of opposing players.
7. When throwing the ball, always ensure that the throw is hard enough.

Tips for competition

1. Keep focused on the play in front of you when the ball is not at your end of the field of play.
2. Keep your eyes on the ball, not the players.
3. Have a backup goalkeeper in case of injury or too many goals being scored.
4. Always be aware of your position on your line.

2

Physical Performance

The implementations of the mental skills produce athletic performance enhancements, even in elite athletes. Any extra effort or physiological cost does not accompany improvements. It is proposed that the teaching of these and similar skills must become part of an athlete's experience if performance standards are to be improved further. Psychology is the study of behavior, it being both covert and overt.

It is relatively easy to investigate overt behaviors accurately and reliably and to employ independent verification of phenomena, but when it comes to covert behaviors, such as thoughts and emotional interpretations, the ability to verify phenomena independently is usually thwarted. While it remains possible to manipulate external events and observe behavioral outcomes, functional relationships between environmental psychological factors and performances can be described. It is not scientifically appropriate to attribute outcomes to intermediary events such as thoughts and perceptions when they have not been directly observed. A position on that restriction has been described elsewhere.

Serious Competitive Settings

A serious competitive setting is where the consequences

of performance are most important and strongest for an athlete. Factors that affect an athlete's perception of this setting have been described in the *Sport Pressure Checklist*. Variations in these factors produce performance inconsistencies as well as suggest patterns that predispose excellent performances. In challenging and serious performance situations, it has been found that performance-oriented "strategies" (plans) of specific detail have notable effects on performance consistency and reliability. The need for specific preparations is now commonly recognized in several fields (e.g., business, performing arts) and its founding research so convincing that it is now rarely investigated. However, it is still being neglected in the majority of sporting situations by coaches and sport psychologists. Further, when strategies are formulated primarily by athletes they generally produce the following benefits:

1. reduction in uncertainty and interpretive distractions and the stress of negative situations,
2. enhanced performance consistency,
3. improved coping capacity for problems, and
4. minimized performance deteriorations. Research reports of the value of performance strategies in sports have been published.

1. Performance Segmenting

If an event is of long duration, it needs to be broken into segments. Partitions should be short enough for the athlete to totally concentrate on what needs to be thought of and done in that period. This assists focusing on the completion of successful competition elements. Structuring performances in this manner is called "segmenting." In the U.S. Navy, a similar approach to combat missions is known as "compartmentalizing". Segmenting originates from two sources. First, the goal-setting literature has shown that distant goals have less effect on performance than do more proximal goals. Short-term performance goals that focus on the processes needed for successful behavior enhance performance.

Second, individuals faced with extensive tasks usually break them down into more manageable segments. Botterill noted successful young athletes spontaneously reconstructed an endurance strength-task into shorter performance segments, each having its own goal or goals. A skier overcame difficulties with traversing a slope when attention was shifted to progress by task parts that eventually lead to completion of the total run. World-champion target sportspersons have reported attempting to fire "one shot at a time" during extended shooting contests. Performing artists have intuitively divided long performances into stages (e.g., acts and scenes, movements) so that performance quality can be maintained. Thus, theory and practice support the notion of segmenting extensive tasks for improved performance outcomes.

Manges and Wahl both tested the segmented versus total performance goal-orientation in runners. Using intraparticipant research designs, the value of short-term process goals over terminal (distal) goals was conclusively demonstrated. Manges' three runners improved 2.0-2.7% while Wahl's ranged from 1.1-6.5% with one participant not improving (-0.9%). The performance differences could not be accounted for in terms of altered physiological functioning, a phenomenon noted long ago by Wilmore. The way segments are structured and their content is particularly individual. Differences in segmenting strategies and moderating factors need to be determined to understand this factor more clearly. The anecdotal and goal-theory literature at present is inadequate for fully explaining this phenomenon.

2. Task-Relevant Thought Content

Performance efficiency is reduced by distraction and enhanced by relevant concentration. There are some minor exceptions to this principle (e.g., cognitive interference), but in tasks performed under stressful circumstances, the focus of attention has to be on the processes for completing the performance to achieve the highest level of outcome. This is particularly true in sports. Cognitive concepts such as "attentional focus," "concentration," and "flow" are characterized by a singular task-orientation, although that orientation varies according to the stage and type of activity. "The focus on task-relevant information is intended to ensure that all resources available to an athlete in a competition are used fully and in the most efficient manner possible".

While task-relevant concentration might seem to be an obvious characteristic of performance control, it is surprising how few athletes develop it effectively through normal training experiences. Training seems to develop a form of habitual/practice thinking that does not transfer effective benefits to competitive settings. Intraparticipant alternating-treatments designs have been used to compare "normal/habitual" thinking with sport-specific task-relevant thinking that has been individualized to the participant. The experimental variable in this paradigm is confounded between individuality and task-specificity. Some studies have introduced other unrelated thinking conditions for further comparisons. Group designs do not demonstrate effects as well as single-participant experiments. Task-relevant thinking appears more consistent in influence the higher the standard of the athlete:

– Canadian elite rowers (N = 5) improved an average of 3.5% on an ergometer task.

- Canadian national team cross-country skiers improved an average of 1.96% over a training track lap.
- Norwegian junior national team cross-country skiers improved an average of 2.5% using both skating and classical techniques over a training track lap.

A common feature of these studies was the opportunity for the athletes to individualize the content and nature of their thoughts after receiving instructions. That feature may be a very significant moderating variable. The normal/habitual thinking developed through training and coaching is far from optimal in its effect on performance. Even though coaches commonly claim to teach and stress "technique," it was only after instructions and practice to use self- and activity-specific detailed content that performances improved.

3. Positive Self-Statements (Thinking)

Positive thinking is *the covert utterance of positive self-statements.* Taylor's work showed that under a positive mental orientation, the body's physiology performs more efficiently than when under an aversive or negative mind-set. Positive self-talk is also related to factors associated with improved performance, such as coping, self-concept, and self-efficacy. Dalton, Maier, and Posavac reported the direct effect of negative thoughts on swimming performance. Among 24 junior tennis players during tournament matches it was found that negative self-talk was associated with losing, and players who used and reported believing in the utility of positive self-talk won more points than players who did not.

Positive self-talk was an important part of a game strategy for improving basketball performance, for learning compulsory figures in ice-skating, and for increasing the number of games won from deuce-point in a tennis player. Intraparticipant investigations on the effect of positive self-talk on performance in a variety of settings produced results similar to those of task-relevant thinking:

– Canadian rowers improved from 1.21-2.20% on an evaluative ergometer task.

– A wide range of Norwegian cross-country skiers improved an average of 3.63% over a test distance.

– Superior Canadian age-group swimmers improved from 1.39-2.13% over two distances.

An emphasis on positive self-talk while performing a task enhances performance. This further supports the inadequacy of habitual sport thinking for provoking an optimal training or competitive response. Self-talk is an individual skill that needs to be practiced before it is evaluated for influence. The general level of effect is marginally less than that of task-relevant thinking, but that is not surprising considering it usually does not entertain direct effects on skill economy. Rather, it sets the "atmosphere" for efficient physiological functioning which then has to be translated into efficient movement patterns. There are certain characteristics of positive self-talk which are recommended for use in practical situations.

Positive self-statements should not be trivial, cheerleader-type expressions (e.g., "go, go, go," "let's do it now"). Four appropriate uses in competitions are:

1. encouraging oneself,
2. handling effort,
3. evaluating segment goals, and
4. general positive self-talk to maintain atmosphere.

It should be spread throughout a strategy. It could be most effective when second-person phrasing is used (e.g., "you," "your"), which produces a perception of control over oneself. The dynamics of positive self-talk in sport settings need to be delineated further.

4. Mood Words

Another form of covert vocabulary involves particular words that emote or energize the individual. Language has basic words which, when said or thought with appropriate feeling and emphasis, have some movement or emotional outcome. They cause a physical reaction in the body. Some languages/cultures use these words more frequently (e.g., Italian, Arabic) than others (e.g., English). Performing artists frequently use simple words emoted in a particular way to promote a behavior that expresses a mood. Mood words require no translation. The expressive thinking of words should produce a feeling appropriate for some performance capacity. If a feeling does not occur, then the content is inappropriate and will be ineffectual. Mood words can reflect various performance capacities.

Typically, a list of monosyllabic synonyms for strength, power (force), speed, agility, balance, and endurance are presented to an athlete. The athlete selects from the lists, or augments personal words that have a similar meaning, the capacities and words that are meaningful to him or her. Those words are then inserted into a performance strategy at the time and during the appropriate task-relevant thoughts when they will be most effective. For example, a rower taking the catch in a stroke might think "BOOM" as a way of elevating the power of that part of the stroke. Rowers have reported that this does increase performance over thinking normally or imaging what is intended. That talk is more effective than imagery during performance has been reported.

Mood words of this type increase the effectiveness of thinking. When one wants to be powerful, thinking words that make one feel powerful will increase the actions of power. Rushall reported unpublished data on a grip-strength test with four Canadian rowers. Three thought-content conditions were used:

1. normal thought content as a control,
2. the utterance of a phrase that had the correct meaning but was unrelated to the emotional state needed to be strong (e.g., the words "exert force"), and
3. the utterance of mood words, such as "crush," "grind," etc., of the athletes' choosing.

All athletes recorded the strongest grip under the emotive mood word condition. Mood words enhance performance marginally better than either task-relevant content or positive self-statements.

Task-relevant content, positive self-statements, and mood words presently are perceived to be the structures that should be employed as thought content during a segmented competitive performance. They should be integrated into a meaningful dialogue by each athlete, and practiced, performed, and evaluated for effect and possible improvement. Their inclusion in training programs is not difficult, and practice could constitute "sporting homework" in a fashion that is not possible with other performance factors. The magnitudes of the performance enhancements reported in controlled research settings with high-level athletes makes the use of thought-content skills an imperative for athletes wishing to maximize their performance and for coaches seeking to optimize their effectiveness.

These four psychological determinants of performance produced enhancements and alterations in a large number of the studies and participants considered. Performance improvements occurred without any notable extra perceived exertion, increase in direct measurements of physiological parameters, or other increased thought dynamics, such as the degree of concentration or "trying harder". These mental activities are a "painless" avenue for assisting athletes to improve. When athletes are exposed to these skills and evaluate their effects they are particularly enthusiastic about their value and use. Psychology offers many performance determinants, only a few being addressed here.

It needs to be recognized that psychology becomes more important, the higher the standard of competitor. It has been reported that psychological factors are better discriminators of high-level performance capacity than physiological measures. For example, Silva, Shultz, Haslam, Martin, and Murray found that psychological variables discriminated Olympic wrestling team qualifiers from nonqualifiers better than physiological variables. Psychology has a major role to play in determining the levels of performance achieved in competitive settings. Athletes should be appraised of the techniques and provided practice opportunities for their implementation as part of the evolving professions of coaching and sport psychology.

Psychological Factors

- *Intelligence*: Ability to interrelate perception of the environment into mental constructs, based on past experienceand education
- *Creativity*: Ability to establish new ways of doing things which are unexpected
- *Alertness*: Mental preparedness to adjust rapidly to changing situations
- *Motivation*: The ability to push the body towards a goal
- *Discipline*: Concentration to the exclusion of external and internal stimuli

Emotions

Emotions can be defined as brief positive or negative feelings occurring in response to meaningful or important situations, which can influence mood states. Basic emotions such as fear, anger, joy and surprise are commonly experienced in sport, although complex mixes of emotions are often evident. Positive emotions can help sustain motivation and enable us to approach events with enthusiasm and energy.

Negative emotions, by contrast, are linked to avoidance behaviours and withdrawal. Emotions in the sporting arena can be triggered by many things personal to an individual, including memories, conversations with other people, seeing the competition venue, weighing up the opposition etc. Researchers have studied emotions in order to determine why they occur and what impact they have on behaviour.

At first it was thought that emotions were simply the result of physiological changes, since physiological symptoms, such as increased heart rate, were commonly observed in such reactions. To test this theory, scientists injected volunteers with the so-called 'stress' hormone epinephrine (adrenaline) to see if emotions could be generated in the laboratory. A small minority of participants reported feeling genuine emotions (usually sadness) while most reported physiological changes (to be expected after administration of adrenaline) and 'as if' emotions - feelings closely associated with being happy, sad or angry, but not the 'real thing'.

Subsequent research demonstrated that emotions could be induced by directing participants' thoughts to emotional triggers, such as deceased relatives (sadness) or past achievements (pride). In summary, research in these areas has shown that both physiological arousal and the cognitive interpretation of that arousal are important in determining the emotional response. During the lead-up to an important competition, the body starts to prepare for the demands to come by releasing hormones such as epinephrine into the bloodstream, setting in motion the physiological changes associated with increased arousal (sometimes referred to as the 'fight or flight' response).

In addition, changes occur in the attentional system, as athletes become more focussed and alert, with increasingly active minds. This overall increase in arousal can be your best friend or your worst enemy: and the key to achieving an appropriate mind set is to analyse the changes in a rational manner and channel your emotions in a positive direction.

Many elite athletes associate increased arousal with excitement as the body readies itself for competition, and use it as a cue to focus on pre-planned routines. This positive interpretation of the arousal response usually leads to more positive emotions and optimistic outlooks. Conversely, some athletes interpret physiological changes like an increased heart rate as anxiety, worry and apprehension , with a negative impact on emotions that is not conducive to good performance. The most important thing to remember is that your interpretation of physiological changes directs your emotional response. However, the relationship between thoughts and emotions works in both directions: although emotions are the result of cognitive interpretations, they can also impact on your thoughts, giving rise to a vicious circle of negative thoughts and emotions.

The good news for athletes who experience unhelpful emotions before competition is that you can gain more control by altering your focus of attention. The next time you feel these unwanted changes occurring try going through the following psychological routine:

- Tell yourself 'this is my body preparing me to perform well', and repeat the affirmation as necessary;
- Try to recall an image of yourself either winning or performing well, and connect this with the feelings you experienced at the time.

You will need to practise this routine on a regular basis in order to establish it as a habitual response that will help you feel more composed and energised before competitions. If negative images jump into your mind during this time, try to visualise the most successful athlete in your sport and the way he or she runs, competes, enjoys performing - in short every positive thing about them; Then visualise yourself with similar positive attributes. Even experienced athletes get nervous and irritable before competing, and a little tension (as long as it is controlled) is often necessary to inspire maximal performance.

The techniques outlined above will not remove all the tension, but they should help you to channel your emotions more positively, which is what top athletes have to learn to do. The difference between winners and losers often boils down to coping skills, in that some athletes have learned to cope with competitive situations better than others. It is important to challenge the belief of some athletes that emotions and mood states are simply reactions to external events; in fact, the athlete has considerable capacity for control in this area. A recent study by Stevens and Lane identified a number of strategies employed by athletes to regulate their moods.

Although unique strategies were employed for specific mood dimensions, results indicated that 'changing location' and 'listening to music' were among the most commonly used strategies. Various research studies have demonstrated the ability of music to impact on emotions and mood by either calming or stimulating the individual as required - although careful consideration is needed in the selection of appropriate music. Listening to music or engaging in a mentally active process, such as a crossword, can help to stop the mind wandering in the hours leading up to competition, although immediately beforehand athletes need to be completely focused on the task in hand.

Having worked with sportsmen and women who have experienced emotional disturbance prior to competing, it is clear to me that mental preparation needs are highly. The common approach that we have found successful is to develop with each athlete a coping response that becomes automated and can be consistently applied in changing circumstances. Such a coping response puts the athlete in control by creating a familiar psychological comfort zone regardless of whatever is going on in the external environment.

One of the biggest triggers for anxiety is uncertainty, which is, of course, inherent in all sporting events. The key principle for the athlete is to control the things you can control but not to waste energy on things you can't control. Many top athletes have found, to their cost, that giving attention to how opponents might perform or how technically good others were in the warm-up has a negative impact on their focus.

The one thing you can control is your own preparation, so that should have your full focus. By developing consistent routines and ways of coping with distractions, uncertainty can be reduced and you are less likely to be negatively affected by external factors. Because athletes have varying requirements, it is impossible to standardise the pre-competition preparation. However, you may wish to adopt some of the ideas below in creating your own pre-performance strategy to achieve the desired emotional state. These ideas are all designed to be put into practice in the hour before competition, although the principles can be adapted for other times.

Physical Preparation

The warm-up period can be an important psychological aid as well as preparing the body for the rigors of competition and helping to prevent injury. Remember the comfort zone? By developing a relatively stable warm-up routine, including mobility work, stretching and increasing deep muscle temperature, uncertainty can be reduced and the athlete's attention directed to appropriate cues, such as quality technique and body awareness. The development of routines in sport has consistently been shown to be important in directing attentional focus to important cues, so aiding performance.

Although during last summer's major athletic events it was impossible to observe what was going on inside the minds of the sprinters, you could clearly observe the regularity of the warm-up routines and the intense concentration written on athletes' faces prior to taking their marks. These routines are not haphazard, but have been systematically designed to promote optimal functioning in the final few minutes before performance. Golfers have routines that allow them to prepare in the same way for each shot, as do some rugby place kickers, and tennis players before serving.

The key to any routine is that it provides the athlete with control and directs attention to the important cues. Coaches and athletes should work together in deciding the key attentional cues and the sequence in which these should occur. Such routines are the opposite of superstitious rituals that take control away from the performer, as with superstitions outcome is essentially believed to be controlled by sources other than the self.

Mental Preparation

The mental aspects prior to performance should involve focussing on what you are going to do during the event. This can include specific strategies, and the establishment of optimal attentional focus. Some athletes will like to use imagery to recall positive past experiences and generate a sense of confidence. Imagery is a very flexible method to employ prior to competition but it needs to be used correctly for maximum effect. Imagery is not just a form of visualisation, but moreover an all sensory experience that should involve the kinaesthetic sense, emotions and auditory experiences to increase the impact.

Many people use imagery to simply see themselves winning but it can be employed to imagine good technique, coping with difficult situations, recreating emotional feelings and rehearsing the up-coming event in the mind. Imagery is a powerful technique since the brain interprets the imagined scenarios very literally, so directly enhancing such psychological variables as confidence. Always keep imagery sessions short and simple just before competition.

Tailoring the imagery to the desired outcome is essential, so if you want to improve your mood, imagine a realistic scenario that makes you feel good. For more advice on incorporating imagery into your preparation, you may like to read a very practical book entitled In Pursuit of Excellence. Mental preparation can include the repeated use of positive self-statements (affirmations) such as 'we have trained hard, and am in great shape'.

Sports Psychology - Thought Control

When it comes to running - or any other endurance sport - your mind can be your biggest asset or your worst enemy. Enjoying your training and achieving your best performances is not simply down to physical conditioning: your mental states and, particularly, the thoughts that run through your mind can affect the way you feel during exercise.

In fact the nature and quality of your thoughts can make the difference between winning or losing, enjoying or hating your training, and may impact on your decision to stay with an exercise programme. Much of this scientific evidence comes from studies of marathon runners. Neuroscientists have shown that athletes have thousands of thoughts running through our minds each and every day. Athletes spend a large percentage of their time thinking sport-related thoughts, but most of these are unplanned and random. The first step towards becoming more organised and purposeful in your thinking is to become more aware of them.

Techniques for Dissociation

- *Music* - This can generate positive thoughts, improve your mood state and distract you from the physical demands of your sport. But be careful not to get too distracted if you are running in a busy area;
- *Counting game* - Count the number of blue cars you see, or the number of dogs of post boxes. Be inventive;
- *Alphabet game* - Work through from A to Z for a chosen category, such as women's names or countries;
- *Rainbow game* - Try to notice as many colours as possible while you work out: aim for all the colours of the rainbow;
- *Active fantasy* - Imagine yourself as a lottery winner and decide how to spend your winnings.

Avoid thoughts relating to your work, jobs you have to do and anything problematic, as this can increase tension. Try to be creative and have fun with dissociation. It can help you relax and enjoy your sport even more.

Association and dissociation

Association involves focusing on bodily sensations and monitoring any changes - usually internal - that occur. Breathing rate and muscular sensations provide physiological cues that allow you to pace yourself with a view to avoiding or minimising pain. By contrast dissocation is about directing attention away from bodily sensations by a form of distraction designed to reduce the athlete's awareness of fatigue or effort. This can be achieved by many means, including music. However, more 'active' strategies like counting tasks or the alphabet game might be more effective.

When trying to decide which strategy might be best for you, it is important to consider your personal situation, preferences and goals. For example, most athletes perform training runs at a slower pace than they use in competition, making body monitoring less essential. A better goal for training might be to relieve boredom and monotony, in which case dissociation, with active mental processing, might be most beneficial. Dissociation may also benefit athletes who want to improve their endurance by running or exercising for longer at moderate intensities. However, because dissociation works by distracting the mind, it might work against an athlete setting an ideal pace for optimum performance. The reason why association appears so important in competition is that, by monitoring his bodily responses, an athlete can ride that thin line between pushing for maximum performance and overdoing it.

Association involves entering a more concentrated state when you can react to changes within your body.

And focusing on internal states like rhythmical breathing can help you feel more relaxed during physical activity. But, on the down side, there is some evidence of a link between association and injury; some athletes, it appears, choose to associate with pain and fatigue-related symptoms and end up pushing themselves too hard.

Most successful elite marathon runners have been shown to combine associative and dissociative strategies when planning their thoughts. There are times, especially in races, when you need to be very aware of your own physical state and of events in the external environment. However, there are also times when you can plan to 'switch off' and give yourself a break from the mental demands of competition or training. The best thing is to construct a plan with your coach, exercise leader or even a more experienced fellow athlete. Try to decide between you what is the best approach for you, and plan what you will be thinking about during the race or training sessions. For a 30-minute training run you might decide on cyclic phases of thinking- e.g. 10 minutes of body monitoring, 10 minutes of alphabet game, then more body monitoring to the end. It's all perfectly logical once you get started: you wouldn't leave your physical preparations to chance, so why allow your thoughts to crop up in random fashion.

Techniques for associative body monitoring follow this three-stage plan:

- *Focus on your breathing:* controlled, relatively deep rhythmic breathing is the key to relaxation. When you breathe out, try to imagine the tension leaving your body;
- Try to remain relaxed while running (or cycling or swimming), but be aware of tension and fatigue in your muscles. It's often a good idea to start from the head and work down, giving each area or group of

muscles your attention. If you notice tension, try to focus on a cue word, such as 'relax' or 'easy' and try to let the tension flow out of the muscles;

- Keep your pace in line with the information you gain from body monitoring. You might, for example, increase the pace if you feel very positive.

Repeat the monitoring constantly or, alternatively, take some time out for dissociation. You might also reinforce your mood by telling yourself how well you are doing and that you need to keep working hard and remain focused.

Suicide and Physical Activity

Physical activity especially vigorous aerobic exercise - has been shown to alleviate depression. Might it also reduce the risk of suicide, which is linked with depression? This is the hypothesis a pair of US scientists set out to test with a major questionnaire survey of nearly 5,000 college students, for whom suicide is the third leading cause of death. Students were classified according to whether or not they participated in any college sport teams. They were further grouped into five categories relating to their level of activity in the week preceding the survey, as follows:

- *Frequent vigorous activity* - exercise that made them sweat and breathe hard for 20 minutes or more on six or seven days;
- *Vigorous activity* - as above for three-five days;
- *Moderate activity* - a combined total of one or two days of vigorous activity and five or more days of walking or cycling for 30 minutes a day;
- *Low activity* - some activity but less than amounts typically recommended for health and fitness gains;
- *No activity* - the 'control' condition.

Students were characterised as suicidal if they indicated that during the past 12 months they had seriously thought about attempting suicide, made plans about how they would attempt suicide or actually attempted suicide. The results revealed distinct - and puzzling - gender differences in the association between activity and suicide, although the actual prevalence of suicidal behaviour among male and female students was similar. In terms of sports participation, there was a trend in favour of a protective effect, with male non-participants being 2.5 times more likely to report suicidal behaviour than participants and female non-participants 1.67 times more at risk - the latter finding being only of borderline statistical significance.

But when it came to activity levels the differences were more stark. For men, low activity was the only clearly protective level, with participants at almost half the risk of suicidal behaviour of those with no reported activity; the men in the three more active groups did not differ significantly in reported suicidal behaviour from the controls. Women, however, exhibited a completely different risk profile, with those reporting frequent vigorous activity having twice the risk of suicidal behaviour of the control group and moderately active women being 1.76 times more at risk. Women in the other two activity groups had slightly - but non-significantly - higher odds of suicidal behaviour than the controls.

These very different findings caused the researchers to engage in a great deal of head-scratching, having hypothesised at the outset that sedentary students of both sexes would run the highest risk of suicidal tendencies. They were especially puzzled by the finding that the association between physical activity and suicidal behaviour in women was independent of distorted weight perceptions that might drive them to exercise obsessively.

Future research should attempt to identify other factors that may be mediating an association between physical activity and suicidal tendencies among college-age women.' Meantime, they suggest that health professionals are in the best position to recommend increased physical activity when appropriate and to determine when such activity is being used excessively or inappropriately in order to mask problems that may require intervention.

Mental Stress

Mental stress can hurt your performances in a variety of different ways. It can raise heart rate and oxygen consumption, harming your exercise efficiency and causing particular workout and race speeds to feel tougher than they actually should. It can increase muscle tension, reducing stride lengths (if you are a runner) and making your legs and arms considerably less 'springy' and powerful.

On a cognitive level, stress prevents you from 'mentally managing' your tough workouts and races; instead of relaxing and focusing on the task at hand, you are preoccupied with stressful thoughts and emotions, so the quality of your performance decreases. If you feel stressed-out before and during your competitions or hard training sessions, what can you do to control the stress, and thus increase your chances of performing at your highest-possible level?

Sport psychologists have proposed a number of different stress-managing techniques over the years, but one of the most successful has been something called 'stress-inoculation training'. Developed in the late 1970s and early 1980s by Donald Meichenbaum, a psychologist at the University of Waterloo in Canada, stress-inoculation training takes its name from the fact that it exposes individuals to stress in manageable but gradually increasing amounts, thereby enhancing 'immunity' to stress for the persons practising the technique. The key, however, to stress inoculation is not simply that stress levels are increased in a governable way during training; athletes also learn skills for coping with psychological stress and enhancing performance, including the development of productive thoughts and self-statements and the utilization of centring strategies.

There are usually three stages in the overall stress-inoculation process: A conceptualization phase, in which an athlete becomes more aware of how positive and negative thoughts, self-talk, and imagery influence performance, a rehearsal period, during which an athlete learns to use centring, positive self-statements, and other coping skills, and an application phase, in which the athlete actually practises his/her skills, first in low-stress situations and then in settings in which stress levels are gradually increased.

Banishing Unsuitable 'headwork'

Stress-inoculation training was originally developed for the public-at-large, but psychologists quickly realized that it could be applied to sports settings. They knew that many athletes unwittingly respond to stress with maladaptive thoughts and images which greatly hinder performance. Once such athletes understand how their unsuitable 'headwork' is keeping them from reaching their potentials, they begin to eagerly construct new self-statements and images which can have a profoundly positive impact on their performances.

Scientific studies concerning the effects of stress-inoculation training on exercise capacity have generally been positive: In one study, two sessions of stress-inoculation training per week for 5.5 weeks improved the running economy of eight male collegiate cross-country runners. Stress-inoculation training has also been linked with improved performance during abseiling (descending mountain faces) and lower stress levels during squash competitions, and it has been particularly effective at boosting the performances of gymnasts. Not too surprisingly, a number of sport psychologists have examined the effects of stress-inoculation training on basketball players, particularly with regard to free-throw shooting, which is often a high-stress activity within the game.

Stress inoculation improved both free-throw and field-goal shooting, and a second investigation (carried out with just three players, however) determined that free-throw shooting accuracy increased from 50 to 88 per cent and self-statements changed from 86-per cent negative to 71-per cent positive after just 10 hours of stress-inoculation training. In practical terms, here's how stress inoculation works:

The Application Phase

Once you have developed positive self-statements and are better at centring and attentional control, you're ready to apply your new strategies in increasingly stressful situations - leading up to your big competitive event(s) of the year. Remember that stress-inoculation training doesn't initially relieve stress; in fact, in a study carried out with competitive gymnasts, the athletes performed better after going through stress-inoculation training, even though their anxiety levels were initially higher during competitions than they had been prior to the 'inoculation'. Don't be alarmed that the stress is not magically going away; in fact, you can use the 'somatic stress' (higher heart rate, higher breathing rate, greater muscle tension) which you might feel as a positive: when you experience it, simply say 'All right, my body is getting ready for a high level of performance.'

Cognitive anxiety (the mental stress you are feeling) will be relieved gradually over time, as your new strategies steadily enhance your ability to perform. For an athlete, there is no better antidote to stress than good performances. The athlete who is stressed out about racing is transiently relieved when he tells himself that he will never race well, but he is permanently and positively relieved when he begins to have solid races and set PBs. Basically, to apply your new stress-managing skills effectively, you would be wise to set up a moderate-length test race which you can carry out on your own.

Practise your positive self-statements, centring, and attentional control during the weeks leading up to this 'race', and then perform to the best of your ability. A few weeks later, enter a low-key contest outside your immediate geographical area, where you will know few of the other athletes (not knowing anyone makes attentional control easier), and use your skills again prior to this race. As the weeks go by, gradually enter more and more stressful races (i.e., races where you want to do fairly well, competitions in which you do know the other competitors, etc.).

Generally, your stress-managing skills will increase enough as time goes by so that you will be able to perform well at these races, in contrast to when you were not managing your stress. At your big event of the year, you will be in much better control of your mind and body - and ready to give yourself a chance to have a great race. If your problem is not the stress of racing itself but a within-race problem such as losing speed in the last portion of a marathon, the positive self-talk, centring, and attentional control will also work, and you'll need to use them leading up to and during a workout which duplicates the stress of marathon day.

A training session in which you run moderately for 20 miles or so and then 'take off' at marathon pace for three to four miles will be helpful, and so will all training sessions which require you to run at goal marathon pace while tired. If you use stress-inoculation training correctly along with your regular training, you can 'inoculate' yourself with the positive focus and self-statements which will make it possible for you to perform at your highest-possible level.

Any look at "*Sports science for the millennium*" must consider the fact that by its nature, there are no major breakthroughs in sports science, such as vaccines and antibiotics in medicine, or the genetic code in biology, or atomic theory in physics, or the big-bang in cosmology. Sports science in general consists of constant refinements or improvements across a broad front; a front that includes training, tactics, techniques, skills, equipment, biomechanics, psychology, chronobiology, nutrition, management and physiology - as well as all the medical aspects.

It was a special event. The attack on the world 10,000m record had been publicised worldwide, and the satellite sports channels had unique coverage. Steve Coe, the challenger, - grandson of a famous father, whose own world 800m record had lasted for almost as many years as Steve had been alive - had put in three periodised sessions daily for the past 24 months under his coach Harry Anderson, specifically to prepare for this attempt to be the first to run under 24 minutes for the distance. Luckily, or he would not have been attempting what he was about to do, Steve had been conceived with a genetic advantage in terms of his response to training. Athletes, otherwise equally endowed physiologically, may respond differently to the same training, because, as Professor Bouchard and colleagues discovered at Laval University, Quebec, some are genetically programmed to produce a better response to the same stimulus.

Good sleep was considered important for maximising the natural growth hormone training-response, and the sex itself for raising androgen levels. Both sets of hormones had an anabolic effect in helping to optimise the muscle response to training stimuli. Breaks and short holidays were considered vital, as was reasonable intellectual stimulus in the form of music, drama, poetry and general conversation.

Coaching Interventions for Athletic Excellence

In coaching literature, Martens, Haslam and Bloom, Durand-Bush, Schinke and Salmela have noted that the relationship between coach and athlete is complex. There is extensive literature outlining the challenging interpersonal dynamic between coaches and athletes. Martens and Wishnietsky and Felder noted that coaches are often unable to reach their athletes due to personal shortcomings in communication such as impatience and the lack of understanding. Adding to the complexity of the dyad's relationship, Seligman and Rettew and Reivich have noted that athletes also vary in terms of how they perceive and subsequently respond to coach criticism based on their personal interpretation patterns.

Though coaches and athletes alike might not consider the root of such difficulties in the heat of the teaching - learning moment, there are reasons why their relationship is so complex, and in some instances, trying. Some of the factors that underlie the behavioral exchange between coach and athlete reside in the moment.

However, there are also other historical factors that underpin the perceptual screens of coaches and athletes alike. Seligman has noted that peoples' perceptions and subsequent explanatory patterns are acquired based on what was learned in childhood from parents and teachers.

Schinke and da Costa recognized that formative interactions with earlier coaches also influence the athletic expectations of sport performers. It seems conceivable that momentary perceptions and responses in the present have their basis in past experiences and interactions. Thus, it is essential for coaches and mental training consultants to understand the current and historical aspects underlying the communication exchange between coach and athlete. In so doing, it is argued herein that coaching and mental training consultants can foster improved interpersonal dynamics and the increased likelihood for personal and athletic growth. Regardless of whether readers are mental training consultants or coaches, the consideration here is to understand how to work through interpersonal dynamics and develop athletes as performers while concurrently mentoring them on a more general level.

Imago Therapy

Imago Therapy is a process of communication developed by Hendrix. Its underlying assumption is that the challenges people experience when interacting with one another are linked to how each has been hurt or oppressed in childhood. Emphasis is placed on teaching individuals to sensitize others to the manner in which they were hurt, and then in collaboration, to create an environment of safety to explore these experiences. The exploration first takes place through a process termed the "conscious dialogue." The foundation of the skill rests with each person learning to mirror, validate and empathize with the other's experience. The crucial premise, and hence recipe for success, lies in one partner's understanding that it is essential to accept and therefore understand the other's reality. To communicate at their utmost potential, coaches must learn how to borrow the lens through which their athletes view the world, while also, remaining conscious of how they as coaches react to such perceived experiences. For the sake of clarification, this process has previously been called "reflectivity" by social psychologists including Parker and Bruner.

Using a feedback process that was built on the foundation of the dialogue derived from Imago Therapy, it will be shown how coaches and other sport practitioners can work optimally with athletes. There is a number of beliefs regarding why Imago Therapy can contribute to coaching practice and athletic performance. First, there is an underlying assumption that there is ample opportunity to exercise a conscious dialogue process for coaches with their athletes.

Coaches spend a lot of time exchanging thoughts and experiences with their athletes. When the time is invested working on the athlete's personal and athletic development concurrently, then the result will be a synergistic form of growth in both areas.

Second, it is the belief, based on the work of Seligman, that the areas in which the coach and athlete experience strife with one another may be directly linked to the manner in which the athlete [and sometimes the coach] have been oppressed or hurt in their own lives. If, for example, the possibility is embraced that some athletes have chosen the path of performing in front of a large numbers of people due partially to an unmet need for recognition in childhood, such information is useful for a coach to be conscious of and active in addressing. Alternately, if an athlete's partial motivation to perform is based on an overwhelming need to compete with others, and this is a life theme for the athlete, that information could also be deemed useful in gaining a deeper understanding of the athlete and how to work with him or her.

Gaining developmental information about each athlete is important in order to improve understanding and pedagogical delivery. Ultimately, improved athlete awareness can help the coach to select a method of communication and feedback that will be more likely to be heard and integrated, within the context, and within general life for that matter, in a positive way.

AHTLETE'S STRUGGLE WITH CONFIDENCE

Hendrix elaborates on six major stages of childhood development, which he believes largely influence the person on an individual and relational level; attachment, exploration, identity, competence, concern and intimacy. The attachment stage addresses the extent that the individual experiences acceptance or rejection from parents during infancy (0-18 months). The exploration stage addresses the extent that the individual was encouraged by parents to explore aspects in his or her environment while a toddler (18-36 months). The identity stage uncovers whether people were encouraged by their parents to assert themselves in social contexts during their third and fourth years. The competence stage is depicted through the actual willingness to exert effort and ability within achievement settings, and its basis is contingent on the previous three stages of development.

Concern is the first developmental stage where people learn how to relate to others outside of their parents or caregivers. Intimacy, the final stage, addresses the individual's resulting long-term relational ability with a partner, and its basis is linked to previous experiences during earlier developmental stages. In terms of personal development, the competence stage occurs during the 4-8 year age span. The ability of individuals to feel masterful in their environment and their world is, according to Hendrix, directly linked to retrospective factors experienced during childhood. Taking this premise to sport, something that Seligman has already teased at, athletes who feel competent and powerful in a performance environment undoubtedly have received a parent or caregiver's value during their earliest achievements.

These athletes may have been noticed for their accomplishments received target specific praise for their successes in and out of sport. The adaptive-competent athlete most likely received unconditional love as a child for efforts, despite the mistakes made. In addition, a caregiver, whether a parent or early coach, who was conscious of nurturing competence in a youngster, may also have purposefully provided concrete efficacy information regarding how to correct mistakes. The underlying intervention was to ensure that explanations and subsequent understandings for performance variance were explained by potentially controllable and impermanent factors.

The aforementioned adaptive intervention is in contrast to methods that critically disempower the individual via permanent and personal explanations for sub-par performances, or basing acceptance largely on successful and impermanent performances. Hendrix maintains that the individual who receives selective praise from a caregiver who demands and only notices excellence internalizes the message "do not make mistakes." Such messages are often translated into a fear of failure. Hence, it can be assumed that this might be part of the reason why some athletes are scared to fail and cannot withstand the ego damage from sub-par experiences where others can. There is a second adaptation to wounding in the athlete's competence stage. If a parent withheld instruction or ignored the child who did not excel, the message internalized might well have been "do not be too powerful, there is only enough room here for one of us to win and it is not you."

According to Hendrix, such an individual may operate from a place of fear of assertion affecting their level of success in life, and so, in sport. We believe that these are the athletes who tend to perpetually find themselves one step behind the proverbial gold medal because winning was not internalized as part of what they were accepted for and identified with. For coaches and other central coaching staff working with such athletes, conscious healing means noticing and accepting the assertive aspects of the athletes in an effort to connect them with their personal power, or agency. This sort of intervention might seem complex, but there is a concise means of achieving it.

The application of Imago Therapy to coaching may be viewed as such: In a relationship where coach and athlete are connected, there exists a potential degree of safety for the athlete. With this sense of security athletes' unresolved issues can surface as they attempt to heal unresolved experiences. Situations and feelings, which remind athletes of previous experiences, will trigger positive and negative affect [feelings] in the present. Such feelings, already recognized by Seligman, will typically come from explanations of past experiences. Fear of failure originating from the parent-child relationship may resurface into feelings of inadequacy, threat, and guilt as athletes relate with their coaches.

If believed that such a preoccupation could detract energy from the athlete's potential, it can become one potential coaching role to remain sensitive and intentional in communication. With a view toward building trust, coaches, and even coaching staff, can consciously give their athletes what they are craving on an emotional level; target specific praise for achievement, unconditional acceptance despite performance glitches, concrete and personally uncritical information to correct mistakes, and thus, a promotion of the athlete's personal agency.

The concept of coach intervention and our personal adaptation of an interactive approach take into account the link between the athlete's mind, heart and body and coaching interaction as a complex and interconnected system. It is assumed that peoples' minds, souls and bodies are intertwined in a world with others, as many adherents of social learning theory including Bruner, Bandura and Seligman agree. Hence, the underlying Imago adage developed by Hendrix seems applicable; individuals are born in relationships, they are hurt in relationships, and they need to heal through relationships. It is this adage that underpins the philosophy and rationale for coaches intervening with the athletes that they aspire to mentor as part of their role.

Understanding the Athlete's Feelings

One word, specific descriptions should be provided during the affect-based component of the performance review. An exchange of affect-based information allows the coach and athlete to understand the reasoning behind a specific reaction or create an opportunity for further exploration of emotions that are either detracting or enhancing from the athlete's competence. Conversely, a coach can use this opportunity to communicate to the athlete his or her sense of fatigue for example, so as to prevent a misconception that occasional temper or impatience was a personal issue aimed at the athlete. This point is increasingly crucial depending on the extent of earlier ego damage experienced by the athlete during childhood and other formative moments.

Therefore, a collaborative discussion on feelings and responses can provide the coach with a better understanding of where and to what extent their athlete's insecurities reside. Open discussion can also provide coaches with an opportunity to explain what they meant in their instructional criticism so that it is not internalized (or attributed) as any form of permanent, personal or pervasive flaw on the part of the athlete. On both accounts, the improved dialogue between coach and athlete can only add to the coach's credibility and success via the athlete's confidence.

In addition to images, somatic responses and feelings, the acknowledgement of performance can become another source of useful confidence-building information. Athletes can list numerous positive, specific, and measurable things they like about their performance. This might be a challenge for elite and aspiring athletes providing they have been conditioned to be perfectionists, and as a result, they have learned to criticize themselves openly at will. In addition, when athletes have relished their performances, others might have previously discouraged them from "bragging." How can performers be expected to enjoy and duplicate success when they are not allowed to acknowledge with what is going well? This is a noteworthy point considering that Bandura has repeatedly confirmed that the primary source of confidence is the self-acknowledgement of past correct performances.

If the mandate is confidence building, it is necessary for athletes to go against what, for some, has been socially engrained, and acknowledge positive personal experiences. It is imperative for coaches to provide numerous positive, measurable, and specific examples of feedback to the athlete. Given the professional credibility of most coaches, verbal persuasion and even positive facial expressions can add to the competence of a confidence-depleted athlete. This, too, carries forward from Bandura's aforementioned research on self-efficacy. Part of the mandate of a conscious coach, then, is to ask athletes to mirror or paraphrase feedback so as to increase probability that confidence-building information has registered intellectually and emotionally as part of the self-referent thought process.

Effect of Growth Gift

A "growth gift" is the final competence building component that should be given by coaches to their athletes, and by athletes to themselves. The growth gift, much like all other forms of feedback, should be positive, measurable and specific. An effective growth gift captures the individual's essence while simultaneously encouraging the potential for personal growth. An example of a growth gift for athletes who have difficulty experiencing their success or digesting praise, may sound like this: " For the next month, every time you practice your sport and someone pays you a compliment, mirror the compliment back to him or her. Accept the praise and say thank you while feeling the joy of appreciation."

The growth gift encourages the athlete to acknowledge the correct elements in their performance. This form of cognition is provided as a substitute to the ongoing rumination and dissection that Schinke and Seligman have noted seems to be prevalent for many athletes as they strive for excellence. Schinke and Seligman have found that too much critical thinking about what is going wrong in performance serves as a contributory factor to helpless - despondent behavior. What the growth gift seems to contribute to the development of athletic competence is an ongoing awareness for the athlete of that which is right and worth persisting toward in sport. The coach's role in this regard is to ensure that a growth gift is provided to the athlete on a consistent basis so as to ensure that competence develops in a synergistic way over time.

Second Generation Cognitive Science

In psychology, decision making, whether it is initiated or motivated by a conscious or non conscious estimation of the contingencies of reinforcement, biological sensitivities, or mentalistic agencies such as will, need, or desire is generally accounted for apart from the patterns of neural activation that are responsible for translating motivating events into behavior. The actual neural and somatic processes that activate behavior are generally not considered as having a significant influence on how behavior is decided. Decision making is thus 'disembodied', since a consideration of bodily influences would not increase the predictive power bestowed by the behavioral road map provided by environmental contingencies, biological sensitivities, or just good old common sense. In contrast to the fixation on of behavioral, social, genetic and otherwise disembodied motivating entities that comprise most of what we call the psychology of motivation, cognitive psychology is primarily concerned with the physiological, biochemical, and morphological content of mental states, and how those states are integrated to produce vision, perception, attention, awareness, etc.

In other words, cognitive science emphasizes how mental processes are activated, not why they are activated. This bifurcation of psychological perspective into a separate emphasis on motivation and activation variables has historically separated cognitive science from those disciplines in psychology such as analytic, social and behavioristic psychology that are concerned primarily with how behavior is instigated or motivated. Within the last twenty years however, a new generation of cognitive scientists has begun to regard this divide as artificial, and has recognized that motivation and activation are tightly bound, and that each informs and explains the other. This position, also called bio-behavioral or second generation cognitive science, has found elegant and forceful advocacy in the works of the psychologists John Donahoe and David Palmer, the philosopher Mark Johnson, the linguist George Lakoff, the neuro-psychologist Antonio Damasio, and the immunologist Gerald Edelman. Their general position is that language, behavior, and value itself it strongly rooted in sensori-motor or bodily processes, and that activation in itself does influence motivation.

Thus sensori-motor and neural activation patterns underlie basic processes of reinforcement, create the basis of language through metaphor, continually influence behavior as emotion, and provide the basis of value and consciousness. However, the complex activation patterns that underlie language, emotion, and value do not in themselves implicate how decision making at its most rudimentary is performed. And here is the critical point. If decision making, if reduced to its molecular correlate of activating attentional processes in itself adds value to behavior, then no behavior can be reliably predicted without a consideration of the activation processes that make behavior possible. Moreover, if this is true, then many of the long held concepts in social psychology, behaviorism, and sociobiology must be reconsidered, reinterpreted, or abandoned.

On a molecular (neural) level, the shifting of attention that occurs as initiated by a sudden change in an environment-behavior (perceptual) relationship is isomorphic with the liberation of the neurotransmitter dopamine in synaptic clefts between coactive pre- and post synaptic neurons. The functional role of dopamine is to stabilize active neural representations in the frontal cortex, to label stimuli with appetitive value (i.e. it feels good), and to provide advance reward information before behavior occurs. Finally, dopamine is released in response to perceived deviations from learned predictions in future reward, or is sensitive to the perceived salience of responses and their consequences (i.e. response contingencies).

In other words, dopamine acts to make thinking processes more efficient and is essential to the process of reinforcement. If these hypotheses are true, then specific response contingencies (particularly variable ratio or 'gambling' schedules of reinforcement) may be hypothesized to signal frequent and consistent deviations in reward prediction, and these deviations will correlate with the consistent and elevated release of dopamine and the felt experience of elation or pleasure. This prediction has been recently borne out by a recent experiment that demonstrated that the increased release of dopamine occurs during the performance of a goal directed motor task: a video game. This result is underscored by an extensive record of self reports that relate ecstatic states to environmental contingencies that require a rapid attentional shifting between salient cognitive precepts.

A specific response contingency (gambling or video game playing) demands a rapid shifting of attention, but multiple concurrent contingencies involving similar behavior that lead to different rewards may do the same thing. If activation patterns (attention) are specific to prediction error, then the continuous prediction errors that sustains attention and the corresponding release of dopamine are inherent in the stimulus context that creates that prediction error, and not in the stimulus itself. Thus extrinsic motivators (money, power, sex, etc.) always include an intrinsically motivating component (pleasurable alertness) that is critically dependent upon how those extrinsic events are arranged to follow behavior. Thus extrinsic and intrinsic motivation are not separate entities, but are individual aspects of the same motivating or learning process. This explains the favor we give to behaviors that have a great deal of unpredictability, such as sports, gambling, and perhaps play writing.

The leads to a critical hypothesis: Objects do not reinforce, but rather the perceptual relationships denoted by those objects. These relationships occur virtually, and always represent as-if relationships and their corresponding prediction errors. That is, an object does not have to be possessed, but be potentially possessed. Reinforcement theory, as defined through modern cognitive science, contrasts with theories informed by behaviorism, sociobiology, economics, and even social psychology that correlate happiness with physical objects. Humans do exist to maximize value, but if value is determined by potential rather than actual events, then value can only be maximized by engineering social environments that provide multiple concurrent rewards for differing aspects of behavior, and inculcating through education our ability to perceive those rewards.

In other words, perfectly engineered societies are merely the societies we admire anyway, such as the idealized models represented by ancient Greece, Renaissance Italy, and Shakespearean England. These societies provide the multi-modal reinforcement for any variety of endeavor, from art to music to sports, but as importantly, they provide the means whereby we may easily perceive the potential approval of the an audience, a girlfriend, posterity, or a Queen. And the Shakespeares of the world, as well as its musicians, artists and saints come about because they are well reinforced by what they do, and this because they can empathize about the world.

Squat Exercise Through Psychological Modeling

Squats, perhaps more than any other resistance exercise must be performed properly. The considerable amount of weight used, in such a multiple joint movement, can result in a variety of injuries to the knees and lower back. However most of these injuries occur when people squat with improper form and technique. Many misconceptions concerning the squat are brought about by ignorance and false information. Adaptations to squatting include but are not limited to the following:

1. Muscles are strengthened far beyond the norm, making injury less likely to occur.
2. Bone density and strength are increased; especially if the stress is applied longitudinally (This is accomplished best by following the outline on proper technique in the subsequent paragraph).
3. Ligaments, tendons, and connective tissues are increased in thickness, viscoelasticity, and tensile strength, making injury far less likely.

Since the squat is a full-body exercise, it elicits one of the highest hormonal responses provided by resistance exercises. Hormonal actions that influence the adaptations to the squat exercise include, but are not limited to, improved force production, stimulation of cartilage growth, and enhanced size. Performing the squat exercise with proper technique is crucial in order to benefit from these favorable adaptations.

Teaching proper form to a student requires visual demonstration by the instructor. The literature in the area of motor skill performance as it relates to or is affected by modeling primarily considers visual perception of the modeled information as a mediating variable on behavior, but what ensues between perception and behavior does not appear to be fully addressed. Apparently, a myriad of intermediary components is essential in transforming the patterns of movement demonstrated by the model into appropriate actions to be accomplished by the learner. These components will be discussed following a brief description of proper technique in executing the barbell squat exercise.

Squatting with proper technique ensures that the quadriceps, biceps femoris, gluteals, and erector spinae receive an overload stress appropriate for development of muscular strength and hypertrophy.

Modeling

Modeling is an effective means of conveying relevant information to facilitate an observer's motor skill acquisition. The literature in the area of modeling primarily considers visual perception as a mediating variable on behavior. Visual demonstrations of motor tasks are retained by the learner in the form of cognitive representations, which may be construed as "mental blueprints" providing an essential link between perception and action. The brain not only categorizes these non-language representations; it also builds successive layers of categories such as shape, movement, and sequence. In this way, the learner organizes visual information, events, and their relationships. The significance of the modeling process lies in its effect on the behavior of the observer.

Particular events and attributes are singled out for observing and describing what exactly ensues between perception and action. So, it is crucial to demonstrate proper technique to the observer in the most effective manner, especially when one considers the many people in various weight rooms that are using bad technique, thereby setting a bad example to those observers. It is evident that the observer somehow retains the modeled action and can later replicate what was seen in the absence of verbal instruction. When the trainer gives too many verbal cues, it causes the trainee to think about too many things. This may result in confusion and attenuate performance. Too many instructions make it difficult for the student to totally isolate one strategy from another.

In doing so, some of the information is lost. It may be that the student is using various combinations of strategies and cannot be focused into using the most effective one. Therefore, it is important that verbal instruction be as clear and parsimonious as possible. The trainer should demonstrate the squat exercise with the learner standing behind him or her. This type of visual modeling facilitates motor skill reproduction. Bandura suggests that behavior is mediated by exposure to the model and that repeated exposure to the model will improve the quality of the cognitive representation which will, in turn, facilitate performance.

The concept of modeling is presumed to be controlled by four sub-components: "Attention", a conjecture that people cannot learn much by observation unless they attend to, and perceive accurately the significant features of the modeled behavior. "Retention", where it is submitted that people cannot be influenced by observation if they do not remember it. "Motor reproduction process", which is the conversion of symbolic representations into appropriate actions. "Motivation" which proposes that people are more likely to adopt a modeled behavior if it results in rewarding consequences.

According to Martens, Burwitz, and Zuckerman, the successfulness of the modeling process is limited by the difficulty of the motor task. This relationship between modeling and performance is predicated on two circumstances: an accurate perception of what is to be accomplished by way of strategy or technique, and the ability of the learner to reproduce the demonstrated action. Why are some people better at solving math problems than others, and why are other people better at performing motor tasks the first time they attempt them? Owing to the disparity in motor performance among clients and trainees learning to use free-weights may be a result of certain individuals generating false assumptions from the way in which they process and record the modeled information. Imagery perceptions are as important in understanding modeling as non-imagery perceptions are for understanding mathematics. These perceptions give the student a reference point from which he or she can improve performance.

The instructor should give immediate visual feedback by demonstrating the movement with an emphasis on correcting existing mistakes or replaying videotape of the student's performance, thereby providing visual assessment of the motor task in a timely manner. According to Adams, this knowledge of results enables the observer to correct errors in movement technique. The greater the accuracy of the cognitive representation of the modeled action, the greater the skill acquisition will be in the subsequent reproductions of it. This is consistent with the schema theory proposed by Schmidt, which states that sensory consequences and actual outcomes, for a given set of initial conditions, could be related by the subject. This expected sensory consequence for an intended movement could be generated even if that expectation required interpolating among previous entries in order to perform a novel movement.

Psychological Perspective in Human Performance

Psychology is the study of behavior, it being both covert and overt. It is relatively easy to investigate overt behaviors accurately, reliably, and to employ independent verification of phenomena, but when it comes to covert behaviors, such as thoughts and emotional interpretations, the ability to independently verify phenomena is usually thwarted. However, it is still possible to affect covert behaviors without actually observing them. While it remains possible to manipulate external events and observe behavioral outcomes, functional relationships between environmental psychological factors and performances can be described.

It is not scientifically appropriate to attribute outcomes to intermediary events such as thoughts and perceptions when they have not been directly observed.

A serious competitive setting is where the consequences of performance are most important and strongest for an athlete. The pre-competition and competition ingredients are unusually complex with the performance characteristics supposedly reflecting the benefits of training. Factors that affect an athlete's perception of this setting have been described in the *Sport Pressure Checklist*. Variations in these factors produce performance inconsistencies as well as suggest patterns that predispose excellent performances. In challenging and serious performance situations, it has been found that performance-oriented *"strategies"* (plans) of specific detail have notable effects on performance consistency and reliability. The need for specific preparations is now commonly recognized in several fields (e.g., business, performing arts) and its founding research so convincing that it is now rarely investigated. However, it is still being neglected in the majority of sporting situations by coaches and sport psychologists.

Further, when strategies are formulated primarily by athletes they generally produce the following benefits:

1. uncertainty and interpretive distractions are reduced;
2. the stress of negative situations is reduced;
3. performance consistency is enhanced;
4. the coping capacity for problem situations is improved; and
5. performance deteriorations are minimized.

Research reports of the value of performance strategies in sports have been published. Thus, the preparation of what is to be done and thought of during a sporting contest has strong validity for enhancing athletic performance as it does in other human endeavors. It remains important to describe elements that constitute effective performance strategies when used in a competition.

If an event is of long duration, it needs to be broken into segments. Those partitions or segments should be short enough for the athlete to totally concentrate on what needs to be thought of and done in that period. This assists focusing on the completion of successful competition elements. Structuring performances in this manner is called "segmenting." In the US Navy, a similar approach to combat missions is known as "compartmentalizing" (e.g., TOP GUN). Segmenting originates from two sources. First, the goal-setting literature has shown that distant goals have less effect on performance than do more proximal goals.

Short-term performance goals that focus on the processes needed for successful behavior enhance performance. Second, individuals faced with extensive tasks usually break them down into more manageable segments. Botterill noted successful young athletes spontaneously reconstructing an endurance strength-task into shorter performance segments each having its own goal or goals. A skier overcame difficulties with traversing a slope when attention was shifted to progress by parts of the task that eventually lead to completion of the total run. World-champion target sportspersons have reported attempting to fire "one shot at a time" during extended shooting contests. Performing artists have intuitively divided long performances into stages (e.g., acts and scenes, movements) so that performance quality can be maintained.

Thus, theory and practice support the notion of segmenting extensive tasks for improved performance outcomes. Manges and Wahl both tested the segmented versus total performance goal-orientation in runners.

Using intrasubject research designs, the value of short-term process goals over terminal or distal goals was conclusively demonstrated. The performance differences could not be accounted for in terms of altered physiological functioning, a phenomenon noted long ago by Wilmore. Segmenting performances is a recommended procedure for performance strategy construction. It has recently been hypothesized that segments need to be shorter, the more intense the activity. The way segments are structured and their content is particularly individual. Differences in segmenting strategies and moderating factors need to be determined to understand this factor more clearly. The anecdotal and goal-theory literature at present is inadequate for fully explaining this phenomenon.

The need to concentrate on task-relevant thought content to complete a task proficiently is no longer investigated. It is a tenet of psychology that performance efficiency is reduced by distraction and enhanced by relevant concentration. There are some minor exceptions to this principle (e.g., cognitive interference), but in tasks that are performed under stressful circumstances, the focus of attention has to be on the processes for completing the performance if the highest level of outcome is to be produced. This is particularly true in sports. Concepts such as attentional focus, concentration, and flow are characterized by a singular task-orientation although that orientation varies according to the stage and type of activity.

For sports, it is important that athletes learn to use task-specific information in their thought structures that will focus on the performance itself. "The focus on task-relevant information is intended to ensure that all resources available to an athlete in a competition are used fully and in the most efficient manner possible". While task-relevant concentration might seem to be an obvious characteristic of performance control, it is surprising how few athletes develop it effectively through training experiences. What seems to be developed is a form of habitual/practice thinking that does not transfer effective benefits to evaluative or competitive settings.

A common paradigm for assessing thought-content effectiveness is to perform an intrasubject alternating treatments design comparing "normal/habitual" thinking with sport-specific task-relevant thinking that has been individualized to the S. The experimental variable in this paradigm is confounded between individuality and task-specificity. Some studies have introduced other, unrelated thinking conditions for further comparisons. In the Crossman and Selkirk studies, group experimental designs were used. They provided no opportunity to develop the mental skill of using particular forms of thinking under the stress of maximal effort to exhaustion. It appears that the design did not allow effects to emerge.

Once intrasubject designs were employed, which allowed learning to occur, effects became quite prevalent. It also appears that task-relevant thinking is more consistent in its influence the higher the standard of the athlete. A common feature of this group of studies was the opportunity for the athletes to individualize the content and nature of their thoughts after receiving instructions. That feature may be a very significant moderating variable in these impressive results.

The disturbing feature of obtaining such impressive performance changes through instructions to use a particular mental skill is that the normal/habitual thinking developed through training and coaching is far from optimal in its effect on performance. Even though coaches commonly claim to teach and stress "technique," it was only after instructions and practice to use self- and activity-specific detailed content that performances improved. One has to ponder what would be the eventual performance outcome if the nature of task-relevant thought content became a large part of habitual performance thinking.

Positive self-statements

The definition of positive thinking is the covert utterance of positive self-statements. There are two main theoretical bases for this advocacy. The first is quite general. It relies heavily on Taylor's work which showed that under a positive mental orientation, the body's physiology performs more efficiently than when under an aversive or negative mind-set.

The effect of self-talk on performance of 24 junior tennis players (mean age 15.4 yr) during tournament matches was examined. It was found that negative self-talk was associated with losing and that players who used and reported believing in the utility of positive self-talk won more points than players who did not. Positive self-talk has been an important part of a game strategy for improving basketball performance, for learning compulsory figures in ice-skating, and increasing the number games won from deuce-point in a tennis player.

The results are similar to those of task-relevant thinking. An emphasis on positive self-talk while performing a task enhances performance. This further supports the inadequacy of habitual sport thinking for provoking an optimal training or competitive response. Self-talk is an individual skill that needs to be practiced before it is evaluated for influence.

The general level of effect is marginally less than that of task-relevant thinking but that is not surprising considering it usually does not entertain direct effects on skill economy. Rather, it sets the "atmosphere" for efficient physiological functioning which then has to be translated into efficient movement patterns.

The value of positive self-talk is further substantiated by its association with factors related to enhanced performance. It is a skill that needs to be taught as part of a coaching program and integrated with task-relevant thinking. The not-so-subtle effect of engaging in positive self-talk is that it is intrinsically reinforcing to the user. Thus, once it is initiated as an important part of a training program, athletes are very willing to continue with its practice. There are certain characteristics of positive self-talk which are recommended for use in practical situations. Positive self-statements should not be trivial, cheerleader-type expressions (e.g., "go, go, go," "let's do it now"). Four appropriate uses in competitions are:

1. encouraging oneself,
2. handling effort,
3. evaluating segment goals, and
4. general positive self-talk to maintain atmosphere.

It should be spread throughout a strategy. It has been suggested that it is most effective when second person phrasing is used (e.g., "you," "your"). The use of second person appears to produce a perception of control over oneself. However, some athletes prefer first person expression. The dynamics of positive self-talk in sport settings need to be delineated further. There are theoretical, experimental, and practical reasons for employing positive self-talk in competitive performances.

The psychological determinants of performance produced enhancements and alterations in a large number of the studies and Ss considered. Performance improvements occurred without any notable extra perceived exertion, increase in direct measurements of physiological parameters, or other increased thought dynamics, such as the degree of concentration or "trying harder". These mental activities are a "painless" avenue for assisting athletes to improve.

When athletes are exposed to these skills and evaluate their effects they are particularly enthusiastic about their value and use. Coaches have largely remained resistant to using mental skills training. They too readily fall back on physical conditioning, skill performance, and/or game strategies as the important emphases for training. It is not the trained state or level of skill that is displayed during practice that is the major issue for coaching, but rather, the teaching of the mental skills so that those factors can be displayed under the stress of competition.

To ignore mental skills training of the type discussed is a dereliction of a duty of coaching. Psychology offers many performance determinants, only a few being addressed here. It needs to be recognized that psychology becomes more important, the higher the standard of competitor. It has been reported that psychological factors are better discriminators of high-level performance capacity than physiological measures. Psychology has a major role to play in determining the levels of performance achieved in competitive settings. Athletes should be appraised of the techniques and provided practice opportunities for their implementation as part of the evolving professions of coaching and sport psychology.

Personality, Emotions, and Health

Psychological factors are involved in causing and in healing many ailments of the body. Some researchers are just discovering these connections scientifically, although Chinese medicine was based on this idea 3000 years ago. A public television series and a book by Bill Moyers, *Healing and The Mind,* document in an interesting way the new mind/body methods of treating pain, stress, cancer (at least the emotional aspects of having cancer), etc. The impact of our emotions on our physical health is called

Mind-Body medicine. They are beginning to learn about emotions influencing our body, e.g. sexually abused women develop a smaller hippocampus. Psychotherapy and self-help, if effective, produce physical changes... we may not know where the changes are but there are no ghosts in the body.

What does "no ghosts in the body" mean? It means that real, physical events carry out or mediate these mind-body connections. Most scientists believe that no thought, no feeling, and no mental change ever occurs without something physical changing in the body. For example, when long-term stress weakens an organ in the body, like the heart, the stress is physically present for months in some form in the brain, in the general nervous system, and in the weakened organ.

Likewise, when a discussion in therapy or use of a self-help method improves some physical condition, the change mechanism between talk (or method) and the illness takes place physically somewhere in the body—nerves associated with thoughts change in the brain, messages are sent in the nervous system, conditions of the muscles change, hormones flow, the immune system activates or shuts down, etc.

There is no mystical magic here. It may seem like magic to you when you are able to influence your thoughts, i.e. neuronal action, which in turn may affect our feelings, then your physical health, then your psychological health, etc. But every action has a physical component (no ghosts) and is lawful and potentially understandable. In case you are thinking that psychological factors are a minor part of "medicine" or health care as we currently know it, consider this: the seven top health risks are behavioral—smoking, overeating, drinking & drugging, injuries, suicide, violence and sexually transmitted diseases. Seven of the nine leading causes of death, such as auto accidents, have important behavioral components. Health is a complex matter and the current professionals on both sides are ill prepared to understand both mental and physical health.

Changes are needed! Perhaps we need a new profession that understands both psychological/relationship problems and physical illnesses. Perhaps we need to automate the initial psychological/medical diagnostic evaluation, so that everyone can easily get an annual check up. Perhaps everyone also needs to educate themselves so that self-diagnosis and self-care is much more thorough and effective. A fascinating 1995 finding from the 1921 Terman study of 1,528 bright California children: going through your parents' divorce as a child (before 21) and/or going through a divorce yourself as an adult may shorten your life by perhaps as much as four years! In addition, certain personality traits, such as conscientiousness vs. irresponsibility, are also powerfully related to longevity.

Stress and personality factors influence how long we live as much as blood pressure, cholesterol level, or exercise-diet factors. These are not minor factors in your life. Likewise, a survey of 6,307 HMO patients found that 10% had anxiety that had not been treated (15% had been treated for anxiety). These untreated anxiety patients (80% also had untreated depression) had suffered marked reductions in general functioning, health, and well-being, resulting in their utilizing a high level of primary medical care. Science can't yet calculate how much the millions of untreated psychological disorders are costing us. Current thinking is: if we can express our emotions, talking openly or acting out our feelings, we can sometimes improve our health.

If we can relax, meditate, let ourselves be touched by others, or establish warm, caring relationships with others, sometimes we get better or get worse more slowly. Heart disease has been reversed by diet, exercise, meditation, and a support group. Women with breast cancer meeting with a support group lived twice as long as similar women who were not in such a group. We need human contact, with it we live longer, e.g. married cancer patients survive longer than unmarried ones. Between 10% and 30% of patients diagnosed as having psychological disorders are later found to have a physical or neurological problem. This highlights the need for referrals by psychotherapists to medical specialists.

Likewise, physicians should refer many of their patients to psychological-psychiatric specialists. For decades family physicians have estimated that 2/3rds of all the illnesses they treat are psychogenic, i.e. caused by psychological factors or stress. A 1995 report said 75% of complaints brought to MD's were psychological. It has been found that stress contributes to heart disease, strokes, cancer, breathing problems, accidents, cirrhosis of the liver, suicide, and many other leading causes of death. So, why is the treatment of most illness, physical and mental, still in the hands of very expensive MD's who have little training in dealing with psychological factors? Because our old laws and health insurance companies have enabled doctors to continue to monopolize health care and because science, until recently, has shown relatively little interest in treating psychogenic disorders.

Physical complaints can be, of course, clues to physical disorders, but pain and fatigue can be clues to psychological problems too. The pain is just as severe, regardless of whether the cause is physical or psychological. In the sections above about sources and effects of stress, we observed the stress-health connection. It works both ways: stress causes physical problems and physical factors cause emotions, e.g. the hormones in PMS cause tension, irritability, sadness, etc. PMS can be reduced by psychological self-help and chemicals.

Hippocrates, 400 years before Christ, thought certain personal-emotional traits were related to specific diseases. Dependable and conscientious young people live as much as four years longer than impulsive, undependable, self-centered people. People more prone to cancer tend to be depressed and/or worriers; they suppress their anxiety and hostile feelings, avoid conflict, act unassertively (overly patient) and feel hopeless; they long for closeness but feel abandoned in important relationships or at work, and just don't handle stress well.

People prone to get heart disease tend to be angry, impatient, and aggressive but sometimes avoid expressing their anger openly; they have repeatedly been annoyed and upset with people opposing them or getting in their way, and they resent not having the power to remove such people; they are suspicious and cynically distrustful, feeling no one cares; they are often trying to get away from someone who has hurt or disappointed them. Both the cancer-prone and the heart disease-prone persons feel tense and fearful. Many bad, unhappy things have happened in their lives which they think they were unable to prevent.

A few simple questions about these traits can supposedly identify the cancer or the heart disease prone person. Moreover, Eysenck says that psychotherapy—and I'd add perhaps self-help—can change a person's personality enough that serious disease can be prevented! Wonderful! What are we waiting for? Eysenck and Ronald Grossarth-Maticek provided "treatment" designed to help these patients

1. express their feelings,
2. learn to relax and handle stress,
3. overcome their passive-dependent nature, and
4. gain greater self-control.

Both kinds of "at risk" patients were taught to relax and overcome their fears (via desensitization), to be more confidently assertive but less angry and aggressive, to see themselves as able and actually be more in control (less passive-dependent or helpless), to express and release pent up feelings, and to know how to handle difficulties in their lives. The individual therapy involved 30 hours, but groups and shortened therapy lasting only 6-8 hours were also tried. The results of this therapy were impressive—the death rates 13 years later in the untreated groups are twice as high as in the treated groups. If 6 to 30 hours spent learning psychotherapy or self-help methods can reduce stress and increase the happiness and length of life, then we had better develop world-wide training programs for everyone soon. There is accumulating evidence that optimistic-pessimistic thinking (attitude) is also related to health.

Positive thinking, especially a belief in your ability to control an illness, is associated with good health and good performance in school and at work. Pessimists can learn to change their thinking; some will need professional help. For decades, the psychoanalysts have thought that complaining and psychological sickness were due to an excessive need for love and attention, stemming from feelings of neglect or criticism as a sensitive, needy child. Most psychodynamic therapists would try to uncover these old, still unsatisfied needs for love and bring them to the light of day, then they will go away.

3

Exercise Domain

Physical inactivity now constitutes one of the major behavioural risk factors to health in modern society. In view of this evidence, promoting physical activity is clearly an increasing public health priority. Physical activity engagement involves a complex interaction between biological, environmental, social, and psychological influences. Examining the motivational determinants of exercise behaviour has become a prominent topic in exercise psychology.

One theoretical approach to human motivation that is receiving increasing attention in the exercise domain is self-determination theory. Essentially, human motivation varies in the extent to which it is autonomous (self-determined) or controlling. Behaviours and actions that are autonomous are initiated freely and emanate from within oneself. In contrast, when behaviour is controlled, it is regulated by an external force.

The individual in this instance feels pressured to engage in the behaviour. There are three forms of motivation exist; namely, intrinsic motivation, extrinsic motivation, and amotivation, which, based on the level of autonomy associated with them, lie oft a continuum ranging from high to low self-determination, respectively.

Intrinsic motivation constitutes the most autonomous form of motivation, and refers to an inherent tendency possessed by all humans to seek out novelty and challenges, to extend and exercise their capabilities, to explore, and to learn. An individual who pursues a goal or activity because it is enjoyable or intrinsically captivating would display intrinsic motivation.

Not all human behaviours can be considered enjoyable, however. To understand how such behaviours are regulated, Self-determination Theory (SDT) proposes extrinsic motivation as an additional motivational force, and a process called internalisation. Extrinsic motivation refers to behaviours that are carried out to attain outcomes unrelated to the activity itself. Internalisation refers to an inherent tendency possessed by all humans to integrate the regulation of extrinsically motivated activities that are useful for effective functioning in the social world, but that are not inherently interesting.

SDT further proposes that the extent to which extrinsic motives are internalised can vary. A multidimensional conceptualisation of extrinsic motivation is hypothesised to exist, consisting of external, introjected, identified, and integrated regulations. These regulations lie on a continuum from lower to higher self-determination and reflect the extent of the internalisation process.

External regulation can be defined as exercising to either appease an external demand or to attain a reward. An example of an external regulation in the exercise domain is "I exercise because my friends and family say I should." Introjection, which is a slightly more self-determined form of extrinsic motivation, involves internalising the behaviour's regulation, but not fully accepting it as one's own. It is a relatively controlling form of regulation in which behaviours (e.g., exercise engagement) are performed to avoid negative emotions (e.g., anxiety, guilt), to support conditional self-worth, or to attain ego enhancement. Identified regulation reflects a more autonomous form of extrinsic motivation and reflects participation in an activity because one holds outcomes of the behaviour to be personally significant, although one may not enjoy the activity itself. For example, an individual who exercises because he or she values the benefits of exercise would display identified regulation in this domain.

In addition to specifying the different types of motivational regulations that may guide behaviour, SDT also details specific conditions that are responsible for more or less self-determined motivation. Specifically, SDT assumes that all humans possess three basic psychological needs; that is, the need for competence, autonomy, and relatedness. The need, for competence implies that individuals have a desire to interact effectively with the environment, to experience a sense of competence in producing desired outcomes, and to prevent undesired events.

The need for autonomy reflects a desire to engage in activities of one's choosing and to be the origin of one's own behaviour. Finally, the need for relatedness involves feeling connected, or feeling that one belongs in a given social milieu. Essentially, SDT suggests that the most self-determined forms of regulation will guide behaviour when the needs are satisfied. In contrast, low self-determination is a consequence of a thwarting of the three basic needs.

According to Deci and Ryan, SDT also specifies that differential levels of psychological need satisfaction in a given domain will result in diverse cognitive, affective, and behavioural consequences. Furthermore, need satisfaction has been postulated to influence outcomes indirectly via the promotion of different types of motivational regulation. It is assumed that intrinsic motivation will engender the most positive consequences, followed by identification.

However, some research findings in physical activity settings —as well as in other domains, such as politics and education—have been less conclusive regarding the positive implications of intrinsic motivation compared to other self-determined forms of regulation. Wilson et al. provided evidence suggesting that among participants recruited to engage in a 12-week structured exercise programme, identified regulation was a stronger predictor of self-reported exercise behaviour than was intrinsic motivation, although both regulations predicted exercise behaviours, exercise attitudes, and physical fitness. In addition, introjected regulation has been shown to be correlated positively with strenuous exercise behaviour in some studies, but not in others.

Ryan proposed that the characteristics of the situation in question will determine the extent to which intrinsic and internalised extrinsic regulations will produce positive behavioural outcomes. With respect to the latter, in contexts in which the activities undertaken are important, but may lack in intrinsic appeal, it is assumed that the innate tendency to internalise the role of such activities will be witnessed. In view of the considerable value that society bestows upon exercise for health aesthetic gains, research demonstrating that introjected and identified regulations positively predict exercise behaviour may indicate that, for some individuals, exercise engagement is maintained via the process described by Ryan. That is, exercise behaviour constitutes an externally motivated activity that requires internalisation to initiate and sustain action.

An additional tenet of SDT relevant to the current investigation concerns the social context in which individuals operate. According to SDT, autonomy-supportive contexts are conducive to need satisfaction and ensuing self determined motivational regulations. Such contexts are characterised by the minimisation of controls by significant others, the understanding of other people's perspectives, and the provision of choices that guide and facilitate the decision-making process.

Supporting these propositions, Wilson and Rodgers found that among female students and staff enrolled in a team-based intramural physical activity event, perceived autonomy support from friends was associated positively with intrinsic motivation and identified regulation. Furthermore, Standage, Duda, and Ntoumanis recently demonstrated that, among secondary school physical education students, an autonomy-supportive climate was related positively to satisfaction of the need for competence, autonomy, and relatedness, which, in turn, predicted greater self-determined motivation. However, as far as the present authors are aware, no study has considered the implications of an autonomy-supportive environment provided by an exercise class leader.

The present research study also examines whether, as assumed in SDT, an autonomy-supportive context provided by an exercise class leader corresponds to greater intrinsic motivation and identified regulation via the support provided for the three basic psychological needs. Based on the propositions of SDT and previous research in the physical, educational, and political domains, the researchers hypothesise first that positive relationships will be observed between psychological need satisfaction and identified and intrinsic motives; and a negative link will emerge between psychological need satisfaction and introjected and external regulations. Second, identified and introjected regulation and intrinsic motivation are expected to predict exercise behaviours positively and to mediate the relationship between psychological need satisfaction and exercise behaviours. In turn, external regulation is hypothesised to predict exercise behaviours negatively and to mediate the relationship between inadequate psychological need satisfaction and more negative behavioural outcomes. Third, it is predicted that perceived autonomy support (PAS) provided by the exercise class leader will be related positively to satisfaction of the three basic needs and self-determined motivation. Finally, PAS is also hypothesised to predict intrinsic motivation and identified regulation via satisfaction of the basic psychological needs.

METHOD

Participants (N = 369; 173 male, 192 female, 4 unspecified) ranged in age from 16 to 64 years (M = 31.86, SD = 11.28). The majority (88.7%) of the participants were White. One hundred six of the participants reported taking part in regular exercise classes, and thus constituted the subsample with which they examined relationships between PAS, need satisfaction, and motivational regulations. The subsample ranged in age from 16 to 62 years (M = 30.24, SD = 10.32).

An a priori power analysis, conducted using GPower, ensured that these sample sizes were sufficient to yield adequate statistical power for all statistical procedures planned and subsequently conducted in the current study. More specifically, to detect a significant finding (at the .05 level) at a desired power level of .95, a minimum of 143 participants was required for analyses conducted on the total sample, and 41 for the substudy analyses.

Measures

Psychological need satisfaction was measured via the 21-

item Basic Need Satisfaction at Work Scale, adapted by the authors to make it relevant to the exercise domain. This 21-item scale is based on a 15-item measure developed by Kasser, Davey, and Ryan to tap reported autonomy, relatedness, and competence in the work' domain. In the development of the original 15-item measure, some items were taken from the Intrinsic Motivation Inventory, support for which has been garnered in the physical domain. The 21-item Basic Need Satisfaction at Work scale exhibited alphas of .73 for competence, .84 for relatedness, and .79 for autonomy in a sample of U.S. workers.

The 21-item scale utilised by Deci et al., includes six items that measure competence, eight items that measure relatedness, and seven items that measure autonomy need satisfaction. Following the stem "Please indicate how true each of the following statements is for you, given your experiences of exercise," participants responded to each item on a 7-point scale ranging from 1 to 7.

Behavioural Regulation in Exercise Questionnaire. Participants completed the BREQ, which is a 15-item self-report measure assessing the reasons why people exercise. The BREQ includes scales assessing external, introjected, identified, and intrinsic regulations. Following the stem "Why do you exercise-" participants responded to each item on a 5-point scale ranging from 1 (not true for me) to 5. Previous research supports the BREQ's multidimensional four-factor structure, the invariance of this factor structure across gender, and the internal consistency of each subscale.

Godin Leisure Time Exercise Questionnaire. The GLTEQ was used to assess self-reported exercise behaviour. The GLTEQ contains three questions assessing the frequency of mild, moderate, and strenuous exercise engaged in (for a minimum of 15 min) during a typical week. Exercise behaviour scores can be calculated by multiplying weekly frequencies of strenuous (e.g., running, vigorous gym workout), moderate (e.g., easy cycling), and mild activities (e.g., easy walking) by 9, 5, and 3 METS (units of metabolic equivalence), respectively. An overall exercise behaviour score is calculated by summing the weighted product of each question as follows: (mild x 3) + (moderate x 5) + (strenuous x 9). Based on its correlations with objective indicators of exercise and physical fitness (e.g., exercise monitor and maximal aerobic capacity test scores), a previous study has concluded that the GLTEQ is a reliable and valid measure of leisure time exercise behaviour.

Perceived autonomy support. PAS from the exercise class leader was measured using a short (6 items) version of the original 15-item Health Care Climate Questionnaire. The original scale assesses participants' perceptions of the degree of autonomy support provided by a relevant health care provider and includes items such as "I feel that my health care provider provides me with choices and options." In the current study, the term "my health care provider" was replaced with "my exercise class leader," and participants were asked to respond to items in reference to the exercise class in which they participated most commonly. Participants responded to each item on a 7-point scale ranging from 1 (strongly disagree) to 7 (strongly agree). Previous studies using the original HCCQ revealed a one-factor solution measuring PAS and an alpha value of .95.

Procedure

The current research was approved by the ethics subcommittee of a university in the United Kingdom. Participants were recruited in a number of different settings, including sports clubs, public leisure centers, private fitness clubs, shops, and supermarkets in the West Midlands, UK. Participants were approached by the first author, who explained the purpose of the study, and were asked if they were willing to complete a multisection questionnaire packet. Those who agreed to take part provided their informed consent.

The first section of the questionnaire assessed psychological need satisfaction via exercise, motivational regulations, and exercise behaviours. Those participants who reported taking part in regular exercise classes completed an additional section of the questionnaire tapping PAS provided by the exercise class leader in the class in which they participated most commonly.

Results

Data were screened according to the recommendations of Tabachnick and Fidell. Four multivariate outliers were removed from the sample based on the Mahalonobis distance criterion, leaving a final sample of 369 participants. Examination of the assumptions associated with regression analyses (i.e., normality, linearity, and homoscedasticity) suggests that there were no particular problems in the data. More specifically, inspection of a scatterplot of the residuals indicates that both linearity and homoscedasticity assumptions were tenable.

To explore whether the data were marked by multicollinearity, both variance inflation (1.96-2.28) and tolerance (0.44-0.95) values were examined. No particular problems were found, since the obtained values are within acceptable limits. In addition, based on Belsley and Belsley, Kuh, and Welsch's suggestions, the condition indexes (CI) and variance proportions factors (VPF) for all multiple regression analyses were explored. Using the criterion proposed in Pedhazur, in no instances when the CI was greater than 10 did the VPF values observed exceed 0.50 for two or more predictors, suggesting that there was no collinearity in the data.

Reliability analysis and descriptive statistics

Internal consistency estimates and descriptive statistics were computed for all variables (Table 1). Reliability analyses indicate that, in general, internal consistency coefficients were greater than .70. However, the alpha values observed for two of the need scales were marginal: autonomy, a = .65; and competence, a = .65. Thus, results based on these variables should be interpreted with caution.

All participants engaged in at least some form of mild exercise. The mean level of total self-reported exercise was higher than that reported in previous studies examining the propositions of SDT in the exercise domain. Autonomy was the most highly satisfied need, followed by relatedness and competence. Intrinsic motivation was the most strongly endorsed exercise regulation, closely followed by identified regulation.

Exercise regulations, and exercise behaviours

Pearson correlations were computed between age, gender, autonomy, relatedness, arid competence need satisfaction, each of the BREQ subscales, and reported exercise behaviours. Small to moderate negative, correlations were observed between all three psychological needs and external regulation. Autonomy was correlated negatively with introjected regulation. Small to moderate positive correlations were observed between all three psychological needs and identified regulation and intrinsic motivation. Small to moderate positive relationships also emerged between the three needs and strenuous and total exercise behaviour.

Autonomy correlated positively with moderate exercise. No significant correlations emerged between the needs and mild exercise. Small to moderate positive relationships were observed between introjected and identified regulation and intrinsic motivation and strenuous and total exercise behaviour. None of the motivational regulations were correlated with mild and moderate exercise.

Total and strenuous exercise behaviours

Separate regression analyses were carried out to predict total and strenuous self-reported exercise from psychological need satisfaction and motivational regulations. Mild and moderate exercise were not examined because they did not correlate with the needs or the, regulations. Preliminary MANOVA revealed significant age and gender differences in exercise behaviours: age, $F(6, 686) = 8.51$, $p = .00$, Pillai's trace = .14; and gender, $F(3, 361) = 4.38$, $p = .01$, Pillai's trace = .04. In view of these results, as well as the fact that the existing literature has linked these characteristics to exercise behaviour, they controlled for their influence in the first step of the regression. By doing so, we could determine whether the theoretical constructs embedded in SDT accounted for additional variance in exercise behaviour above and beyond important demographic variables. Needs were entered in the second step of the regression, as they are postulated to affect behavioural outcomes indirectly via motivational regulations, which were entered in the final step.

As seen in Table 1, 18% of the variance in total exercise behaviour was explained by this model. Two of the variables contributed independently to the prediction of total exercise behaviour; namely, age and introjected regulation. Six of the variables contributed independently to the prediction of strenuous exercise behaviour: gender, age, competence, external regulation, introjected regulation, and identified regulation. This set of predictors predicted 32% of the variability in strenuous exercise behaviour.

Table 1: Summary of Hierarchical Regression Analysis Predicting Total Exercise Behaviour From Gender, Age, Psychological Needs, and Motivational Regulations

Independent variable	*Adj.* R^2	β	t
Step 1: $F(2, 344) = 13.10, p < .00$	.07		
Gender	- .03	- 0.56	
Age	–.26	–5.06	
Step 2: $F(5, 241) = 10.84, p < .00$	.13		
Gender	.01	0.13	
Age	–.24	–4.60	
Autonomy	.09	1.59	
Relatedness	- .04	- 0.58	
Competence	.22	3.51	
Step 3: F(9, 337) = 9.22, p < .00	.18		
Gender	- .03	- 0.68	
Age	–.21	–4.02	
Autonomy	.09	1.55	
Relatedness	–.03	–0.41	
Competence	.12	1.72	
External,, regulation	.09	- 1.58	
Introjected regulation	.15	2.46	
Identified regulation	.14	1.89	
Intrinsic motivation	.06	0.82	

The regression procedures of Baron and Kenny were employed to examine potential mediation effects. Three basic steps are proposed in establishing mediation: (a) the predictor variable (i.e., psychological need) must have an effect on the criterion variable (i.e., exercise behaviour); (b) the predictor variable (i.e., psychological need) must have an effect on the mediator variable (i.e., motivational regulation); and (c) the mediator (i.e., regulation) must affect the outcome (i.e., exercise behaviour), after controlling for the predictor (i.e., psychological need). To establish complete mediation, the effect of toe predictor on the outcome should be zero in the third step of the analysis. Partial mediation occurs when this effect is reduced, but remains statistically significant.

Given that SDT assumes that the three psychological needs coexist, it was decided that it made theoretical sense to include all needs in the same step and not to examine them independently. They followed the same logic for the motivational regulations. Examining Step 2 of the regression analyses results for total and strenuous exercise (Tables 1), it is apparent that competence was the only need to predict behavioural outcomes and thus meet Baron and Kenny's first criterion for establishing mediation.

Testing Baron and Kenny's second criterion for establishing mediation, competence was found to be a significant predictor of identified regulation ((3 = .46, p = .00), but none of the other regulations (these results are not included in Tables 1). Identified regulation was a positive predictor of strenuous, but not total exercise; thus, these findings rule out the possibility of mediation effects with regard to total exercise.

With respect to Baron and Kenny's third criterion for establishing mediation, the standardised beta coefficient for competence dropped from .36 to .23 (both ps = .00) when strenuous exercise was being predicted and the motivational regulations were entered into the regression equation, suggesting partial mediation. Using the Goodman I version of the Sobel test, as recommended by Baron and Kenny, partial mediation was confirmed. The reduction in the effect of competence on strenuous exercise behaviour as a result of identified regulation was significant (z = 2.56, p = .01).

One hundred six participants reported being members of an exercise group. Relevant data were screened according to the recommendations of Tabachnick and Fidell. No problems were found. The assumptions associated with multiple regression analysis (i.e., normality, linearity, and homoscedasticity) were examined, and again no problems were observed. Inspection of residual scatterplots indicates that both the linearity and homoscedasticity assumptions were tenable for all regression analyses. Furthermore, an examination of the variance inflation (1.011.65), tolerance (0.61–0.99), CI, and VPF values revealed that the data were not marked by collinearity.

Reliability analyses indicate that internal consistency coefficients were above .70 for all variables, except for autonomy (a = .64) and competence (a = .65). Thus, the present results based on these variables should be interpreted with caution. PAS scores ranged from 1 to 7 (M = 4.82, SD = 1.46).

Autonomy was the most highly satisfied need (M = 5.25, SD = 0.82), followed by relatedness (M = 5.16, SD = 1.03), and then competence (M = 5.07, SD = 0.90). Intrinsic motivation was the most highly endorsed form of motivation (M = 3.65, SD = 1.00), followed by identified (M = 3.61, SD = 0.82), introjected (M = 2.20, SD = 0.95), and external (M = 1.38, SD = 0.51) regulation.

Pearson correlations

Pearson correlations were calculated to examine relationships between age, gender, PAS, psychological need satisfaction, and motivational regulations. Low positive correlations were observed between PAS and autonomy (r = .26), and between PAS and competence (r = .27). A moderate positive association was observed between PAS and relatedness (r = .45). In addition, low and moderate positive correlations were observed between PAS and identified regulation ($r = .22$), and intrinsic motivation ($r = .36$).

As positive correlations were observed between PAS and identified regulation and intrinsic motivation, hierarchical multiple regression analyses were conducted with each of these regulations as the criterion variables. Age and gender were entered in the first step of the analysis. PAS was entered in the second step, and each of the psychological needs in the third step.

Test of mediation

The hypothesised mediating role played by psychological need satisfaction in the relationship between PAS and motivational regulations. PAS predicted intrinsic motivation, and thus met Criterion 1 of Baron and Kenny's procedures. PAS also significantly predicted autonomy ((3 = .28, $p = 01$), relatedness ((3 = .46, $p = .00$), and competence ((3 = .28, $p = .01$) need satisfaction via exercise, and thus met Baron and Kenny's second criterion for establishing mediation.

Competence was the only need (i.e., mediator) to predict intrinsic motivation (i.e., criterion variable) after controlling for the effect of PAS. After controlling for the effect of competence on the relationship between PAS and intrinsic motivation, the beta coefficient for autonomy support dropped from .35 ($p = .00$) to .23 ($p = .02$), suggesting partial mediation. The Goodman I version of the Sobel test revealed that this effect was significant ($z = 2.59$, $p = .01$).

Self-Determination Theory Framework

This framework is the study of Nikos Ntoumanis (University of Birmingham). This study examined whether contextual and personal motivational variables, taken from self-determination theory, could predict student cognetive and affective experiences in school physical education (PE). A theoretical framework that is being increasingly used to study motivation in PE is self-determination theory. SDT distinguishes among three types of behavioural regulation with varying degrees of self-determined motivation: intrinsic motivation, extrinsic motivation, and amotivation. Intrinsic motivation represents the highest degree of self-determined motivation and refers to situations in which individuals freely engage in activities that they find interesting and enjoyable and that offer the opportunity for learning.

In contrast, extrinsic motivation is evident when individuals perform an activity because they value its associated outcomes (eg., public praise, extrinsic rewards) more than the activity itself. Three types of extrinsic motivation have been measured in classroom education and in PE. These are identified regulation, introjected regulation and external regulation. Identified regulation represents behaviours with high degree of self-determined motivation. Individuals with high identified regulation have internalised the value of certain behaviours that they perform out of choice but without necessarily enjoying them.

For example, some students may participate in PE because they value the importance of exercise for their health. Introjected regulation describes extrinsically motivated behaviours which have been only slightly internalised and which are performed out of feelings of guilt or shame. For example, some students may participate in PE in order not to let their parents down. Last, external regulation represents the lowest degree of self-determined motivation and, refers to behaviours carried out in order to attain tangible rewards (e.g., social status among peers) or to avoid punishment.

The third type of behavioural regulation described by Deci and Ryan is amotivation. Whereas both intrinsic motivation and extrinsic motivation represent different degrees of volition, amotivation represents the absence of motivation. Amotivation is evident when individuals lack the intention and willingness to engage in a particular behaviour. It often results from feelings of incompetence and uncontrollability and is frequently linked up decisions to drop out of PE or school altogether.

The antecedents and outcomes of the different types of motivation have been described by Vallerand in his model of motivation. According to this model, a number of social factors can impact on the various types of motivation via the satisfaction of the fundamental human needs for competence, autonomy, and relatedness. Social factors that satisfy these needs Will promote self-determined forms of motivation. In contrast, social factors that undermine these needs will result in controlling motivation and amotivation. In turn, the various types of motivation can predict a number of cognitive, affective, and behavioural outcomes. Usually, intrinsic motivation and identified regulation predict the most positive outcomes, whereas amotivation and external regulation predict the most negative outcomes.

An important behavioural outcome that has been assessed in classroom education and sport is persistence (or drop out). For example, Vallerand et al., found support for a motivational model of high school drop out in a sample of 4,537 Canadian students. The results of structural equation modeling analysis showed that the degree of autonomy support provided by parents, teachers`, and the school administration influenced students' reported satisfaction of their needs for competence and autonomy (relatedness was not assessed). In turn, these two need satisfaction variables positively predicted an index of self-determined academic motivation. Finally, the more self-determined the students were the less likely they were to intend to drop out of high school. These behavioural intentions positively predicted (β = .24) students' actual drop out behaviour a year later.

Two studies have replicated the prospective design used by Valleranil et al. to examine drop out behaviour (or persistence) in youth sport. Pelletier et al. used a prospective 2-year design to examine persistence in competitive swimming in a sample of predominantly adolescent Canadign swimmers. The results of structural equation modeling analysis showed that swimmers' perception of coaches' autonomy support positively predicted self-determined motivation (intrinsic motivation and identified regulation), and unexpectedly, introjected regulation. In contrast, swimmers' perception of coaches' controlling style predicted swimmers' amotivation, external regulation, and introjected regulation.

Self-determined motivation predicted participation in swimming at two follow-ups (10 and 22 months later). Introjected regulation was a positive predictor of persistence at 10 months, but not at 22 months. External regulation and amotivation were negative predictors of persistence at the second follow-up and both follow-ups respectively. Last, mean comparisons between persistent and drop-out swimmers showed that the former, compared with the latter, had higher intrinsic motivation and identified regulation and lower external regulation and amotivation. No differences in introjected regulation were found. Pelletier et al. did not assess the three psychological needs postulated by SDT to mediate the effects of social factors on motivational regulations. Furthermore, autonomy support is only one aspect of the means by which coaches influence athletes' motivational experiences and behaviours.

In a subsequent study, Sarrazin et al. also tested a motivational model of drop out of sport (handball) with a sample of 335 French female adolescents. This study integrated aspects of SDT and achievement goal theory. Sarrazin et al. examined the social factor of motivational climates, that is, whether coaches are perceived to evaluate and reward their athletes on the basis of task (self-referenced) or ego (comparative) competence criteria. The results of structural equation modeling analysis showed that a taskinvolving motivational climate was more conducive to the satisfaction of the three psychological needs compared with an egoinvolving climate. Of the three need satisfaction variables, autonomy (and, to a much lesser extent, competence and relatedness) predicted an index of self-determined motivation.

In turn, the latter negatively predicted behavioural intentions to drop out of handball. Twenty-one months later, 22% of the handball players dropped out of their sport. The path from behavioural intentions to drop out behaviour was moderate (β = .55). Comparison of mean scores between persistent players and drop outs showed that the former perceived the motivational climate as being more taskinvolving, experienced greater satisfaction of their three psychological needs, and reported higher intrinsic motivation and lower amotivation and intentions to drop out.

The studies by Pelletier et al. and Sarrazin et al. are interesting because they clearly show the importance of contextual and personal motivational factors in predicting drop out behaviour in sport. However, it is important to assess multiple outcomes, and not only intention and behaviour, in order to have a more comprehensive understanding of how personal and environmental factors affect individuals' motivational experiences. Furthermore, both studies, as well as the study by

Vallerand et al., relied exclusively on self-reports which inadvertently inflate common method variance.

Admittedly, from a theoretical viewpoint, self-reports are more appropriate. This is because SDT argues that student perception of significant others' autonomy support is a more important determinant of their motivational experiences compared with "objective" measures of autonomy support. Furthermore, self-reports are needed to assess students' motivational regulations as well as the degree to which their needs have been satisfied. However, in terms of student behaviour, some more "objective" measures (e.g., teacher ratings) can be used.

In sum, the primary purpose of the present study was to expand on previous studies on dropout by looking at multiple antecedents of self-determined motivation and how the latter can predict a number of important consequences, including dropping out of or participating in optional PE programmes. More specifically, although most of the past research has restricted the examination of sociocontextual antecedents of motivation to autonomy support (or the lack of it), this study also assessed the extent to which PE teachers emphasised task-involving criteria for success and promoted cooperative learning.

Research by Ntoumanis has shown that the emphasis PE teachers place on individual improvement criteria (e.g., mastering new or difficult skills) can result in student competence need satisfaction reducing the controlling nature of interpersonal ability comparisons. In addition, the promotion of learning via student cooperate can result in stronger feelings of relatedness, among students. In terms of the motivational outcomes assessed, besides intention and behaviour which were measured in previous studies on drop out, this study also assessed levels of negative affect, concentration in the class, and effort. These variables were chosen because they have been shown to be indicators of student interest and investment in learning.

An SDT-based motivational model was tested that hypothesised that the degree to which PE teachers supported their students' needs would predict the latter's need satisfaction. The indicators of need support were autonomy support, teacher emphasis on individual improvement criteria, and promotion of cooperative learning. It was also hypothesised that student need satisfaction would predict an index of self-determined motivation. In turn, it was expected that self-determined motivation would negatively predict negative affect and positively predict student levels of concentration and effort in the class as well as their intentions to participate in optional PE. Last, it was expected that behavioural intentions would positively predict actual behavioural choices.

In terms of mean differences between participants and nonparticipants, it was hypothesised that the participants would rate their past experiences in compulsory PE as more adaptive. More specifically, it was expected that the participants would report that their teachers used more task-involving criteria for success, and were more autonomy supportive compared with the teachers of the nonparticipants. Furthermore, the participants were expected to report greater need satisfaction, more self-determined motivation, and less controlling motivation and amotivation compared with, the nonparticipants. Last, the participants were predicted to report more adaptive affective, cognitive and behavioural experiences in compulsory PE.

Method

The participants were 460 (girls n = 145; boys n = 315) British 15-year-old school students from eight schools in the north of England. Almost all students were Caucasians. As explained in the Procedure below, follow-up information regarding participation status was obtained from 302 of those students. With the exception of the confirmatory factor analyses that used the full sample, all other analyses reported in the Results section used the subsample of 302 students.

Measures

Learning Climate Questionnaire. The short form of the LCQ (6 items) was used to measure student perceptions of the autonomy support provided by their PE teachers. The wording of the items was adapted to be applicable to PE classes. An example item is "My PE teachers encourage me to ask questions." Each item was measured on a 5-point scale (1 = strongly disagree; 5 = strongly agree). Williams and Deci reported that an exploratory factor analysis of the long form of the LCQ (15 items) produced one factor that had a Cronbach's alpha coefficient of .96.

Perceived Motivational Climate in Sport Questionnaire-2. Two facets of a task-involving motivational climate were measured with a PE adaptation of the PMCSQ-2. These facts were the emphasis by the PE teachers on individual criteria for student improvement and the extent to which the teachers promote cooperative student learning. An example item of the former factor is "In this PE class, the PE teacher makes sure students improve on skills they're not good at." An example item of cooperative learning is "In this PE class, students help each other learn." Both factors were measured on 5-point scales (1 = strongly disagree; 5 = strongly agree). Evidence for the validity of the PMCSQ-2 has been provided by Newton et al. In the same study, both factors were shown to have adequate internal reliability coefficients.

Basic Need Satisfaction Scale. This is a 21-item questionnaire that taps perceptions of competence (6 items), relatedness (8 items), and autonomy need satisfaction (7 items). The scale was used by Deci et al. to measure need satisfaction at work, but it was modified in the present study to assess need satisfaction in PE. Example items are "I feel that I can make a lot of inputs to deciding what to do in PE" (autonomy), "I really like the students I exercise with in PE" (relatedness), and "I have been able to learn interesting new skills in PE" (competence). All factors were measured on 7-point scales (I = not at all true; 7 = very true). Deci et al. reported adequate alpha coefficients for the three factors with a U.S. sample; however, with a Bulgarian sample, the alphas for relatedness and autonomy were low (a = .57 and a = .57, respectively).

Self-Regulation Questionnaire. To measure the different types of motivation postulated by SDT, a questionnaire presented by Goudas et al. was used. This questionnaire adapted to PE the Self-Regulation Questionnaire, which measures intrinsic motivation, as well as identified, introjected and external regulations in the classroom. Furthermore, Goudas et al. adapted to PE the Amotivation subscale of the Academic Motivation Scale. The students in the present study responded to 20 items measured on scales ranging from 1 (strongly disagree) to 7 (strongly agree). Each item followed the stem "I take part in PE . . ." Example items are "because PE is fun" (intrinsic motivation), "because I want to improve in sport" (identified regulation), "because I would feel bad about myself if I did not" (introjected regulation), "so that the teachers will not yell at me" (external regulation), and "but I cannot see what I am getting out of PE" (amotivation). The adapted SRQ has been used in various studies in PE and has been shown to have clear factor structure and high internal reliabilities with the exception of introjected regulation whose alpha coefficient is usually slightly below .70.

Negative affect in PE. Four adjectives that measure negative affect (e.g., "disappointed," "embarrassed") were used to assess typical negative affect experienced by students in PE. These adjectives were taken from Ebbeck and Weiss. Each adjective was assessed on a 5-point scale ranging from 1 (never) to 7 (always). Participants responded to the stem "In this PE class I feel . . ." Ebbeck and Weiss have provided psychometric evidence for the use of these items in youth sport.

Concentration in the PE classes. Three items were written in the present study to measure students' concentration in PE classes. An example item is "In PE, I concentrate on the skills/tasks I have to do." Each item was assessed on a 7-point scale (I = strongly disagree; 7 = strongly agree).

Intention to participate in optional PE. Two items were written in the present study to measure students' intention to participate in optional PE classes in the following school year. An example item is "I intend not to do PE next year." Each item was assessed on a 7-point scale (1 = strongly disagree; 7 = strongly agree).

Teacher rating of students' effort. The PE teachers were asked to provide an overall rating of each student's levels of effort in PE. For each student, one PE teacher provided a single rating on a 7-point scale (1 = no effort at all; 7 exceptionally high levels of effort). The PE teachers were told that an objective of the study was to assess how hard the students try to improve their skills and whether they "give their beat" during PE lessons.

Procedure

Informed consent was obtained from the participants and the head teacher of each school. The questionnaires were administered at the start of a PE lesson. Prior to questionnaire administration, the students were told that their responses would be kept confidential add, that hey could decline to participate or withdraw at any time. The questionnaires were administered in late spring and early summer to 460 fifteen-year-old students. In the fall of the same year, the schools were contacted and were asked to confirm whether the students had enrolled on an optional Year 12 PE programme.

In Great Britain, after the age of 16 years, participation in PE is optional. Academic-that is, science-based PE programmes offered by some schools to 16-year-olds were not targeted, because the purpose of this study was to focus on health-enhancing physical activity programmes. To protect anonymity, the students were matched on the basis of their dates of birth, gender, and school identification. It was possible to obtain information for 302 students, of whom 171 chose to enroll in an optional PE programme. There are various reasons that it was not possible to obtain information for the remaining 158 students': (a) Some students dropped out of school altogether; (b) others relocated to a different part of the country; and (c) some students moved to a different school in the same area, but the new school declined to provide the necessary information.

Results

Confirmatory factor analysis using the full sample of 460 participants was carried out for all scales to examine their factorial structure. To evaluate model fit, the two-index presentation strategy was used. According to this strategy, the standardised root-mean-square residual (SRMR) should be used along with one or more incremental or absolute fit indices to evaluate the fit of the confirmatory factor model. Hit and Bentler found that, among all fit indices, the SRMR (a) is the most sensitive to misspecification in both simple and complex models and (b) is less sensitive to sample size and violations of distributional assumptions. According to Hit and Bentler, a value close to .08 for SRMR, combined with a value close to .95 for the comparative fit index (CFI) and a value close to .06 for the root-mean-square error of approximation (RMSEA), is indicative of good model fit.

For brevity reasons, the results of the confirmatory factor analyses are not presented here but are available on request. All scales were found to have satisfactory fit indices with the exception of the Need Satisfaction scale whose fit indices were very poor: Sattora-Bentler χ^2 (186, N = 460) = 838.60, $p < .001$; SRMR = .11; CFI = .70; RMSEA = .10. Inspection of the modification indices and the standardised loadings suggested the removal of all negatively worded items. Therefore, these items (3 from each BNSC subscale) were excluded from any further analyses. The revised Need Satisfaction scale had a satisfactory model fit: Sattora Bentler χ^2(186, N = 460) = 838.60, $p < .001$; SRMR = .06; CFI = .93; RMSEA = .06.

Descriptive statistics and internal reliability coefficients for the 302 participants are presented in Table 5. The descriptive statistics and alphas for the full sample of 460 students were almost identical and are not presented here. According to Table 5, the participants' mean scores were slightly above the midpoint for all variables with the exception of amotivation, external regulation, introjected regulation, and negative affect: The teachers' average ratings of student effort were moderate to high. The alpha coefficients for all the subscales were satisfactory with the exception of competence need satisfaction and introjected regulation, whose reliabilities were marginal.

The intercorrelations among the need support factors and among the need satisfaction factors were moderate in size. Of the three need satisfaction variables, competence had in general the highest correlations with the need support factors. The three need satisfaction variables were positively correlated with self-determined motivation regulations and negatively with amotivation and external regulation. Negative affect was correlated positively with amotivation and external regulation and negatively with self-determined motivation regulations. The opposite pattern of relationships was observed between concentration, future intentions, participation status, and the motivational regulations.

Motivational Differences Between Participants and Non-participants

A secondary purpose of this study was to examine differences between those who chose optional PE and those who did not in terms of need support, need satisfaction, motivational regulations, and certain motivational outcomes in the previous school year. As previous research has shown mean gender differences in many of the variables under investigation, and because chi-square analysis indicated that significantly more boys opted for PE, participation status was examined in conjunction with gender.

Four two-way multivariate analyses of variance (MANOVAs) were carried out to examine participation and gender differences in need support (autonomy support, cooperative learning, individual improvement), need satisfaction (competence, relatedness, autonomy) motivational regulations (intrinsic motivation, identified regulation, introjected regulation, external regulation, amotivation), and motivational consequences (negative affect, teacher ratings of effort, concentration, future intentions), respectively. An advantage of MANOVA over a series of analyses of variance is the protection against inflated Type I error stemming from multiple testing. In each MANOVA, following a significant omnibus test for main effect or interaction, Bonferroni adjustments were carried out to further protect against Type I error.

With regard to need support, only the main effect for participation status was significant: Hotelling's t = 0.04; F(3, 295) = 4.28, $p < .01$; partial $\eta^2 = .04$. Follow-up analysis showed that the participants, compared with the nonparticipants, reported significantly higher perceptions of teacher emphasis on student individual improvement criteria. No differences in autonomy support or cooperative learning were found In relation to need satisfaction, there were significant effects for participation status: Hotelling's *t* = 0.08; F(3, 293) = 7.83, p < :001; partial $\eta^2 = .07$; gender: Hotelling's *t* = 0.05; F(3, 293) = 4.04, $p < .01$; partial $\eta^2 = .05$; as well as for the interaction between age and gender.

Hotelling's t = 0.03; F(3, 293) = 2.85, $p < .05$; partial $\eta^2 = .03$. The only significant gender difference in need satisfaction was found with regard to relatedness with the girls scoring higher than the boys. An interesting interaction also emerged between gender and participation status predicting autonomy need satisfaction. Whereas male participants and male nonparticipants had very similar scores in autonomy need satisfaction (M = 4.08 and M = 4.12, respectively), female participants had substantially higher scores than female nonparticipants (M = 4.59 and M = 3.84, respectively).

The MANOVA for motivational regulations showed significant main effects for participation status: Hotelling's t = 0.16; F(5, 290) = 8.99, $p < .001$; partial $\eta^2 = .13$, and gender: Hotelling's t = 0.09; F(5, 290) = 5.02, $p < .001$; partial $\eta^2 = .08$, but the interaction effect was not significant. More specifically, the participants were less amotivated and more self-determined compared with the nonparticipants. Surprisingly no differences in controlling motivation were found. Furthermore; the boys scored significantly higher on intrinsic motivation than did the girls. Last, with regard to the motivational outcomes assessed in this study, the MANOVA revealed a significant main effect for participation status only: Hotelling's t = 0.17; $F(4, 281) = 11.96$, $p < .001$; partial $\eta^2 = .15$. The participants reported stronger intentions to opt for optional PE in Year 12, and their efforts in the class were rated higher by their teachers than were the efforts of the nonparticipants. No differences in negative affect or concentration levels were found.

The results also showed that need satisfaction predicted self-determined motivation. This is in accordance with SDT, which postulates that the satisfaction of the needs for competence, autonomy, and relatedness is essential for intrinsic motivation and self-determination. Furthermore, in agreement with Vallerand's model, self-determined motivation was found to predict positive motivational outcomes. More specifically, self-determined motivation positively predicted levels of concentration in the class. This finding makes conceptual sense, because students who enjoy PE or appreciate its value will pay more attention to the teachers and will concentrate on the tasks at hand, compared with those who feel pressured or amotivated to participate in the lesson.

Furthermore, self-determined motivation was a negative predictor of negative affect and a positive predictor of student effort. These findings also make conceptual sense since individuals with high self-determined motivation do not feel guilty, pressured, or bored to participate in PE. Similar relationships between self determined motivation and negative affect indices have been reported by Ntoumanis and by Standage, Duda, and Ntoumanis. The positive path between self-determined motivation and effort was also theoretically expected.

Although internally controlling regulations can also predict what Ryan, Koestner, and Deci labelled ego-involved (i.e., means-end) persistence, this is usually the case in experimental situations and for relatively short periods of time when one's self-worth is at stake. However, over the course of a school year, self-determined motivation is needed to sustain high levels of effort. The relatively weak path between self-determined motivation and effort might be due to a number of reasons. First, teacher ratings were obtained as opposed to student self-reports, reducing common method variance, which inflates the strength of relationships. Second, it is possible that, for various reasons, teachers did not hold accurate perceptions of student effort. Third, a multi-item rating scale could have improved the reliability of the teacher ratings and could have potentially increased the size of the path coefficient between self-determined motivation and student effort.

One of the most interesting parts of the model was the significant path coefficient between intention to participate in optional PE courses and actual behavioural choices. The path was positive, indicating that holding positive behavioural intentions, based on need satisfaction and self-determined motivation, can lead to actual decisions to be physically active in PE. The size of the path coefficient was moderate in size-larger than the one reported by Vallerand et al. but smaller than the coefficient reported by Pelletier, Seguin-Levesque, and Legault.

An explanation for the modest size of the coefficient is that when the students reported their intentions to join optional PE programmes in the following school year they were not aware of the type of sport activities that would be offered. Perhaps if they had been aware of the type of available activities, then the path coefficient would have been stronger. In addition, the modest path coefficients might reflect changes in students' priorities that, took place after the spring data collection. Students in this age group start preparing for school examinations that can influence their future admission to university programmes.

Therefore, it is possible that some students might have decided to invest more time preparing for such exams as opposed to enrolling in optional physical activity programmes. From a public health perspective, it is important that future research examine whether the majority of students who do not participate in optional PE programmes adopt a sedentary lifestyle or whether they remain physically active in sport clubs outside schools. Obviously, in the latter case, there is not much cause for concern. However, children who report negative experiences in PE because of low perceived ability, overemphasis on competition, or social evaluation concerns are unlikely to be physically active in or out of school.

Self-referenced criteria, which are promoted in task-involving motivational climates, are relatively controllable. Therefore, students who are evaluated and rewarded on the basis of such criteria are likely to report high levels of effort and persistence. Spray also found that participants in optional PE courses reported significantly higher perceptions of task-involving climate in compulsory PE compared with nonparticipants. There was also a nonsignificant trend in the present findings, indicating that participants perceived higher levels of autonomy support in the past by their PE teachers.

While autonomy support might benefit students who have some experience with particular sport activities or skills, it might be less effective with students who lack sport experience. In such situations, supporting student autonomy will have little effect on their motivation unless there is a certain degree of guidance and structure from their PE teachers. Reeve also argued that student motivation is optimal under conditions in which teachers provide optimal structure along with high autonomy support. Therefore, it would be informative if future studies examined whether autonomy support and structure can play a complimentary role in promoting motivation in PE classes.

Perceptions of competence are very important in PE because variations in physical ability level can be easily observed. Therefore, those students who feel physically competent are more likely to find PE interesting and fun, and, given the choice, will continue to participate in PE (hence, the medium effect size for competence need satisfaction). Relatedness is also important because young people often form friendships through their sport participation. Last, the participants reported greater autonomy need satisfaction compared with the nonparticipants. However, this difference was overshadowed by a significant gender by participation status interaction which indicated that autonomy need satisfaction was related to differences in participation status in females only.

Prusak, Treasure, Darst, and Pangrazi have also highlighted the role of gender when examining autonomy and choice in PE classes. The authors argued that adolescent girls are particularly underserved by traditional PE offerings, but their motivation can be increased if they are offered choices. The participants were also significantly less amotivated and more self-determined compared with the nonparticipants. This finding is in line with existing results in the literature.

The participants, compared with the nonparticipants, exhibited more effort in the class during the previous school year and had stronger behavioural intentions to participate in PE. The finding that students who chose optional PE courses had in the past received higher ratings of effort from their PE teachers makes intuitive sense. However, it is not clear the extent to which a behavioural confirmation process was in operation. For example, it is possible that students who were perceived by their teachers to be self-determined were rated higher by their teachers or were given more attention compared with less self-determined students. Increased teacher attention may well explain why self-determined students exerted more effort and were more likely to choose PE compared with students whose teachers perceived them to be less self-determined. Ratings of student effort by independent observers could be used in future studies in conjunction with teacher and student ratings. The results of this study also showed a nonsignificant trend indicating that participants reported lower negative affective experiences in compulsory PE compared with nonparticipants. In the SDT framework, emotions are considered as sources of information that precede and energise behaviour.

Negative affective experiences in PE, such as boredom or anxiety, have been previously related to amotivation. Further research is needed to examine whether such negative affective experiences are also associated with future behavioural choices. The lack of significant differences in concentration levels between participants and nonparticipants could be due to the possibility that, even though some students may lack intrinsic interest in PE, they have to retain some levels of concentration during the class because of the interactive nature of many sport skills. Future research could use more sensitive measures of concentration that will assess the frequency with which students are distracted by nonrelevant stimuli and thoughts during lessons.

Similar to the findings of Pelletier et al., very few significant gender differences emerged in the variables of interest. Specifically, the boys, compared with the girls, reported significantly higher intrinsic motivation and lower relatedness need satisfaction. However, all associated effect sizes were very small, indicating that gender did not play a contributing role in the present findings. Nevertheless, chi-square analysis showed that boys were more likely than girls to opt for optional PE. This finding could be due to the fact that PE activities are traditionally oriented toward competitive team sports, which boys tend to favour.

Although causal inferences cannot be drawn from this study, the results are useful because they are in line with findings of previous studies on dropout. Besides the noncausal nature of the presented evidence, a further limitation of this study is that the analysis did not take into consideration the nested structure of the data. Unfortunately, no information on student classes was obtained. Although schools could hoe been used as a contextual variable, such analysis would have produced an inaccurate estimate of the variation at the contextua level, because of the very small number of schools.

Future research with larger numbers of contextual units should employ multilevel structural equation modeling to examine the drop-out model at both the between- and within-group levels. Future research should also examine the contextual factors that determine the extent to which PE teachers will provide need support. Furthermore, the reciprocal effects of teacher motivation on student motivation should be investigated in the context of PE. Also, in addition to teachers, the influence of peers on student motivation should be examined. Research about how peer interactions affect children's motivation in youth sport and PE is limited.

4

Sports Fitness

Fitness is affected favourably or unfavourably by the influences which contribute to, or detract from, all of the functioning parts of the organism and the organism as a whole. To attain and maintain fitness, one must live the intelligent life, making constant adjustments to one's environment and accepting the responsibility of changing it when such change is needed.

This means a rational programme of activity, an adequate and balanced diet, ability to control psychological and physical stimuli and to resolve the resultant stress that they cause, prompt and competent medical care, and, of course, a sound philosophical basis for coping with contingencies for which no planning can be made.

In short, the intelligent life means rational judgements tempered with human emotional overtones which add both spice and grandeur. Physical education is generally concerned with specific aspects of fitness dealing with physiologic competence. This is not to indicate that such concern can be placed in a vacuum called "physical" or "the body" and be treated in isolation from the whole. But it does imply that physical educators mainly and by tradition use as their tool for total fitness the neuromuscular aspects of man and attempt to condition him though activity for the stress he will inevitably meet.

Physical education's concern with fitness is functional rather than anatomical, although both areas are interrelated. Our scientists, philosophers, holists, educators, better-informed physical educators, and even our poets have pro-claimed that there is more to fitness than muscle strength. A conference of such people described fitness as "that state which characterizes the degree to which the person is able to function." This implies the ability of each person to develop his potentialities most effectively.

In addition, the conference agreed that fitness is maintained at a high level only if motivation is continuously present! An inner desire is required; the activities which produce fitness must have meaning. The conference listed seven mutually interdependent components of fitness:

1. Optimum organic health consistent with heredity and the application of present health knowledge.
2. Sufficient coordination, strength, and vitality to meet emergencies, as well as the requirements of daily living.
3. Emotional stability to meet the stresses and strains of modern life.
4. Social consciousness and adaptability with respect to the requirements of group living.
5. Sufficient knowledge and insight to make suitable decisions and arrive at feasible solutions to problems.
6. Attitudes, values, and skills which stimulate satisfactory participation in a full range of daily activities.

7. Spiritual and moral qualities which contribute the fullest measure of living in a democratic society.

The term physical fitness has a questionable connotation, numerous attempts have been made to evaluate "the functional capacity for the task". Both muscular performance and organic function have been used as criteria for measuring fitness. Obviously, anatomical fitness, meaning possession of all the parts and organs of the body which are necessary for the task, is basic.

Physiological fitness means skillful performance and rapid recovery, and psychological fitness implies emotional stability, drive, intelligence, motivation, and educability. Ideally, a fitness test should take into account all of these aspects of fitness. Lacking such, people have had to assess themselves against standards of so-called normal structure, control, and psychological elements in approaches to tasks, and then to measure how much work a person can do in a limited time and observe what happens to the body during and after the task.

The fit man usually shows the following physiological advantages over the unfit man of the same height and weight when both are performing the same piece of moderate work which both can sustain in a steady state: lower oxygen consumption, slower pulse rate during work, larger stroke volume of the heart, lower blood lactate during work, and faster return of blood pressure and heart rate to normal after work.

If both a fit and an unfit man are performing the same piece of exhausting work which neither can sustain in a steady state, the fit man usually shows longer duration of effort before exhaustion, higher oxygen consumption, slower maximal heart rate, larger stroke volume, higher blood lactate and faster return of blood pressure and heart rate to normal after work. Since there is always a syndromic reaction to an exercise bout in terms of cardiorespiratory function, a relatively accurate measure of functional fitness can be obtained by evaluating the response of a single factor.

Post exercise heart rate has been used most often to measure this particular syndrome and hence to measure functional fitness. One of the most valid. reliable, and easy to administer tests of physical fitness in terms of heart recovery rate is the Harvard fatigue Laboratory Test of Physical Fitness, usually referred to as the Harvard Step Test.

It appears that "physical" fitness can be maintained only be continuing to train muscularly at atleast a minimal level. There is no "easy" way to fitness. Lying on a vibrating couch, being massaged, or riding an electrically driven bike, will do little to maintain physical condition. Active, dynamic exercise is the only way to organic efficiency. Such exercise results is strength, agility, flexibility, coordination, and ultimately endurance.

Physical fitness programmes rely heavily upon running, vigorous sports, and gymnastics, for fitness is a "do-it-yourself" matter. Functional integrity and well-being are achieved only as one remains active. Fitness can be lost as quickly as it is gained. The current way of life in the United States does a great deal to discourage organic fitness on the part of children as well as adults.

The rubber tire has replaced shoe leather electronic conveniences have replaced shoulder girdle muscles, and a life of non-movement has replaced the vigorous activity of the past. It seems quite feasible that those who have matured in a world which does not encourage gross body movement will have to pay the penalty in terms of weakness and softness. Obviously, there is no standard fitness for all; fitness is "neither a fixed standard nor an average, but rather an objective," It varies according to sex, occupation, hereditary pattern, and level of interest. What is fitness for one may well be softness for another.

Physical education has the unique opportunity to help people attain an organic well-being through activity—an opportunity that no other discipline has. Physical educators would be less than true to their heritage and would be ignoring their responsibility if they did not consider such fitness as essential by-product of their particular programme. However, let it be noted that the intelligent physical educator should be discreet in his enthusiasm for a "unique contribution" for there is real danger in equating physical education with physical fitness alone. The two are not interchargeable terms in spite of the fact that total fitness is one of the basic aims of all education.

Fitness Characteristics

Organic fitness is acquired by undertaking a specified amount of physiological work which must be continually increased in terms of resistance and speed. Only through overload can the body be adequately conditioned. If training is systematic. Certain specific results may be anticipated: there will be systemic change in the body an functional change in individual reaction.

Systemically, training should result in a respiration adjustment that increases the expan-sion of the chest, slows down the rate of breathing, and deepens inspiration and expiration. Usually, oxygen is more readily available to the blood; the trained person seems to need less air than the untrained. The minute volume of the person who is trained has a tendency to decrease while the oxygen absorption tends to increase.

The endurance of the respiratory muscles is raised, so that the discomfort of chest restriction felt during exercise is reduced. Alveolar tissue tends to form new elements. There is a marked hypertrophy of the diaphragm muscle. Each of these respiratory adjustments makes the respiratory system more efficient. Since there seems to be evidence that respiration is the keystone to endurance, efficient respiratory patterns are an essential aspect of total fitness. It should also be noted that the lungs cannot store oxygen, and the use of oxygen by athletes has no known physiological advantage.

The circulatory system is dramatically influenced by exercise. The capillaries in the active muscles multiply, allowing the muscles to have a larger blood supply. Capillary increase takes place not only in the active muscle tissue but in heart muscle and in the motor area of the cerebral cortex. All of this enriches the circulatory process and contributes to the efficiency of the total person. Severe and persistent training results in hypertrophy of the heart beyond the limits usually acknowledged as normal. There is nothing alarming about this enlargement.

The term which is sometimes applied to it, athlete's heart, is to be valued rather than feared. Like any other muscle, the heart gets larger through exercise, and this hypertrophy has organic integrity. It is a normal result of intense activity. Heart size is related to thoracic circumference as well as hereditary factors.There seems to be a tendency for sports which require long endurance to enlarge the right side of the heart, while intensive brief exertion produces its greatest change on the left side of the heart.

With training there is a reduction in the heart rate. The heart beats more slowly but more powerfully. The increased stroke volume offsets the decreased heart rate so that really more blood is sent out with each stroke. As a result of the greater minute volume, the heart is able to pump larger amounts of blood to the active muscles during exercise and so permit more muscular endurance. During exercise it is possible for the minute volume of the blood to increase as much as ten times.

Exercise raises the velocity of circulation flow through cardiac adjustment and skeletal muscle contraction. During training, systolic blood pressure has a disposition to rise; increased diastolic pressure after exertion is the usual systemic identification of many conditioned athletes. the frequency of heart rate during exercise bouts is a linear relationship with the work load: the heavier the load, the harder the heart must work. The only exception to this rule occurs when the physiological work load calls for a sustained contraction such as the press in weight lifting. This contraction has a tendency to hinder the return of the venous blood to the heart. Holding the breath, which usually accompanied sustained contraction, increases intrathoratic pressure and thus also inhibits venous return. As a result of training, the heart returns to its homeostatic level more quickly after exercise.

The heart rate is governed by a small node of very specialized muscle, the sinoauricular node or the "pacemaker," which discharges the rhythmic impulses initiating the heartbeat. The nerves supplying the heart are autonomic and are classified as the vagus nerve and the sympathetic nerves. The slow rate of the trained person is due to what may be described as increased vagal tone. Emotional states cause a stress syndrome which characteristically increases the heartbeat. This psychic response is usually evident in the first few minutes of exercise and may even be manifested as a result of anticipation of exercise. It is not known whether this reaction is caused by adrenal secretion or not, but it can be surmised that the physical and emotional stress in exercise augments the heart rate.

Therefore, athletes who are anticipating play are quite normal in having a faster pulse rate. In addition, there is evidence to indicate that carbon dioxide and temperature can change heart rate, as does a change in the blood oxygen content. At any rate, the trained individual appears to have a greater capacity to endure the discomfort of some of these cardiac changes than does the untrained individual. Also many of these cardiac changes seem to facilitate oxygen transport, which is absolutely essential to the endurance of any working muscle.

It would be wise to sum up the efforts of physical activity upon the heart since this is one of the most misunderstood of all the organic factors.

1. Strenuous exercise will not damage the heart of normal integrity.
2. Exercise will tend to increase the size of the heart but this is not a dangerous phenomenon; it is desirable.
3. No matter how heavy a load the normal heart is asked to carry, the load will not injure the heart fibres and will not exhaust the heart's reserve.
4. Training or conditioning slows down the rate of the heart but increases the volume of blood expelled with each stroke, thus causing the transport of oxygen to muscular tissue to be more efficient.
5. Heart hypertrophy may occur from causes other than exercise. These are usually pathological and involve valvular leaks which require the heart to pump more forcefully to clear itself of regurgitated blood.
6. There is some medical opinion to support the idea that even a damaged heart needs activity over and above a resting beat, in order to regain its strength.

7. Athletes who collapse owing to strain of a contest may do so for one or more reasons—*e.g.* psychological stress, deteriorated arteries, respiration exhaustion, heart damaged by disease—but there is no evidence to show that athletics themselves can cause dilation or other abnormalities in heart action. Strenuous physical exercise and hard manual labour do not cause, or predispose to, heart disease; that such activities do not cause abnormal cardiac hypertrophy and that athletes do not develop early disability and die because of exercise they indulged in while in school.
8. There is some evidence to show that coronary heart disease may be related to lack of exercise.
9. The heart and blood vessels of children develop in proportion to each other and not disproportionately, as was once thought. The onset of fatigue in the adolescent is not due to insufficient cardiac development.
10. Unless medical diagnosis contraindicates, strenuous activity facilitates circulatory well-being.
11. The weight of evidence which indicates that coronary disease may be related to tobacco usage is imposing.

These statements carry certain implications that should be heeded by the physical educator.

- The heart is strengthened and made more efficient by the vigorous running, climbing, and swinging activities of childhood. The human being thrives best on activity of a large, purposeful sort. The heart is one of the first of the vital organs to feel the effects of the slow, inactive life. Its efficiency is reduced and its endurance is lowered. Sedentary living and certain diseases are two great enemies of the heart, the avoidance of both is important to physical well-being.

- Competitive athletics are not harmful to the heart, and there is no reason to suppose that strenuous school and colleges sports will damage hearts of normal integrity.
- Like all other muscles, the heart is subject to fatigue. Young people should not be forced to extend themselves past the normal stopping point for the sake of "school spirit," "the championship," or "the good ol' coach." When young athletes tire, they should be allowed to rest, and no coach or teacher in his right mind should invoke the "do or die" spirit. Rest is an important part of the individual's adaptation to activity and should be provided in ample amounts during strenuous athletic contests. There is no particular wisdom in continually driving athletes to the point of all-out effort and total exhaustion.
- Participation in most forms of physical education activities, including competitive athletics, should be severely limited, if not wholly prohibited, during periods of illness. There can be no justification for following, much less asking, a player to participate in a game when he is ill. Athletes do not like to be thought of as "quitters" or "chicken," and they do not wish to let the team down. In addition, they sometimes think that the team will fall to pieces without them. The plain fact is that infection and illness are always enemies of the heart. The best medical judgement indicates that it is usually best for the player to remain out of action until he is well, thus keeping the heart from damage and allowing it to do its part in the normal protective process which goes on most efficiently while the organism is at rest. It must be remembered constantly that physical education exists for the benefit of the participant and not to reward the greedy and unprincipled who tend

to excuse their actions on the premise that they are "making men out of softies." No victory, no school or college, surely no contract or salary of any coach or teacher is worth the risk of damage to one player. The game is for the good of those who play.

- Every participant in physical education and in competitive athletics should have a heart examination at sufficiently frequent intervals to guide the teacher in placement of the students in activities. The information thus gathered, from whatever competent medical source, must be as accurate as possible and must be used by the physical education personnel. If only limited activity is desirable, a programme of such activity should be developed. If a student should be excused temporarily from all activity, something else in physical education should be provided. At no time should the physical education teacher attempt to diagnose the heart condition himself and certainly he should not controvert the judgement of a physician. It is completely reprehensible to ignore advice from the medical doctor and allow or encourage the student to play in spite of a heart condition which indicates otherwise. Physical educators should work cooperatively with the medical profession by informing physicians of the approximate energy cost of certain activities. All physical educators should be ready to suggest activities suited to those students who are restricted in either the intensity or the scope of their participation.
- There is ample reason to support the traditional restriction of tobacco during training and during all of childhood and adolescence.
- There is no reason to believe that older persons cannot tolerate vigorous activity for fear their hearts

will not be able to adapt to it. As long as the heart is undamaged by disease, there is no need to fear heart failure because of exertion at middle age or beyond. Obviously, for the middle aged participant as for the youth, conditioning must be a part of any participation programme. One should return to activity gradually, purposefully increasing the work load in terms of resistance and speed each day. If a same programme is followed the most mature individual can expect to "come back" to the point where he can obtain fun and satisfaction from athletics.

Blood Composition

The blood chemistry undergoes some rather interesting changes as a result of training and conditioning. There is some controversy as to whether the alkaline reserve is increased, but certainly the rate of lactic acid formation is reduced; thus the blood lactate concentration is lower in the trained than in the untrained. During exhausting exercise bouts, the former seems to be able to tolerate higher lactate concentration in the blood than the latter. This toleration seems to have a relationship to endurance.

Under certain conditions of very intense work, some of the lactic acid that enters the bloodstream is eliminated by the kidneys, and it is possible to find sodium lactate in the urine for some time after exercise. Training increases the red blood corpuscle count—the red bone marrow becomes redder. Prolonged, extensive muscular effort can cause the destruction of red blood corpuscles to the point of anemia, but usually the red bone marrow is so developed during training that any normal destruction of red blood corpuscles is corrected.

The white blood cells do not seem to be affected by training, although there is a decrease of eosinophils, which are leucocytes, as a result of the stressors of activity and activity anticipation. The specific gravity of the blood has a direct correlation with the erythrocyte picture. It increases during periods of exercise, then drops below normal immediately following the work, only to rise to its homeostatic level again. Various trials of moderate exercise do not have a pronounced effect on the blood sugar, but if there is great emotional involvement or the trial is particularly strenuous, the blood sugar does rise. When the exercise is prolonged, the blood sugar has a tendency to drop.

There are some reasons to believe that level of blood sugar has some effect on endurance; the closer to normal the blood sugar level the better the individual's condition. However, blood sugar cannot be augmented instantly, and the use of honey and sugar immediately before or during a game is questionable. In general, a fitness programme does not cause drastic changes in blood chemistry, but training does appear to increase tolerance for any blood changes there are.

Training improves muscle tone. This does not mean that the muscle automatically hypertrophies, although it may, but the sarcolemma of the muscle fibre thickens and toughens and the amount of connective tissue within the muscle increase. It is thought that the number of muscle fibres does not increase as a result of training, although each fibre may hypertrophy. In addition, the fit individual gains in muscular strength and endurance: his phosphocreatine content rises, and the active muscles maintain a very red colour, probably due to increased hemoglobin content. This improved transportation of blood to the muscles undoubtedly facilitates the gain in endurance. Consequently, as man gets stronger he can do more and thus continue to increase his strength.

The improvement in skill patterns of the trained individual argues well for some essential change in the central nervous system. It has been suggested that the transmission of the nervous impulse over the motor end plate is aided by training, also that the chemical mediums at the synapses change to improve nervous response. If such is true, it might explain why it is possible to improve coordination and to change reaction time to a certain extent.

Although only certain muscles are used in any one specific exercise, the entire body responds via the nervous system. Thus, the tonic neck reflex is employed in exercise demanding all-out hand grip effort. In fact, many of the muscular mannerisms employed by athletes under great strain are probably really "assists" given via the central nervous system to facilitate the task at hand. There seems to be just reason for facial grimaces during certain exercises of exertion, and the trained individual employs these extraneous actions frequently.

Exercise has little influence on the digestive ability of the organism. However, intense and prolonged exercise does temporarily inhibit gastric acid secretion and peristalsis. This inhibition often causes one to feel as if he had "lead in his stomach" and may well have contributed to the time-honoured rule that there shall be no swimming until one hour after a meal. Stomach distention may interfere with diaphragmatic breathing and this cold certainly affect exercise. Training does not "improve" one's digestion except as the abdominal muscular action assists in normal peristalsis. Conditioning is important to fitness. If the conditioning is regular and systematic, utilizing the principle of overloading to insure maximum effort, the following results should take place in reference to the systemic function of the organism:

1. Breathing will become slower and deeper, thus enabling the athlete to undertake more work without being winded.

2. The increase in capillaries and greater availability of oxygen will make the athlete less susceptible to muscular fatigue.
3. Greater mechanical efficiency, resulting from cardiorespiratory adjustments, will increase the participant's endurance.
4. There will be a circulatory adjustment with a lower heart rate and larger stroke-volume. This will permit strenuous exercise without throbbing and palpitation of the heart.
5. There will be a more rapid return of the heart rate and blood pressure to their homeostatic levels, which will speed up the athlete's recovery from fatigue and quickly ready him for subsequent play.
6. Adjustment in the blood chemistry will allow the individual to tolerate greater amounts of lactate in the blood and thus to withstand fatigue better.
7. There will be improved muscle tone, resulting in greater muscular strength and endurance.
8. Some muscular hypertrophy will occur as a result of muscular contraction.
9. There will be an improvement in skill patterns with resulting neuromuscular facilitation; consequently, techniques will become easier as they are practiced.

Besides systemic changes, many functional changes will occur as a result of improved physical well-being.

Fatigue is a natural condition. It was once described as being caused principally by the lactic acid produced by muscular contraction. However, such a simple explanation is inadequate, for fatigue is a very complicated phenomenon. It is now thought the organism never really reaches a point of complete fatigue, a point which would herald true exhaustion. If such were possible, a fatigued heart or diaphragm would be unable to function and death would follow.

General fatigue is now believed to have a neurological origin, psychic as well as physical. Fatigue is signaled by diminished capacity for doing an assigned task effectively, local tiredness in specific music groups, a general feeling of tiredness throughout the entire body, sleepiness, localized, pain, soreness, stiffness and swelling inability to concentrate and recall, and slowness of comprehension.

All of these symptoms usually are subjectively interpreted, so that fatigue is almost unmeasurable. Indeed, it can really be measured only in terms of changed performance. It seems apparent that if all else has been kept constant, fatigue is the most important factor in causing performance change.

In physical education classes, fatigue may be identified in a number of ways. The unskilled student who cannot keep up with the class in the gymnasium develops tiredness and asks to be excused. This fatigue may become chronic, a condition that will be identified with the experience; that is, the very thought of physical education will have the power to make him tired. Or fatigue may be manifested in a state of anxiety by the highly nervous athlete who uses up his energy in his pre-game practice and has nothing left for the playing situation. Or fatigue may taken the form of boredom; standing in the goalie cage, for example, waiting for the ball that never comes, may bring on fatigue that is psychically induced.

The most usual type of fatigue, however, is that found on the gymnasium floor after the basketball game, on the playing field after hockey or football, on the tennis court after the last set or the golf course after the last hole. The player has given his all and is sufficiently exhausted so that he would find it difficult to continue with the activity. Although each of these states of fatigue apparently is brought about by differing circumstances, there is a great deal of similarity in the end result. Boredom, staleness, anxiety, and muscular work create the sensation and it is that sensation which the physical educator must attempt to understand. He should find the following admonitions helpful:

- Fatigue should not be thought of as a purely physical and metabolic state. Of course, muscular work will increase the output of lactic acid, which in turn may adversely affect the end organs of the nerves, which in turn may become less efficient in their operation. But such a physical syndrome is only part of the story. Inability to function is not a simple thing and the psychic evertones are tremendous.
- A feeling of fatigue may stem from a variety of cause besides muscular work. The individual is a whole, and the fatigue can be due to both physical and psychic factors—each dependent upon the other.
- There is a real difference between actual impairment and a feeling of tiredness. In the former, the vital activities of the cells are weakened, sometimes thwarted entirely, by the poisonous end products of the activity, which interfere with the normal function of the muscle cells. Such impairment can be relieved only by rest, sleep or at least a lessening of activity.
- Fatigue may be a part of the general reaction to any stimulus or stressor agent. Possibly fatigue, or an impression of fatigue, alerts the individual to the stressful situation. Then, as the homeostatic level is again reached by resolution of the stressor, fatigue is relieved. Thus, fatigue may be a symptom of homeostatic upset as well as its result.

- "Staleness" among athletes may be largely psychological. The performers may be bored with drill, practice, and the discipline of the training routine. The players exhibit their boredom in weariness, lack of snap, loss of interest, what seems to be lack of endurance, and a disposition toward accidents. This behavior may be due to fatigue induced by boredom: usually it can be alleviated by introducing novelty into practice sessions, by introducing the aspect of fun, and by attempting to remove some of the constant pressures of practice and substituting new, challenging, and untried pressures. There are even times when a day off from practice can do wonders. Frequently the joy, satisfaction, and sense of achievement inherent in sports success are effective antidotes to the fatigue generated by the frustrations of life itself. Over and over it has been observed that men who are employed on manual jobs involving heavy labour find their recreation at the end of the day in such physical activity as a game.
- Some activities produce only moderate fatigue, but in sufficient quantities to be felt. Sitting all day at a desk, standing at a bank window, working over a steam table, selling clothes, checking out groceries in the local supermaker—all these may produce weariness from boredom or from an accumulation of lactic acid and other fatigue products at the distal parts. There has usually not been enough gross physical activity to facilitate the removal of the fatigue products, just enough to produce them. Often, activity involving large muscle action is the best counterbalance. In other words, general fatigue tends to dissipate the products and thus relieve local fatigue.

– Fatigue is less likely to develop if one is engaged in something interesting. If the meaning and value of a task are kept clearly in mind, the entire enterprise is absorbing and socially and psychologically welcome. If there are rewards in status, social approval, or esteem, fatigue is less likely to occur. Conversely, excessive tiredness accompanies the enterprise that is distasteful, unrewarding, or socially unacceptable. It is easy to become tired even at the thought of doing some things; and when tiredness is present, it is difficult to simulate enthusiasm. Too often, this is the picture presented by the teacher: fatigued by papers, meetings, lessons, and discipline, and feeling that the rewards of the job are meager. Sometimes this fatigue can be ameliorated by looking at the job through different eyes. There seems to be some virtue in occasionally donning rose-coloured glasses.

The physical education teacher need be concerned less about fatigue if the games, aquatics, dance, and sports offered are rewarding and challenging. The fatigue factors operate in the long seasons of training which are typical of football and basketball. Long seasons and long practice sessions are frequently self-destructive, and their monotony has turned many a player away from further association with the game. The same danger is prevalent in pushing highly organized games down further in the elementary grades. Many potentially good players are sick of the game before they reach the stage where their skills are really good. Early chronic fatigue is one of the hazards of junior high and elementary school competitive sport. On the other hand, it is essential that these age groups be challenged by activity that it is not boring. Young children are ready for games of intrigue and skill and these need not be the same games that are played at the high school and college level.

- It is possible for the individual, under emotional stress, to expend tremendous amounts of energy without feeling any marked degree of fatigue. The situation must be dealt with in a unitary way. Hormonal stimulation often obliterates the fatigue feeling and work results are phenomenal. This accounts for the effect that a contest has on "pepping up" a team. The relationship of ideas to harmone secretion is very real, and there is reason to believe that the body experiences greater stress from psychic than from physical influences. In moments of emergency one can play with abandon and force, "over his head," as it were. He becomes so enthusiastic and absorbed in what he is doing, his motives are so powerful, that all else becomes secondary and be responds with all out endeavour.
- Motivation tempers fatigue and should be used to reduce fatigue caused by boredom or insecurity. It has been demonstrated experimentally that motivation delays the onset of fatigue and encourages greater work output. The physical education teacher, though making use of this knowledge, should not that there is some danger in increasing work output. If an individual is so powerfully motivated that he does not recognize or heed the ordinary signs of fatigue, impairment may take place. The wise teacher will utilize motivation up to a certain point but will recognize the fine dividing line when it is apparent that additional motivation may do more harm than good.
- Frequent and intense periods of work with adequate rest between them are to be preferred to sustained work with little rest. It is much wiser to hold a practice for fifteen minutes three times during the hour, with five-minute breaks between periods, than to attempt to hold an hour's drill with no break. It is

suggested that a rest period of at least 45 minutes be provided between strenuous events, especially those that are based upon speed, like swimming events or running races in track. Rest is best accomplished in a horizontal position, with the legs elevated. If it is not possible to lie down, mild exercise is better than inactivity. It is better to walk about than to stand or sit.

Fatigue is neither simple nor well understood. Its relation to nutritional states, vision, climatic conditions, variations in grandular secretions, emotionality, sleep, auditory stimuli, and many other factors needs further explanation. Indications are that the capacity for movement will loom larger, not as productive of fatigue, but as the antidote for it, in a modern world which seems predisposed to fatigue. It is not unreasonable to believe that the weariness and boredom which appear to affect many today can be alleviated by physical activity. Teachers must impart those skills in school which will later be used as preventives of fatigue.

Nutrition has a major impact on heart health and physical fitness. Your body needs food for fuel. Like a car, your body won't work well if you do not have a well-balanced mix of fuel. Physical activity can decrease risk factors linked with coronary heart disease; help improve your ability to exercise and do physical work; increase enthusiasm and foster a sense of well-being; release tension and help you relax and sleep; help control your weight; and encourage positive changes in other lifestyle habits.

Good eating habits are the key in helping you achieve these goals. Basically, there are three genetic metabolic types of bodies among human beings: ectomorph, endomorph and mesomorph. Some of us gain weight with difficulty, some of us put on fat easily and some of us put on muscle watching television.

The genetic differences between individuals is great. Body type has little to do with athletic ability or coordination, it simply relates to metabolism and genetic predisposition to gaining fat or muscle or staying lean. Athletic ability and coordination are also tied to genetics but not the body type/metabolism genes. Ectomorphs generally have a very high metabolic rate making it difficult for the to gain both muscle and fat. They are naturally lean individuals. They need less aerobics and should do anaerobic/strength building resistance training with reps in the six to 10 range.

The synergistic exercise programme is adaptable to all three body types. We all need aerobic exercise, however lean. People obviously need less aerobics than heavy people. No matter what your body type the Ultimate Aerobic and Anaerobic Programme will provide an excellent total body workout or an excellent warm up for your specific exercise programme. The combination of lower body aerobics and upper body aerobics provides muscle stimulation with the resultant increased nutrient and oxygen rich blood flow to all the muscles of your body. To ectomorphs some aerobics (20 minutes, three times per week minimum) are required for cardiovascular fitness—low rep 6-10 with heavier weights to gain size—longer rest between sets, two-three minutes.

Mesomorphs need aerobics for cardiovascular fitness (20 minutes, three times per week minimum); a balanced programme of low rep for size and high rep for definition. If a mesomorph's goal includes optimal physical condition, he needs more aerobics. Endomorphs need lots of aerobics to burn calories/fat; higher rep 12-20 with lower weights and short rest intervals, 30-60 seconds between sets.

Aerobics utilising the muscles of the upper body is equally as effective as aerobics for the muscles of the lower body for cardiovascular/endurance training. In activities of daily living upper body endurance and strength are every bit important, or even more, as lower body strength and endurance. The participants in this aerobic exercise and strength building programme experience a complete cardiovascular workout, muscle toning, calorie burning, metabolic enhance-ment, posture improvements, body-shaping and weight-loss in one complete programme.

Current researches recommend strength building, anaerobic exercise combined with an aerobic exercise programme. According to the researches aerobic exercise is essential for weight loss, cardiovascular fitness and body-shaping. Anaerobic exercise is essential for strength building and muscle gain.

Combining aerobic and anaerobic exercise is optimal. Benefits of the ultimate aerobic and anaerobic exercise is optimal. Benefits of the ultimate aerobic and anaerobic exercise programme include: improved endurance, strength, range from motion, balance, posture and coordination. An anabolic and growth hormone-friendly diet should include plenty of animal protein, sufficient good fat and carbohydrates. Such a diet is anabolic and is appropriate for any healthy and active individual.

Take good oils with in 20 per cent-30 per cent total calories. Specific essential fatty acids are needed for most of the body's hormonal functions. The oil must have the proper fatty acid composition and molecular bonding. Metabolism and cellular replication are carried out by a number of processes including many components.

The classes on nutrition were mixed with courses on microbiology, and anatomy and physiology provided credence to the principles of science in nutrition. The microbiology and physiology of tissues at the cellular level documents the complex nature of providing the cells the needed raw materials through proper nutrition and supplementation. The exact nutrients necessary for optimum function change throughout the day.

The nutrients necessary for cellular replication, hormonal secretions, and neural function are not random and unspecific. The numbers of specific nutrients that must be present in the body, simultaneously, and in the proper ratios is phenomenal for the millions of chemical reactions that are occurring constantly and simultaneously in our bodies 24 hours per day. The last three decades were years of fad diets. The late 1970's saw the liquid high protein diets.

Beginning in the 1980s the aversion to any kind of fat began. Then the high carbohydrate diet became the thing. None of these ever made any sense. But marketing and pop-media convinced millions of people that proper nutrition was unimportant and that fad diets were the way to go. As we are in the 21st century, science at the cellular level has changed and complicated much of the previous nutritional philosophy.

Obesity is the biggest health problem facing most of the urban population across the world. More than half of us are over our ideal weight and more than one-third are obese enough to significantly raise the risk of disease and premature death.

Nutrition is one of the greatest weapons against diseases, keeping fats at about 20-30 per cent of caloric intake. Eating five or more servings a day of fruit and vegetables lowers your chances of getting cancer. The advocates of the low carbohydrate, ketogenic diet cringe at the thought of multi servings of fruit. However, moderation is a key to a stable life. Professional body-builders have different goals than a person eating for health.

Persons with extreme weight loss requirements obviously have different needs than the average weight conscious person. Persons striving for a five per cent body fat and rippled abs probably also have different goals than simply enjoying a healthy life. Choose methods of cooking that will retain flavour, colour and nutrients. Steam instead of boiling vegetables.

Avoid cooking at high temperatures and long cooking times. Both extended heat and liquid can destroy or leach out valuable nutrients. Add vegetables whenever possible to ensure your five-a-day intake. Experiment with more vegetable variety in salads, try new vegetable mixes, include some shredded vegetables in casseroles, and add different vegetables to soups and stews. Use chopped red or yellow peppers to 'pep-up' the flavour.

Try vegetable salads and fruit chutneys as accompaniments to meat or poultry in place of heavy sauces. When you use oil, select olive, sunflower or canola oil. Drain off visible fat while cooking, blot pan-fried foods on paper towels to absorb extra grease.

Hormones are secreted by the endocrine system and used at the cellular level for communication between body tissues including the brain, organs, other glands, muscles and other tissues of the body. There are two types of glands that compose the endocrine system: a) exocrine glands and b) endocrine glands.

The exocrine glands secrete their hormones into ducts and body cavities. The glands include sweat glands, oil glands, and digestive glands. The endocrine glands secrete into capillaries to be transported with the blood. These glands release hormones into the bloodstream. The endocrine glands include the pituitary, thyroid, parathyroid, adrenals, pineal, thymus, and hypothalamus.

In addition there are organs of the body which contain the endocrine tissue but that are not exclusively endocrine glands such as the pancreas, ovaries, testes, kidneys, stomach, skin and heart. These hormones, glandular secretions, control many of our short-term and long-term bodily functions. Although hormones are chemically diverse they are constructed from amino acids and cholesterol. They can be divided into three classes: a) amines, b) proteins and peptides, and c) steroids.

Amines are the simplest hormone molecules and are fabricated from amino acids. These hormones are extremely important in metabolism and energy production. Proteins and peptides are long chains of amino acids and are large molecules. Insulin secreted by the pancreas is an example.

Steroids are hormones fabricated from cholesterol. Examples include aldosterone, testosterone and estrogen. Our growth, mood, digestion, respiration, sense of thirst and hunger, sexual functions, fat metabolism and most other bodily functions are all triggered by hormones.

The amount of hormone released or secreted by the endocrine glands is determined by the body's need for that particular hormone at a given time. Once the hormone is secreted into the circulatory system it is transported by the blood to all areas of the body but only specific target cells react to their presence. Target cells contain receptors that respond to specific hormones being transported throughout the body by the circulatory system. There are thousands of receptors in each of our cells.

Each of these receptors responds to a specific hormone's unique amino acid chain or pattern. Once the hormone is bound to the receptor cell a chain of genetically predetermined biochemical events within the target cell occur. The degree to which the target cell responds to the hormone depends on the number of target cells, genetics and the concentration of the hormone.

In effect, the amino acid structure of the hormone is the key and the receptor is a lock. In order for the key, hormone, to fit the lock receptor, the hormone-receptor complex must be an exact match. If for any reason this lock and key do not fit, the cellular binding is disrupted, the hormonal signals are interrupted and the communication is not complete. Hormones also interact with other hormones to price-specific metabolic responses.

In some cases the effect is synergistic, that is, the cellular response is more than the sum of hormones involved (1 + 1 + 1 = 4), they compliment each other. In some cases the effect is antagonistic, one hormone stops or reduces the action of another hormone (1 + 1 = 0). A natural and expected effect of aging is the decrease in function and effectiveness of body structures and tissues. The most obvious are our skin and eyesight.

Glandular function, metabolic function, endocrine system function, immune system function, proteins synthesis, protein assimilation and most other body functions are similarly affected by aging. The effect of this is that the endocrine systems, functional demise can be compared to the 'chemical telephone lines' being down.

The various parts of the body do not properly communicate with each other. The intracellular and intercellular chemical instructions are interrupted and body parts in effect become hormonally isolated from one another. Messages that would normally prompt cellular rejuvenation are never sent or received. Consequently, cells grow old, losing natural healthiness. As we become old, most of our glands secrete less and less of the hormone they are designed to secrete.

There are times when the regulatory systems do not operate properly. As we age this regulation becomes less efficient and hormone levels change. The amount of hormones released by the endocrine glands is determined by the bodies needs for the hormones at a given time. However, the endocrine glands can be stimulated to release more hormones, more frequently. A remarkable amount of data has been compiled that indicates that many of the 'diseases' that the middle-aged begin experiencing, including depression, poor sleep, abdominal weight gain, muscle loss as well as prostate and heart conditions are directly related to hormone/endocrine/glandular imbalances that can be correct with currently available medication and nutritional therapies. Replacing the hormones which decline with age is as important to the treatment of aging as is replacing normal levels of insulin is to an insulin-dependent diabetic.

Women have seen a dramatic reduction in the infirmities of aging, general health improvements, with the increased use of the hormone estrogen as a safe and effective Hormone Replace-ment Therapy. The Human Growth Hormone (HGH) secreted by the anterior pituitary responding to chemical, hormonal instructions from the hypothalamus, is composed of over 190 amino acids arranged in a particular order or chain. If any of these amino acids are not present at the correct position in the chain it is not HGH. If any these amino acids are not present proper cellular binding will not occur.

The endocrine system is composed of a complex network of glands that secrete hormones. Hormones are in effect the chemical messengers of the body. These hormones are essential for the regulation of many of our biological processes. These are the chemical messengers of our body.

Our sense of thirst, hunger, mood, immune system, sexual function, growth pattern and most other biological functions are dependent on the appropriate levels of hormonal secretions by a variety of glands often working in conjunction with each other. There are 22 essential and non essential amino acids which are fabricated into something like 50,000 proteins.

All amino acids can be fabricated from the eight essential amino acids. Some textbooks state that there are conditional amino acids that the body cannot synthesise under certain conditions. Current research indicates that the anterior pituitary can be stimulated with nutritional supplementation and exercise to increase the HGH secretion, and the adrenals can be stimulated to produce more hormones, as can the thyroid and the pancreas. The anterior pituitary under chemical/hormonal instru-ctions from the hypothalamus produces HGH.

HGH blood levels diminish after adolescence, the measured levels decline each decade of our life. HGH is produced throughout our lives but the blood levels go down. Many of the effects associated with aging are associated with declining HGH levels such as thin skin and skin wrinkles; muscle wasting; abdominal fat; cognitive changes; mood changes; decreasing energy; sexual perfor-mance; weak bones; reduced cardiac output, and so on. These conditions are directly or indirectly affected by the decline in HGH levels present in our system.

HGH is critical for tissue repair, brain function, physical health, mental health, muscle growth, bone strength, energy, and any other cellular functions. This decline in HGH level is not irreversible. If you are in your 30s you can stimulate growth hormone release and keep your body supplies from decreasing. If you are in your 40s, 50s, 60s or older there are nutritional programmes to recharge our dwindling supply. If for some reason your body has completely stopped producing HGH, then there is replacement hormone therapy, actual HGH injections. HGH is at its peak during adolescence. It continued to be produced throughout our lives, however in increasingly diminished amounts.

The fact that HGH production is reduced significantly as we age is a major factor in aging. HGH is critical for tissue repair, healing, brain function, physical health, mental health, muscle growth, bone strength, energy and metabolism, and its demise is a major factor in aging. As you can see many of the effects of aging are controlled by the HGH.

Controlling hormone levels is the best way to improve both body composition and to slowdown aging. Hormone levels can be controlled through dietary supplementation of amino acid secretagogues, exercises and prescription medications. Growth hormone promotes and increases in the synthesis of new protein tissue and retards the breakdown of protein tissue that can occur with dietary deficiencies, exercise stress or other factors. Although growth hormone has powerful protein building effect it is probably more potent in its ability to promote the breakdown of stored body fat.

Growth hormone not only stimulates body and muscle growth directly, it also stimulates the body's production of other anabolic growth factors circulating in the bloodstream. The most powerful of these other hormones are the insulin-like growth factors. In addition to stimulating the insulin-like growth factors, the HGH interacts with these hormones in such a way that the net effect of all of them is to produce a reduction in fat tissue while increasing lean tissue/muscle mass. If we consider aging a disease and not just a normal occurrence, it follows that anyone who wants to maintain his youthful vigour and endurance should include an effective growth hormone stimulation therapy as part of his health regiment.

One study conducted by Ralph Paffenbarger and his colleagues involving 17,000 Harvard alumni found that men who burned 500 to 1,000 calories a week on physical activity had a 22 per cent lower risk of death for all causes, while those who expended 2,500 calories a week also added one to two years to their extended lifespan. People who are physically fit, eat a healthy, balanced diet and take nutritional supplements can slice 10 to 20 years off their biological age—the true age that your body should be measured, in terms of function, rather than your chronological age as measured by the candles on your birthday cake.

The goal of hormone replacement is to restore levels to those normally present for several decades during early adulthood. The safe levels at age 30 will remain safe when restored to that same level later in life. Adverse effects from hormone replacement result only from excessive doses or the use of unnatural and synthetic hormones. Hormonal secretions are the basic components in the communication process of the endocrine system.

The secretions are composed of amino acids. Through supplementation of specific amino acids at specific times we can have a great effect, in effect, manipulate the hormonal system. Specific glands use specific and unique combinations of amino acids and nutrients to trigger specific responses and glandular/hormonal secretions.

Amino acids used in the secretagogue stacks are identical to the amino acids present in food. Proteins are composed of amino acids. Egg protein, beef protein, milk protein and soy protein all have different amino acid ratios and composition. In order for the amino acids to be used by the body as protein, all the required amino acids must be present in the gut at the same time.

For a complete protein to be formed is integral to the timing of amino acid secretagogue supplementation. If the secretagogues are present with the essential amino acids the secretagogues will be used as protein instead of HGH releasing secretagogues. In human body, there are eight essential amino acids and 14 non-essential amino acids that can be fabricated from the eight essential amino acids.

From these 22 amino acids, being combined and arranged into varying specific chains, all proteins are fabricated by the human body. These are the basic building blocks that combine into literally thousands of complex protein, amino acid chains. Amino acids are organic compounds with at least one amino group and one carboxyl group. The amino groups include at least one NH_3 molecule. The carboxyl contains at least one COOH molecule. These molecules are combined in long chains to form proteins.

They are precursors to many important micro-molecules such as dopamine, epinephrine, scrotonin, and many other substances critical to health and well being. They are intimately involved in metabolism and glandular activity. Their presence is mandatory for glandular activity. Amino acids are necessary for growth and cellular replication throughout the body. They are a major constituent for muscle, blood, skin, and internal organs.

The proper functioning of the immune system is dependent on the presence of specific amino acids. They control the pathway that allows hormones and enzymes to be released. In addition to being the building blocks of structure, amino acids in effect turn on and off the 'chemical switches' that control our metabolism and body function. Amino acids are involved in everything from our sense of thirst to how our brain functions. Messages from the brain that are sent to various body parts by neurological chemicals called neurotransmitters. These neurotransmitters are responsible for the complex messages and instructions that the brain sends to all body parts.

5

Coaching

Many of the tasks assigned to coaches are too numerous to list, yet many schools expect young college graduates to step into a head coach position. They need to be prepared to handle the complexities of game strategy, unruly parents, demanding athletes, coordination of home and away contests as well as manage budgets. Most coaches need to accomplish these tasks while maintaining a separate career all for a small pittance. These young coaches need a thorough and varied approach to their preparation. A very important factor in establishing a coaching program for college students is to adapt the program to fit with current academic credit load as well as create a program that will best prepare them to handle the intricacies of the coaching world. Including enough material without overwhelming the student is a key consideration.

Coaching Volleyball

Before you can effectively teach the skills and strategies of volleyball, a coach must understand how the athletes learn. Learning physical skills is a process with measurable progressions and goals that change as skill level improves. The learning process must involve both the coach and the athlete. A coach's role is to ensure that proper techniques are presented and that the athletes enjoy their participation in the sport. This requires motivation on the coach's part and on the athlete's part.

Both coach and athlete must have an understanding of why they are involved in the sport volleyball. That means that a coach must know why he/she is teaching the selected skills and also investigate the expectations and goals of the athletes involved in the program. When these variables are clearly understood and accepted, learning can begin to take place. For simplicity, three stages of learning are recognised and labeled beginning, intermediate, and advanced.

The goal of the beginning stage of learning is to develop an understanding of the concepts, principles, and mechanics involved in volleyball. The principles of execution should be established. Drills aimed at developing this level of understanding emphasize mechanics rather than the integration of the skill into playing situations.

Three important guidelines should be utilised when presenting materials during this phase of learning:

1. Explain the reasons why a skill is executed.
2. Present as few principles as possible without compromising the message.
3. Movements and postures that the athlete will do naturally do not need to be discussed.

This phase of the learning process should be the shortest of the three. A coach will want to move on to game-related skills as soon as possible.

Practice or Intermediate Stage

During this stage, the focus is on learning to perform the skills. Coaches will spend most of their skill-teaching time in this phase, especially if they work with young or beginning volleyball players. Because players will begin to refine a motor program for performing a skill, the learning environment should parallel the competitive environment as closely as possible.

This final stage of learning assumes that skills have been established in set, game related motor patterns. The player can at this phase focus on tactical applications. The subtleties of tempo control and ongoing competitive adjustments can be addressed. Although skill refinement is a goal of this phase, refinement is accomplished through a focus on playing the game.

To meet the needs of the athletes in each of the phases of learning, a coach will need to develop a teaching plan. Each coach will have different individual strengths and weaknesses that will make this teaching plan unique from any other teaching plan. However there are several important issues that should be addressed when devising a teaching plan.

- Assessing fitness and skill level
- Developing a seasonal plan
- Planning practices
- Selecting drills
- Selecting an appropriate teaching style

There are many principles of teaching and each school of thought about teaching modifies the concepts. The following list of principles have universal acceptance and have been found to be successful.

- Keep any presentation simple by using carefully chosen words.
- Use as few words as possible. Be sure to use consistent, memorable, and meaningful cues.
- Demonstrate the skill frequently. Visual instruction often has more impact than verbal instruction.

- Describe the desired end result and encourage the athletes to explore ways of achieving that result as long as the technique is biomechanically correct.
- Provide cues, hints, and technical information as needed.
- Communicate clearly why a skill is being taught and why it should be performed in a prescribed manner.
- If possible, answer a question with a question. This process involves players in the learning process by encouraging problem-solving through exploration.
- Make all learning activities compatible with the skill level of the players.
- Keep activities challenging and fun.
- Use drills that duplicate the way a skill will be used in competition.

Teaching Concerns

As a coach presents new skills, additional concerns need to be taken into consideration.

- *Speed of execution* : Each player should perform skills at the fastest speed possible without sacrificing correct execution.
- *Perfection of movements* : Players should strive to perfect their movements, postures, and ball-contact skills during the beginning phase of learning.
- *Effort* : Players should exert maximum effort at all times, during practices as well as games. Remember, a player plays the game of volleyball the same way she practices for a game.
- *Imagery* : Visualising a complete skill give an athlete an opportunity to review correct techniques, cue their motor program, and see a clear image of what they are trying to accomplish.

- *Become a student of the game* : Volleyball is a multifaceted game. In addition to understanding the rules, a coach must understand the elements of the sport and how to teach skills. Take the time to watch other successful coaches. Go to as many volleyball games as possible and watch other teams. Play the sport as experience can be a beneficial teacher. Finally, join a coaches' association and attend the clinics.
- *Teaching and coaching the game* : Before a coach or player can really learn the various systems, theories, tactics and their application to the game volleyball, a coach or player must understand the nature of the game itself. Volleyball has many unique characteristics with which the coach and player must become familiar with before he/she is able to successfully teach and apply the skills.

Volleyball is distinguished by the following elements.

- it is a rebound sport.
- uses intermediate contacts.
- has a congested playing area.
- offers little immediate positive feedback.
- is a game of transition.
- has an imbalance of offense and defense.
- is a noncontact sport.
- is player dominated.
- requires similar skills of all players.
- uses unique skills and playing zones.

It is important that the coach and player understand each of the above elements. The coach and player must learn the importance of the many specific roles a player is responsible for during the course of the volleyball game and each role's significance as it pertains to the total team picture.

The fact that volleyball is categorised as a rebound sport means that players never maintain possession of the ball. Rather, the ball is contacted briefly and then directed to another player. The only exception to this is the serve. In most other sports, athletes can compensate for poor body position at the time of possession by moving into a more advantageous position. Because a player can not catch the volleyball and then move to a better position to release the ball, a player must learn to position themselves correctly before contacting the ball.

Common volleyball strategy encourages the use of three contacts per team possession on each side of the net. Because two of the three possible contacts are not the final contact, controlling the rebound of the ball is important. This need for controlling the ball highlights the necessity of moving into position for an intermediate contact before contacting the ball. In addition to good ball control, cooperation among team members is essential. For this reason, the interaction of players and the development of teamwork are dominant themes in learning the skills of volleyball.

Volleyball is unique in that a high concentration of people play in a small area. The congested playing area makes it vital to organise the positioning of players and their movements. Balanced coverage of all parts of the court is an important goal to achieve before any team or player can achieve any type of success. In achieving balanced coverage, the relationships between players positioned next to each other must be considered. Team dynamics become a prime coaching concern because of the congested playing area.

Because playing volleyball itself offers few opportunities for immediate positive feedback, some difficulties are created in the learning process. Each player needs to be able to identify and perform correct skill techniques and be able to "teach" these same skills and techniques to other players. As players learn to recognise and appreciate the correct execution of the volleyball techniques, those players should make positive compliments to the other players who are demonstrating those correct skills.

The roles of offense and defense can be confusing. Volleyball does have offensive and defensive skills, but they are not as separate as they may appear to be in other sports. The ball does not stop between the time a team takes an offensive role and when it must play defense. And a team may switch frequently between offense and defense without a point being scored or a violation being called. Volleyball players must understand the nature of this game of transition. To be successful, a team must be able to shift between offensive and defensive alignments fluidly.

There are four ways to score a point in volleyball: a service ace, a stuff block, a controlled defensive play resulting in an attack (known as "transition"), and an unforced error. A serve has been described as both an offensive and defensive skill. It is offensive because the server directs the velocity and trajectory of the ball. It is defensive in that the serve is intended to, at the least, disrupt the opponents's offense and, at the most, cancel it. A stuff block is clearly a defensive play. A controlled dig is also defensive and can lead to a point through team offense.

The opponent's unforced errors can be credited to a tough defense that intimidates the other team into attempting shots not usually found in their attack game plan. A team's overall discipline and consistency is reflected in the opponent's errors. It is often said that the best offense is a good defense. This is particularly true in volleyball. Traditionally aggressive offenses are sometimes handicapped buy unforced errors that result in lost opportunities for points. Vice versa, the conservative defense, which simply waits for the opponent to make mistakes, is not likely to produce success. To be successful, teams must strive to be aggressive defensively to create opportunities to score points.

Probably more than any other team sport, the offense has a tremendous advantage. The offense achieves success (by scoring a point or side-out) over 60% of the time.

Volleyball is a team game with a physical barrier (the net) that prevents most direct one-on-one contact. The players are in control of their own games, and in many respects the players control their own success and failure, regardless of the skill level or actions of their opposition. In volleyball players must learn to control their frustrations and aggressions. Volleyball players must play within themselves and compete against self-imposed standards more than compete against opponents.

The rules of volleyball present no time limit. Teams compete until one team scores at least 15 points and has a two point advantage. As a consequence, the last point must be scored by the winning team. A volleyball team cannot run out the clock as in football.

Because no time limit can stop play, there is constant pressure to score points. Players must learn to create opportunities to score points so that they can win a volleyball game. Players waiting for the other team to make enough mistakes to lose a game can produce a loss for their own team.

Volleyball is more a player-dominated game, rather than a coach-dominated activity. Communication between the coach and athletes is restricted. As a result, a team must prepare thoroughly before each competition. Players must also learn to adapt to the changing situations that occur throughout a volleyball game without relying on the coach's comments.

The rules of volleyball require that players rotate to each of the six positions on a volleyball court unless a substitution for them occurs. Therefore, volleyball is dominated by the theory that all players must become equally skilled in all phases of the game. Having a team in which all players are equal in all respects has been the goal of coaches for years. Unfortunately, this is an unattainable goal for most coaches. Players must understand the rotation concept, the limitations of specialisation, and the rules of the game. Each player must become familiar with playing in all portions of the court and must be equally comfortable in the front or back row.

Players need to also understand that even though coaches try to train all the players to be perfect in all the skills, this task is almost impossible in the real world situation. There are simply not enough hours available to train everyone equally well. Consequently, most coaches will teach all the skills to everyone but will work within the rotation rule to build limited specialisation.

Running, shuffling, sidestepping, diving, rolling, and various combinations of these skills comprise the movement skills used in volleyball. It is during practice time that the athlete learns to perform a series of movements that will lead to a successful execution of a skill without having to think about each step. Further, the underhand pass is unique to volleyball. In most sports, the ball is contacted with the feet, the hands, or an implement of some sort. Because contact is made with the forearms, special eye-arm coordination is required.

Finally, in volleyball, there are two additional unique zones of play. Most sports are played at a level between the top of the head and the knees, in something we call the middle zone. Volleyball also involves two additional zones. Many balls are played very close to the floor in the LOW zone. For this reason, players must become comfortable diving, rolling, and using flying recovery techniques, all of which are standard skills.

The other zone used in volleyball is the HIGH zone which spans from the top of the athlete's reach to a point 10 feet or more above the floor. Because much of the game of volleyball is played in this high zone, jumping skills are frequently needed. Volleyball is a unique activity in many respects. Coaches and players need to familiarise themselves with the various offensive and defensive schemes permitted in volleyball. Coaches and players need to learn how the skills are applied during the tactics of an actual game. Players need to develop a general proficiency in all the skills and understand the role of limited specialisation in the success of a team's efforts. Players need to understand how their emotions affect their ability to perform in a game and how their feelings and emotions affect the players around them.

Volleyball Coaching

Passing

1. Good passing posture
2. Forearm contact
3. Angle platform to target
4. Simple movement to the ball

1. *Good passing posture*—feet should be set up with the heel toe relationship. This is the heel of the right foot, slightly in front of the toes of the left foot. Knees bent; body bent at the waist with the

shoulders in front of the knees. Knees should be just in front of the toes. Arms should be out in front and straight. It is important that the heels of the hands be together. You can use a hand in hand grip.

- *Drill:* 4 people at the net—tossers—pass to 1st, 2nd, 3rd and then 4th.

2. *Forearm contact,*—Contact the ball between 1 and 6 inches above the wrist, the meaty part of the forearm. If you drop the wrists a little, then a small V should show. The ball should sit there (in the V) softest part of the arms. The passer needs to be relaxed. Let the legs do the work. Platform relaxed and the ball should be absorbed into the arms. Soft pass.
   - *Drill:* 3 people—pass go to the next spot, other person passes
3. Angle platform to the target
   1) Vertical—closer to the target, the more parallel to the floor, the arms need to be. Stay down; the ball will go straight up. If you drop or lower the arms and keep the arms in front, then you can pass the ball farther and on a 45-degree angle.
   2) Horizontal—pass the ball to the right or left by dropping a shoulder. More you drop the shoulder, the greater the angle. Right shoulder down, and then pass right. Left shoulder down, then pass left.

      Drill: 3 shaggers, everyone else pass. Coach tosses the ball, person passes to the shagger, and the shagger brings the ball back to the coach. Start right, then left.
4. Movement to the ball—transfer of weight from left foot to the right foot. Try to step with the right foot if you want to put a little more power on the ball.

The platform must stay controlled and stationary. Work from the legs.

- *Drill:* two people on the other side—shagger—toss the ball over the net, the passer calls and then passes to the shagger. Shagger then goes under the net and drops off the ball, next shagger steps up.

Setting

1. Squat under the ball
2. Basket over the forehead
3. Extend

    1. Squat under the ball—knees bent—sit back into a squat position. The back should be slightly erect. Hips lined up under the ball. Knees are in front of the toes and shoulders behind the knees. Hips under the ball are important.
    2. Basket over the forehead—bring up the hands. Note that the fingers should be pointing out (or away), this aids in the "spring" action. Make the shape of a basket. This should be the same shape as the ball. Bring the hands together, and then spread out the fingers. Then take the fingers apart, keep the palms facing each other (thumbs pointing to eyes), cock the wrist back, just above forehead. The ball should rest on the first two fingers and the upper insides of the thumbs and remaining fingertips.
    3. Extend—extend into the ball using the arms and legs in unison. Legs and arms extend up in direction of the pass. The wrists should flex forward and the thumbs "through" the ball + out.

Drills

- Preset—catch, extend and release.
- Partner toss—catch and pass back. Then toss and pass back.
- Partner toss—long and short, left and right.
  - *Drill*: start at the 10-foot line—run under the net—ball is tossed; the player sets the ball, and back peddles under the net, back to the 10-foot line.
  - *Drill*: set the ball over the net, the people receive it by setting it to themselves and then they set it back over the net to the other person.

Serving

1. Fencer stance
   - Balance important. Lefty or righty?—opposite foot forward.
   - Weight should start on the back foot.
   - Where your opposite foot is facing is where the ball will go.
2. The ball in opposite hand—waist level.
   - Arm outstretched—raise to nose—ball should come up centerline of body
   - Wrist and elbow frozen.
   - Raise your hand above your shoulder + release the ball.
   - The release should be 6—12 inches .
   - As you release the ball, front knee bends—similar to tennis serve.
3. On the hitting arm, the elbow should be high above the shoulder.

- The shoulder should be square.
- The player then must shift their weight from back leg to front leg.
- The back leg should end up with the toe down for balance.
- This should be one fluid motion.

4. Contact the ball at the highest point of the toss (apex).
   - You want to make sure that you contact the middle of the ball.
   - One trick I use is—take the v-ball, find the trademark or the middle, then put your hand over it. Go through your routine.
   - You want to use the heel or middle of your hand to contact the ball.

One other thing—having trouble with one hand toss, try two. It really comes down to with what you are most comfortable.

Hitting

Four keys to hitting are:

1. Approach—body to the ball—2 steps—directional + hop.
2. Pendulum arm—movement of arms up in the air + hand in position.
3. Jump and take off.
4. Ball contact.

1. Approach—footwork—4 step

- Righty approach—Right (small), left, right, together explode.
- Lefty approach—Left (small), right, left, together explode.

- Direction – this is what takes you towards the ball Arms should be in front
- Should be jumping from about 2–3 feet from the net – knees bent When jumping, jump straight up – not on an angle (otherwise into net)
- Angles – outside – 45 degrees – middle – 22 degrees off hand – straight

2. Pendulum arm – on approach – elbows bent On hop (explosion) – knees bent – arms back
3. Jump and take off

   Right foot – heel to toe rock – left foot push off toes

   Arm swing to shoulder level

   Left arm extends up – this is used to spot the ball

   Right arm reaches back; arm extends up, hand open

   Shoulder back (like a hammer) – body opens up to setter

   Arch the back, knees bent with heels back

   Key – stay back and wait for the ball – do not rush!
4. Ball contact

   Left arm thrusts down

   Right elbow leads – right arm reaches high

   Fingers spread out – wrist should be relaxed

   Contact the ball w/ lower 3rd of hand at close to max.

   Reach

   Wrist snap, fingers spread over the ball

   Follow through – right arm down – across the body

   "Reach and snap" – technical term

   Where do you contact on the ball?

   Normally the back center of the ball

When off the net (or those with low touches) under the center of the ball

Those with high reach—over the ball (top)

Drills

Drill tips

1. Hit with topspin down to partner.
2. Have partner hold the ball up high—approach and hit out of hand.
3. Hold ball above the net and hit out of hand.
4. Hit ball from coaches toss (1's).
5. Hit setters set.

Blocking

Sequence should be: watch the ball, pass to setter (make sure there is no setter dump), then focus on the hitter (where are shoulders facing)?

Footwork

- Outside blocker—step—hop—plant—jump (landing should be 2 feet)
- Middle blocker—big step—crossover hop (this saves time—balance is key)

Responsibilities

- Outside hit—outside sets block and the middle seals
- Middle hit—middle sets block and the outside seals

Drills: Approach the net, middle, strong side, etc (blockers move and react) Toss ball to setter—setter sets any hitter (or dumps the ball...) Blocking lines—pair up, footwork and simultaneous jump

6

Psychological Well-being

Anxiety measures taken (trait or state, behavioural, self report, physiological), or exercise regimen invoked (acute v chronic), the results point to a consistent link between exercise and anxiety reduction. Furthermore, a meta-analysis specifically examining studies that distinguish between those who are coping with stress and those who are not concluded that aerobic exercise training programmes were effective in reducing anxiety, particularly among those experiencing chronic work stress.

Their overall effect sizes were comparable with those found by other meta-analyses of the exercise-stress literature, as well as other forms of psychotherapy used to reduce anxiety. At the same time, explicating the variables that mediate the relation between exercise and anxiety reduction has proved problematic, a task made doubly difficult because so few studies specify levels of intensity, duration, and/or length of exercise programme. To date, it can be inferred that most research studies have involved aerobic exercise, with the few studies examining non-aerobic activities-for example, strength/flexibility training-actually showing slight increases in anxiety.

The duration of individual training sessions has been considered across individual studies, with somewhat surprising results. According to recent research, even a single, five minute exercise bout may be sufficient to induce an anxiolytic effect. In terms of the length of training programmes, both clinical and nonclinical studies have shown that the largest anxiolytic effects are noted when programmes have run from 10 to 15 weeks or even longer, with smaller effects observed for programmes lasting less than nine weeks.

Mood State

Numerous studies have investigated the mood enhancing properties of exercise and have shown that exercise can indeed have a positive influence on mood state. At the same time, the early optimism generated by studies of clinical samples has been tempered by the discovery that the effects of exercise on mood state may not be as pervasive as earlier thought. For example, Dishmanand Frazier and Nagyave identified individuals who were not initially depressed or anxious, who failed to match a post-exercise mood enhancement as had been noted with clinical samples. On the other hand, it has also been shown that individuals may self report an improvement in mood state without a corresponding improvement being detected by the psychometric test of mood. These and other methodological concerns have been addressed.

In particular, the fact that most studies examining exercise effects on mood have utilised the Profile of Mood States (POMS) has been criticised because the test was initially validated for use in clinical populations and includes only one positive mood dimension. In the light of these and other criticisms, future reliance on the POMS as the primary measure of mood state in exercise research must be questioned.

A meta-analysis by McDonald and Hodgdon appeared to confirm a clear relation between exercise and positive moods, with significant effect sizes being shown for all six subscales of the POMS. However, more recent research suggests that this relation may be quite complex and demands further clarification. For example, Lennox et al., compared aerobic, anaerobic, and waiting list control groups and found no significant improvements in long term mood states among non-clinical samples. By comparison, other studies found improvements in mood states of female exercisers.

These studies highlight the possibility that gains in physical fitness may operate independently of mood, and hence it may be possible to show physical fitness gains in the absence of mood effects and vice versa. In comparison, acute aerobic exercise has been shown to be associated with significant positive mood changes. Two recent studies examining the benefits of acute exercise have also found mood benefits associated with exercise.

Steinberg et al., compared different intensity (low impact/ high impact) aerobic exercise of 25 minutes duration with a video watching control group and found increases in positive moods and decreases in negative moods after exercise. Another study adopting a slightly different approach set out to determine if a lengthy bout of acute aerobic exercise would attenuate the adverse mood effects induced by prescribed blockers to normal healthy individuals. Results showed that one hour of moderate (50% of maximum) treadmill walking was able to produce mood states comparable with those recorded for participants in placebo trials.

Overall these results do indicate that various forms of exercise, both aerobic and anaerobic, can be associated with an elevation of mood state, particularly for clinical samples, although given the diversity of results it is likely that more than one underlying mechanism may be implicated. The nature of these mechanisms, whether psychosocial, psychological, psychopharmacological, or psychophysiological, has yet to be understood.

Self Esteem

A positive link between exercise and self esteem has been established and in turn this appears to be strongest among those whose self esteem is low. For example, most studies examined global self esteem, which is a relatively stable construct, rather than considering domain specific esteem. Furthermore, few studies have explored changes in self esteem over time, with most focusing on differences between exercisers and non-exercisers at a given point in time.

Self esteem improved with participation in physical activity regardless of physical activity type. However, a meta-analysis that focused solely on self esteem in young children found a greater effect size for aerobic activities. Recent work in this area has tended to focus on the development of valid and reliable measures of self esteem, which in turn is regarded as multifaceted. For example, Foxas developed the physical self perception profile, which distinguishes between global self esteem and physical self esteem and which in turn has been related to factors including body image and sports competence. Subsequent work has been concerned with validation and in so doing has found further support for the notion that physical activity is associated with higher levels of self esteem in younger and older adult men and women.

An emerging viewpoint suggests that the more specific subdomains of self esteem, in particular perceived sport competence, physical condition, attractive body, and strength, may be associated differentially with behaviour in various sports. For example, Sonstroem et al., found that exercise in adult female aerobic dancers was associated with positive evaluations of their physical condition but with negative evaluations of their bodies. However, little can be said in terms of exercise prescription in the development of self esteem or its subcomponents because so few studies have considered such changes over time.

In fact, only one study appears to have considered this in middle aged men in the context of a five month walking programme. The study showed a significant relation between improved aerobic capacity and a measure of physical esteem. Results indicate that the greatest degree of change over time was in the subdomain element of physical condition, and global level self esteem showed the smallest degree of change (although it was still significant).

Premenstrual Syndrom (PMS)

Despite anecdotal evidence pointing to a relation between exercise and PMS symptomatology, and the fact that negative effect, depression, and anxiety, are commonly associated with PMS, only a small number of studies have considered the potential benefits of exercise on PMS. One such study investigated the impact of a 12 week training programme on symptom severity in relation to primary dysmenorrhoea.

Eighteen women who were diagnosed as suffering from dysmenorrhoea were assigned to a training programme which involved a 30 minute walk/jog session three times a week for 12 weeks. Their symptoms were subsequently compared with a non-exercising control group, and it was concluded that this form of exercise had ameliorated symptoms.

This and other examples of early research on PMS has tended to confirm that exercise has a prophylactic effect on a range of symptoms both physiological and psychological. More recently, Choi and Salmon monitored the effect of various frequencies of exercise on PMS in a self selected sample across one menstrual cycle. Low exercise and sedentary groups showed no improvement in symptoms whereas the high exercise group experienced significantly fewer symptoms.

Interestingly, competitive exercisers did not show improvements, perhaps indicating that strenuous exercise may be dysfunctional, and confirming earlier speculations relating to the negative effects of competitive exercising on anxiety and mood state. Likewise, Cockerill et al., found that those who engaged in exercise more than four times a week reported higher tension, depression, and anger, whereas those who exercised two to three times a week had healthier mood state profiles.

As regards the type of exercise that appears most beneficial, a study that considered this looked at 23 premenopausal middle aged women engaged on either an anaerobic (strength training) or aerobic exercise programme which took place three times a week for one hour over a 12 week period.

Participants completed a menstrual symptom questionnaire during their luteal phase once before the start of the programme and once more at its conclusion. While both aerobic and anaerobic exercise were shown to reduce premenstrual symptom severity, aerobic exercise appeared to have a more significant effect on premenstrual depression.

Numerous explanations have been advanced, including the effect that exercise may have on the oestrogen: progesterone ratio. On the one hand, some research has indicated that sportswomen have lower levels of oestrogen than non-exercising women, while on the other hand, other studies have found no differences. An alternative explanation highlights improved glucose tolerance during this stage of the cycle, as the symptoms of poor glucose tolerance are similar to those often reported by women who experience PMS, namely fatigue, depression, anxiety, and increased appetite. According to others, the elevation of endorphin levels before menstruation may be a significant factor, and regular exercise may stabilise or prevent extreme variation in endorphin levels and thus decrease the effects of PMS.

Body Image

In prescribing activity for both physical and psychological benefit, due caution must be taken to ensure that risk factors are not introduced that may attenuate the process of exercise induced psychological health. The gendered nature of physical activity cannot be disregarded in this debate, for while men may enjoy a symbiotic relationship with sport, too often in the past women's sport has been associated with sex role conflict and associated disorders. Despite significant gains in public acceptance and participation, women are still more likely to engage in non-competitive activities such as aerobics and keep fit, which in turn may serve to reinforce the cult of thinness and femininity.

Women consistently score higher than men on measures of self confidence with regard to their bodies and physical competence. Biddle et al, among others, have emphasised the need for exercise promoters to address this issue of poor self confidence among women, and to think carefully about sporting venues and other contextual factors (for example, changing facilities) in order to make women feel more comfortable with their body image during exercise.

Body image itself refers to a multidimensional construct consisting of a set of cognitions and feelings about one's physique. Research shows that body image tends to be less positive among women, and is more closely linked to women's overall self esteem than men's. For example, in a national survey of 803 US women, over half reported globally negative evaluations of their body parts and a preoccupation with losing weight.

The implications of such findings are considerable given that disturbances in body image have been so strongly implicated in the development of eating disorders and clinical depression. Without doubt, physicians who advocate the adoption of exercise regimens must remain alert to these body related concerns when prescribing forms of physical activity.

When training and diet regimens are overly stringent, women in particular are susceptible to three distinct although interrelated disorders collectively referred to as the female athlete triad (FAT). Referring to disordered eating, amenorrhoea, and osteoporosis, FAT is the physical manifestation of a pathological adherence to exercise, often coupled with inappropriate diet.

Davis et al., have described the role that exercise may play in sustaining the cyclical repetitious nature of eating disorders, and have also outlined the manner in which exercise and self starvation may interact as mutual catalysts. Disordered eating practices and a drive for thinness or leanness are often accompanied by psychopathological consequences observable in depressive symptoms such as low energy and poor self esteem.

With these thoughts in mind, caution is required when recommending exercise practices which may provide a link in the chain of disordered eating or which may present itself as a dysfunctional response to body dissatisfaction. A related concept, that of withdrawal from habitual exercise, may also be relevant in the context of attempting to provide exercise prescription. Morgan and colleagues speculate that cessation of regular physical activity could result in dysphoric states-for example, increased anxiety, depression, restlessness, guilt.

Indeed, a number of previous studies would concur with this speculation. However, yet again, despite the intuitive appeal of anecdotal examples, there is a limited amount of empirical research on the topic, and comparison across studies is not possible given the methodological differences surrounding deprivation periods and behavioural measures.

Whether the mechanism for supposed exercise addiction is based on psychological factors (for example, personality types), physiological mechanisms (for example, endorphin dependence), or an interplay between the two has yet to be established. A recent workshop concluded that much more systematic investigation needs to be conducted before definitive conclusions can be made about exercise prescription.

A number of cautions were raised, including doubts about whether the syndrome of "exercise dependence" exists at all except as one facet of an eating disorder, the danger of confusing exercise adherence with exercise dependence and exercise addiction, and that the hypothesis for a "runner's high"-that is, that exercise releases endorphins which produce physiological dependence-is still only a hypothesis with little supportive evidence.

A range of exercise regimens may be able play a therapeutic role in relation to a number of psychological disorders. At the same time, the research evidence to date does not provide unqualified support for the effcacy of exercise, and enthusiasm must be tempered with an acknowledgment of the dangers associated with exercise. Instead, it does suggest that different forms of physical exercise may be palliative in relation to particular conditions.

Whether that exercise be non-aerobic, aerobic, or anaerobic, of short, medium, or long term duration, competitive or non-competitive, team or individual, single or multi session is not always clear, but there are suggestions that different psychological conditions respond differentially to alternative exercise regimens, and recent attempts to develop taxonomies of physical activity and mental health may offer a realistic starting point in attempting to draw together some of the diverse recommendations.

As to explanations as to why more definitive conclusions cannot be reached at this stage, then three factors stand out. Firstly, the research base remains thin, and primary data are not extensive. To overcome this problem there is a need for large scale multidimensional experimental programmes, associated with multivariate analyses of covariance, in order to clarify the complexities of the relations between physical exercise and psychological health. Secondly, it is not yet clear how psychological and physiological processes and functions interact in the determination of outcomes.

The grey areas of confusion are most apparent when dealing with psychophysiological responses such as stress reactivity. Indeed, it could be that cartesian notions of mind-body dualism continue to drive a wedge between the physiological and the psychological.

Greater collaboration between the two disciplines would undoubtedly help this situation. Thirdly, and in a related vein, the primary mechanisms that underlie the relation between exercise and psychological well being remain poorly understood. It would also be fair to say that a great deal of the literature remains descriptive or atheoretical. That is, it is able to describe how exercise and psychological well being interact but it has shied away from asking or exploring why the relation is as it is. Here psychophysiologists have led the field in attempting to provide explanations, including consideration of the influence of catecholamines, body temperature, and endorphins.

Psychosocially, issues relating to lifestyle, boredom, and "time out" have also been implicated but how, when, and where each factor may be involved is once more a matter for debate. In all likelihood, given the complexities of the relations between exercise and well being outlined above, it is unlikely that any single theory, model, or hypothesis will suffice. Instead, multiple perspectives must be employed.

Finally, it is also important to recognise the difficulties associated with adherence to exercise regimens. No matter how beneficial such schemes may be, if there is no willingness to exercise voluntarily then the practical utility of exercise is diminished dramatically. Hence recommendations must be put in context of adherence research. For example, it has been maintained that only 10% of the population is committed to physical activity; 20% will start but not adhere to exercise; 40% will promise to start an exercise programme; 20% need to be convinced to participate in exercise; and 10% are not interested in any form of organised or recommended activity. Such research highlights the deep rooted resistance to taking exercise among large sections of the population, sections that lead essentially sedentary lives, with inactivity rates of 25% and 15% recently recorded for American and British populations respectively, and with the likelihood of even higher rates among those with psychological problems.

In exploring the population's apparent resistance to physical activity, a recent study has considered some of the theoretical models utilised in designing exercise interventions. As with the arguments advanced above in relation to explanations for exercise induced mental health benefits, they conclude that no individual model can sufficiently explain exercise behaviour or how best to intervene.

However, in proposing future directions in the area, it is interesting to note that the authors draw on largely psychological components as offering promise for encouraging greater participation. Specific factors outlined include enhancing self effcacy, increasing enjoyment of the activity, enhancing social support, and promoting the perceived benefits of exercise.

All these arguments aside, general practitioners remain the ideal mechanism by which to promote exercise regimens. At the same time, recent surveys suggest that, despite a generally favourable reception from general practitioners themselves, their role is not without problems, particularly in relation to the referral system, their lack of knowledge of exercise recommendations, and difficulty in evaluating community health promotion schemes. This level of enthusiasm for exercise promotion makes it all the more important that researchers, physicians, and exercise practitioners continue to work together to develop sound guidelines.

General recommendations are now commonly accepted as to the somatic benefits that accrue from exercise; the relation between exercise, fitness, and general cognitive functioning is now also receiving closer scrutiny. Alongside this research activity, now is the time to develop more specific guidelines relating to psychological benefits of exercise, taking due cognisance of psychosocial variables-for example, gender, age, previous mental health, environment-and recognising that the picture that will be revealed will not be as unidimensional as previous work may have implied.

7

Short-term Performance

Many of the determinants for aerobic and anaerobic capacity change with age. Muscle mass, which is central to both aerobic and anaerobic capacity, decreases with sedentary aging, as shown by several investigations. These decreases appear to occur primarily due to the loss of muscle fibers, but are also due to atrophy of individual fibers, particularly fast twitch muscle fibers. Some early research has suggested that there is a selective loss of fast twitch muscle fibers with aging. If true, this selective loss of fiber could result in a relative decrease in anaerobic work capacity, greater than the amount of muscle atrophy. However, more recent work has not confirmed this specificity of fiber loss, and indicates a preservation of muscle fiber type distribution with aging.

In healthy sedentary individuals, VO2 max decreases about 1% per year. This decrease is related to decreased capacity in all of the systems that determine VO2 max: maximum heart rate, stroke volume, and a-v O2 difference. Maximum heart rate declines about one beat per year with age. Although results regarding stroke volume are mixed, most investigations have shown that during exercise, stroke volume decreases with sedentary aging. However, other investigations show that stroke volume is maintained or even increased. Similarly, a-v O2 difference decreases with age in sedentary people. This decrease is related to decreased capillary density, mitochondrial density, and muscle mass.

Early studies of mitochondrial density in skeletal muscle did not indicate any age-related decrease. These findings may have been influenced by the effects of an active older subject population. More recently, however, investigations of subjects that were truly sedentary showed a significant (25-40%) age-related decrease in three mitochondrial enzymes, and in in-vitro muscle oxygen uptake.

Parizcova et al., demonstrated that the number of capillaries per unit of cross-sectional area did not change with age, but that, due to muscle fiber atrophy, there was a significantly lower capillary to fiber ratio in the older subjects. These findings were supported by those of Grimby et al.. More recently, however, Coggan et al., has shown that in truly sedentary subjects, both capillary density and capillary to fiber ratio decrease with aging.

Early studies of age-related effects on the anaerobic enzymes in skeletal muscle showed that the maximal activity of PFK, MK, and ATPase did not change with age, but that LDH decreased significantly. These findings were supported by Aniansson et al., except that they did not find an age related change in LDH. Grimby et al., found no age related decrease in the activity of HK and LDH. More recently, Coggan et al., found no age related difference in phosphorylase, LDH, or PFK. Additionally, resting levels of ATP are not affected by age. Perhaps the most thorough investigation of glycolytic enzymes and aging was performed by Essen-Gustavsson and Borges, who found no age-related change in HK, LDH, CK, or MK. Aside from early findings that LDH was reduced with aging, no age-related decrease in glycolitic enzyme activity or high energy phosphates has been demonstrated.

Creatine phosphate concentrations have been shown to decrease slightly with respect to aging. Moller et al. found a slight (5%) but significant decrease in creatine phosphate in skeletal muscle of men and women 52-79 years of age, compared with younger adults. McCully et al. also found a small decrease in the creatine phosphate to inorganic phosphate ratio using magnetic resonance spectroscopy.

Neural activation of skeletal muscles may change with aging. Evidence to support this hypothesis stems from the finding that specific tension (i.e.; force per unit cross sectional area) is maintained with aging in muscle fibers in-vitro, but not in whole muscles in-vivo. Since neural enervation is maintained with respect to aging, it is possible that "age-related deficiencies of motor function are probably related to other factors, such as those associated with neuromuscular transmission or propagation of nerve impulses".

Smith and Rosenheimer investigated neural transmission velocity and found no age related effects in rats. They concluded that "...motor deficits during aging must be associated primarily with changes in central pathways or at the muscular apparatus." To test that hypothesis, they examined architectural changes to the neuromuscular junctions, and found age-related changes in nerve terminal branch number; the rate of changes in end-plate morphology of all muscles studied increased after 25 months of age. In rats, 25 months is equal to the mean lifespan, so it is unclear whether these changes occur as a linear function of aging, or as an end lifespan event.

The neural signal to fire muscle contraction is maintained with age, but the ability to communicate that signal to the contractile machinery of the muscle may be compromised by changes at the motorneuron endplate.

Figure 2 below presents the effects of aging on the mechanisms of maximal short term performance. The shaded portions represent those systems in which maximal performance or function has been shown to decrease with age.

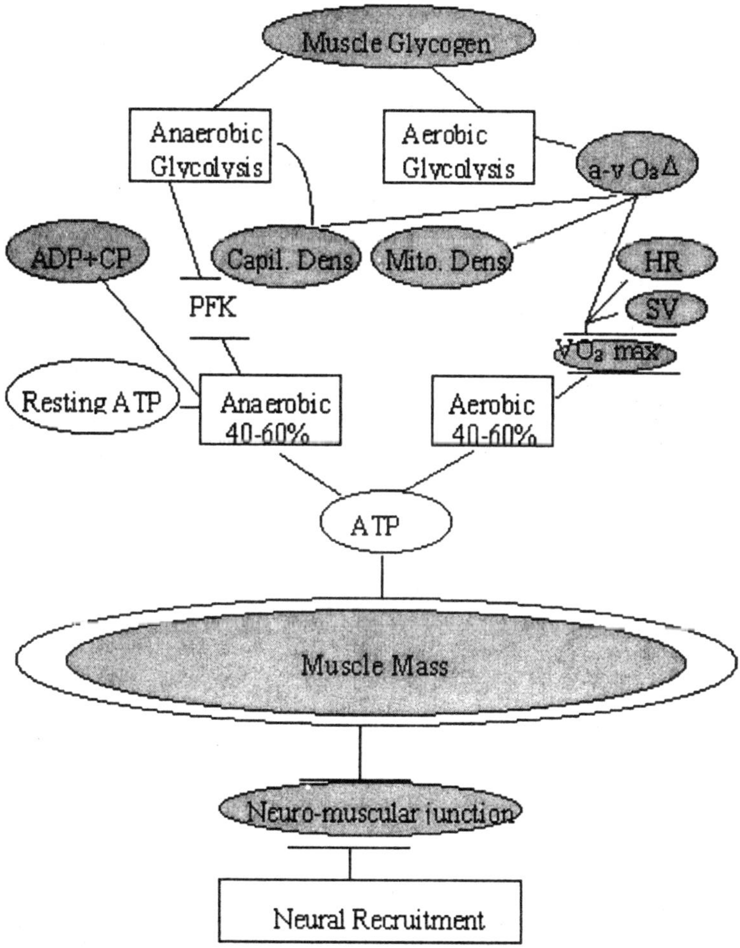

Figure 2

The age-related loss of muscle mass can be ameliorated with strength training. The subjects in the study of Frontera et al., increased muscle cross sectional area by 11% after 12 weeks of intense training, which is similar to the increases experienced by young adults for similar training. The subjects in the study of Brown et al., trained only one arm for twelve weeks, and increased CSA in the trained arm by 17%.

Charette et al., trained older women for 12 weeks. These women increased CSA by 20%. In all these studies, cross sectional area was increased due to hypertrophy of individual fibers, not by restoration of lost fibers. In an animal model study, Klitgarrd et al., found that weight training reduced the age-related decline in rat muscle. In cross-sectional studies of VO2 max, older individuals who maintain vigorous endurance training, experience a decrease of about one-half of one percent per year, compared to younger adults, or about half the decline experienced by sedentary adults. Some of this difference may be related to training between older and younger subjects.

To control for training differences, Hagberg et al, matched older (56 year old) runners for training volume, intensity and 10k performance, with younger runners (25 years old) and still found a 9% difference, or 0.3%/year decrease in VO2 max. However, in a longitudinal investigation, runners who maintained their training over a ten year period did not exhibit any decrease in VO2 max. Several of the runners in this study stopped training and they experienced a 14% decrease in VO2 max. This is interesting in that it is similar to the decrease in VO2 max experienced after only 56 days of detraining. Taken together, these findings suggest that the effects attributed to aging in sedentary individuals and detraining in previously trained individuals may be difficult to separate.

With regard to the components of cardiac output, training has no effect on the age-related decrease in maximum heart rate. However, stroke volume is improved significantly with endurance training. Specifically, training appears to enhance diastolic filling. In one of the best conceived investigations of training and hemodynamic function, Hagberg et al., studied older and younger runners who were matched for performance, training intensity and training volume. Their findings indicate that the decreased VO2 max of the older runners was solely a function of decreased maximum heart rate, and that stroke volume and a-v O2 difference were similar to those of the younger runners.

The age related decline in mitochondrial density may be ameliorated with exercise training. Early studies found little or no change in markers of mitochondrial density. However, these studies used exercise protocols that were relatively low intensity, and were maintained for only a brief time. Also, the subjects in these studies may have been moderately active rather than truly sedentary.

More recently, Coggan et al., screened carefully to obtain a truly sedentary subject population, and employed a vigorous exercise regime for 9 to 12 months. They found that this exercise significantly increased citrate synthase, the best predictor of mitochondrial density (29% in men and 17% in women). Furthermore, masters runners who were matched for training volume and intensity with young runners had similar CS activity. Also, the primary cause of loss of mitochondrial function is thought to be the prolonged effects of oxidative free radical stress, therefore it is possible that chronic intake of antioxidants may preserve mitochondrial density independent of exercise.

The results of investigations of capillary density are similar to those of mitochondrial density. Exercise regimes that involve low intensity exercise for a short period, and those that trained active older people did not increase muscle capillary density. However, Coggan et al., found significant increases in both capillaries per unit cross-sectional area (16% for men and 25% for women) and in capillaries per fiber (26% for men and 38% for women) when truly sedentary individuals performed more intense exercise for a longer period. Furthermore, masters runners who were matched for training volume and intensity with young runners had similar capillary density in capillaries per mm^2 and a greater number of capillaries per fiber. Interestingly, the strength training performed by the subjects of Frontera et al., elicited an unexpected increase in VO2 max, capillary to fiber ratio, and mitochondrial enzyme activity.

Muscle glycogen is increased in young people after exercise training, but has apparently only been investigated once, by Meredith et al.. They showed that a relatively short (12 week), but fairly intense (70% of VO2 peak) training programme produced significant (27%) increase in muscle glycogen content. Even with this increase, the older subjects still had less muscle glycogen than either the trained or sedentary younger men. It remains to be determined if higher intensity or longer duration training would restore muscle glycogen content to levels equal to those of younger people.

The small age related decrease in creatine phosphate may be eliminated with training. Moller and Brandt showed that six weeks of cycle ergometer training increased creatine phosphate levels of 61-80 year old men to those of younger adults. Although the joint effects of aging and exercise on motorneuron endplate structure has not been specifically investigated, we may be able to hypothesise on the effects based on other findings.

Specifically, in the strength training studies cited, the increases in strength are greater than the increase in muscle cross sectional area, indicating an increase in specific tension. It is known that specific tension in muscle fibers in-vitro is maintained with aging but decreased in whole muscle in-vivo, probably due to changes in motorneuron endplate structure. Therefore, we can surmise that the apparent increase in specific tension with strength training is due, at least in some measure, to increased performance of the motorneuron. It should also be mentioned that improvements in expressed strength after training may be in part due to improved coordination and learning.

PRINCIPLES OF TRAINING

There are four training principles.

1. The Overload Principle

We are biological organisms composed of an interdependent assortment of billions of individual cells. It has been said that "every cell in our body is psychological". This may sound crazy, but in a sense it is true. Every cell is in some form or another sensitive to certain forms of stress, and capable of initiating a specific response.

2. The Principle of Specificity

Any sport you pursue places highly specific demands on your body in at least two major ways. First, the exercise will have a very specific pattern of joint and muscle coordination. For a rower, there is absolutely no substitute for rowing. Ditto for swimming. Even when we try to duplicate the basic movement of a sports skill with strength training exercises, the transfer of increased strength to the actual sports movement is often small or absent. In the worst case this type of training can detract from performance of the real skill due to disruption of technique. Second, the exercise will place high metabolic demands on a very specific group of muscles.

For example, running and cross-country skiing appear to involve many of the same muscles, used in a similar movement pattern. Yet, several research studies have demonstrated that there is NO relationship between VO2 max measured by treadmill running and VO2 max measured by cross-country skiing in a group of elite-trained skiers. In contrast, there is a strong relationship between on-snow skiing and performance on a skiing specific test such as the douple poling test. A high endurance capacity in a specific sport requires both 1) high oxygen delivery (cardiac output) and 2) high local blood flow and mitochondrial density in the precise muscles used. The only way to optimally develop the second component of endurance is to train those exact muscles by doing your sport!

One of the keys to success in sport is staying healthy over the long haul. Weight training by itself will almost certainly do nothing for a runner's 10k time, but if weight training maintains muscular balance in her abdominal wall and low back, preventing injury, then it is contributing to her becoming a faster runner. And, cycling isn't running. But if cycling takes the pressure off tired knees and hips on a recovery steady-state day, then it will probably make the next running workout better. Cross training should always be limited to those activities that allow us to do our event-specific training workouts with greater enthusiasm and intensity, or less risk of injury.

3. The Reversibility Principle

If people were as economical as their bodies, we would not have problems with personal debt and excess world waste production. The human body is nothing if not thrifty. The iron and protein in those millions of blood cells that die each day is almost completely re-used to build new blood cells. The body does not build proteins it doesn't need, and it doesn't retain proteins that are no longer needed! For the athlete, the unfortunate consquence of this thriftiness is the rapid reversibility of training adaptations if training is stopped.

4. The Principle of Individual Differences

Last but not least on the list of Training Principles is the Principle of Individual Differences.

TIME COURSE OF TRAINING ADAPTATIONS

Some basic physiological variables that are known to 1) bear a strong relationship on endurance performance in every sport and 2) respond to training.

1. Maximal Oxygen Consumption
2. Lactate Threshold
3. Efficiency

Number 1. is an oxygen delivery issue. A high maximal capacity for blood delivery means higher oxygen delivery and the potential for more muscle to be active simultaneously during exercise. VO2 is primarily limited by the maximum pumping capacity of the heart, and the specific arterial development to the active muscles.

Number 2 is an oxygen utilisation issue. The greater the intensity of work we can achieve prior to the point when we begin to accumulate the inhibiting acidity of lactic acid, the faster sustained pace we can tolerate. The limiting adaptations are the capillary density, fatty acid breakdown enzyme level and mitochondrial density in the specific skeletal muscles used in your sport. Combining elements 1 and 2 gives us the sustainable power output of your "performance engine".

Number 3, Efficiency, links sustainable power to performance velocity. The better the efficiency, the greater the achieved velocity at a given level of energy output. Since, ultimately, we have a limited "engine" size, improvements in efficiency are critical to additional improvements in performance time.

VO2 max is increased significantly after only one week of training. The reason for this early improvement appears to be an increase in blood volume, which results in improved maximal stroke volume. As training continues, VO2max continues to increase, for several months, albeit at a slower rate of improvement. After about 3-4 months of regular exercise, the improvement in maximal oxygen consumption begins to level off dramatically. At this point, it is common to see about a 15-20% improvement in this variable. For example, a hypothetical male (Bjorn) with an initial VO2max of 3.5 liters/min (at a bodyweight of 75kg, that's 47ml/min/kg) may increase to 4.0 liters/min, a 14% increase in absolute VO2. If in the process of training, Bjorn also loses 4kg (close to 10 pounds), then his relative VO2 max will have increased even more (from 3500/75 or 47, to 4000/71 or 56 ml/min/kg). This is a nearly 20% improvement. Unfortunately, after another 6 months of training, it will have increased little more, if any.

If the level of training intensity remained the same after the first 4 months, then no further changes would be expected. If on the other hand, Bjorn continues to intensify his training over the next 6 months, a small additional increase might occur. This increase might be as much as 5 additional percent, bringing our example athlete up from an initial value of 3.5 liters/ min at 75 kg, to 4.2 liters/min at 70kg (he also lost another 1 kg of fat). That's 47 ml/min/kg up to 60 ml/min/kg due to a combination of both increased absolute VO2max (20%) and decreased bodyweight (6.7%), for a total improvement in relative maximal oxygen consumption of 27%. This is actually an unusually large improvement in this variable, but definitely plausible.

At the same time Bjorn's VO2max was increasing due to central and peripheral cardiovascular adaptations, changes were beginning to occur in his skeletal muscles. Initially, an incremental exercise test on a treadmill revealed that Bjorn began to show an substantial increase in lactic acid concentration in his blood while running at 60% of his maximal oxygen consumption.

Remember, his max was 3.5 liters/min. 60% of this is 2.1 l/min. So functionally speaking, 2.1 l/min was his threshold workload for sustained exercise. If he runs at a speed that elicits a higher VO2 than 2.1, he fatigues quite quickly. However, over time, the overload of training induced quantitative changes to begin occurring in his leg muscles. Mitochondrial synthesis increased.

More enzymes necessary for fatty acid metabolism within the muscle cell were produced. And, the number of capillaries surrounding his muscle fibers began to increase. Additional capillaries are being constructed. The functional consequence of these local muscular adaptations is a very positve one. Bjorn's running muscles use more fat and less glycogen at any given running pace. And, the glycogen metabolised to pyruvate is less likely to be converted to lactic acid and more likely to inter the mitochondria for complete oxidative metabolism. Consequently, Bjorn's lactate threshold begins to increase. After 6 months of training, in addition to a higher VO2max, his lactate threshold has increased from 60% to 70% of max, a 17% improvement in an absolute sense, but functionally much more.

Now, the important thing to know is this. While VO2max plateaus quite rapidly, lactate threshold does not. If Bjorn continues to train, and increase his intensity appropriately, his lactate threshold will continue to improve slowly for a longer period. Of course, improvements in lactate threshold also plateau, otherwise elite athletes that have been training for 15 years would have LT's of 100% of VO2 max! But, the time course of adaptation is slower, so the plateau occurs after a longer period of intense training, probably several years

It is also important to remember that the lactate threshold is even more specific to the mode of exercise than the VO2 max. This was exemplified by a study performed by Coyle et al. and published in 1991. In this study, 14 competitive cyclists with nearly identical VO2 max values differed substantially in their lactate threshold determined during cycling. When the cyclists were divided into a "low" and "high" LT groups, it was found that the two groups differed considerable in the years of cycling training (2.7 compared to 5.1 years on average). However, they did not differ in years of endurance training (7-8 years of running, rowing etc.) When the low cycling LT and high cycling LT groups were asked to perform a lactate threshold test while running on a treadmill, the two groups were no longer different. Measured while running, the lactate threshold in both groups averaged over 80% of VO2 max.

The final element of our big three endurance adaptations is efficiency. Efficiency is defined as mechanical work/metabolic work. For example, one (quite good) cyclist can sustain 300 watts power output for 1 hour on a cycling ergometer at a sustained VO2 of 4.3 liters/min. Another rider performing at the same oxygen consumption, squeezes out 315 watts, a difference in efficiency of 5%. Even though both riders have the same "metabolic engine" they have different power output capabilities. You don't do 40k time trials on a lab ergometer, though.

So efficiency makes a difference, often much bigger than the above example. And it also varies among different athletes. That's interesting, but not terribly useful for your training. In highly technical sports like swimming, efficiency differences between beginners and experienced swimmers can be absolutely tremendous. Swimmers already know this full well. In rowing, efficiency also improves dramatically at first, due to gross technical improvements. However, efficiency can also continue to improve after years of training. Dr. Fritz Hagerman followed one group of national class (U.S.) rowers for 8 years, measuring ergometer performance, VO2, lactate threshold, etc. Peak values for maximal oxygen consumption and lactate threshold stabilised after only 2 or 3 years in these hard training athletes. However, performance times on the water and on the rowing machine continued to improve over additional years of training.

Slow improvements in rowing efficiency. One source that is independent of on-water technique may be optimisation of workload distribution among the large muscle mass employed in rowing. Ultimately, the rowers who went on to become national team members and have success at the highest levels were more efficient than their peers.

Cycling and Running

In studies carried out on "Good" vs. "Elite" cyclists carried out by Dr. Ed Coyle and colleagues at the University of Texas, it appears that elite riders sustain higher power outputs despite similar physiological values in part by learning to distribute the pedalling force over a larger muscle mass. In running, fomer U.S record holder in the mile, Steve Scott, was shown to have improved his running efficiency even "late" in his career.

Based on a tremendous amount of both laboratory and "field" data, there are three endurance performance variables reach their peak is 1) VO2max, then 2) lactate threshold, then 3) performance efficiency. Putting it all together, and neglecting for now the negative impact of aging on maximal oxygen consumption.

Obviously, if you are just beginning in an endurance sport, then all three elements will probably improve dramatically, almost no matter what you do! But, if you have been training in sport for a year or more, you must construct your training programme with more and more care to continue making progress in those adaptations that have "room to improve" while maintaining the levels of those that have plateaued or are beginning to. Since for the masters athlete, the option of "just adding another workout" is usually not a viable one, this will often mean finding the right distribution of a limited amount of training time among a variety of workout types.

Understanding Intervals

In endurance training circles, no matter what the sport, Interval Training has become a standard practice. Since the 1960's, interval training has come to be thought of as the key to endurance performance success. In some training programmes, it accounts for 50-75% of the total training volume.

Physiology of Intermittant Exercise

In exercise physiology research, one of the true "Fathers" of the field is Per Astrand from Sweden. Today, Dr. Astrand is still showing up at International Sports Medicine research meetings at the age of 80 or so. His best known contribution, "Textbook of Work Physiology", co-written with Norwegian Kaare Rodahl and now in its 5th edition or so, remains a "must have" for the student of exercise physiology. In the 60s he performed some simple experiments that still have important training implications regarding the physiological impact of continuous versus intermittant exercise.

In a lab setting, a bicycle ergometer serves as a very useful tool for performing exercise studies. We can precisely control the workload that the cyclist must maintain, and since he/she is sitting still, it is easy to perform an extensive array of physiological measurements, such as heart rate, VO2, blood lactate etc. The following experiments were performed using just such an exercise setup.

One subject was made to accomplish a certain amount of work (force x distance, a quantity that can be precisely measured on the ergometer) in 1 hour. This work could be accomplshed either by a continuous bout of exercise at a power output of 175 watts, or by intermittent exercise at a heavier load, separated by regularly spaced rest intervals. A double power output was chosen for this heavier load. Thus the desired work could be acomplished with 30 minutes of exercise at 350 watts within the span of one hour.

At a work load of 175 watts, the subject could easily cycle for one hour continuously. Heart rate was only 134, VO2 was only about 55% of maximal, and blood lactate remained near resting levels. When the subject tried to exercise as long as possible at 350 watts, or double that workload, the exercise could only be maintained for 9 minutes. Heart rate was 190 bpm (maximal), VO2 was at max, and blood lactate had risen to 16.5 mM, an extremely high value indicative of extreme fatigue. If, instead, he exercised at the same 350 watts intermittantly for a duration of between 30 seconds and 3 minutes, always with equal rest, he could perform the desired work within the hour. However, the physiological responses differed tremendously depending on the interval duration.

Interpretation

There are two major points to draw from Dr. Astrand's experiments:

1) Intermittant exercise allows a higher total volume of high intensity work. Performed continuously, the subject could only manage 9 minutes at 350 watts. Performed in 3 minute intervals, he could accumulate over 3 times as much total work (30 minutes, with great effort).

2) When the intervals were 3 minutes in length, the desired work could be accomplished within one hour, at great effort. However, when the work and rest periods were shortened, the physiological strain was dramatically reduced, even though total oxygen uptake during the hour was not markedly reduced. Specifically, if the intervals are less than 2 minutes in length, the physiological workload/stress is severely reduced despite the same total accumulated time (30 minutes here) and same interval intensity (350 watts workload here). If you compare the peak oxygen consumption, HR, and lactic acid concentration achieved during 1 minute intervals with 2 minute intervals in the table above, this difference is easily observed.

Interval training allows us to accumulate a greater volume of stress on the blood pumping capacity of the heart. By using a large muscle mass, we promote maximal stroke volume responses. A high heart rate also is achieved as a function of the intensity. Finally, the periodic elevations and decreases in intensity may create special loading stresses on the heart that are adaptive. For example, during an interval, heart rate climbs high, then at the moment you stop the interval, heart rate immediately starts to drop, but venous return remains high. These exposures to additional ventricular stretch may help trigger ventricular remodeling (bigger ventricle volume). In addition, interval training may create a greater signal for changes in the compliance in the arterial system, but that is just more speculation.

For the untrained, interval training is a way of accumulating minutes of exercise at a higher intensity than our skeletal muscles are initially adapted to tolerate. In the untrained, the heart is better conditioned to endurance performance than the skeletal muscles. Therefore it needs a greater overload to adapt maximally. Intermittent high intensity training is also a powerful stimulus for increasing blood volume, which is a critical adaptation that contributes significantly to improved maximal cardiac output and VO2 max.

The VO2 max is only the 1st wave of change for the endurance athlete. VO2 max plateaus quite early in the career of an adult runner or cyclist who trains hard and regularly (though its exact value will undulate several % from off-season to competitive season).

It is the improvement in lactate threshold, or the percentage of VO2 max that can be maintained without significant lactic acid accumulation. Changes in the lactate threshold occur over a longer time-course than the improvement in maximal oxygen consumption, even if we train regularly. The site of adaptation moves from the cardiovascular sytem to the skeletal muscles. Additional mitochondria are synthesised, new capillaries are constructed, type II b fibers are converted to more fatigue resistant type II a. These adaptations occur progressively over a period of several years. The most powerful stimulus for change in skeletal muscle aerobic capacity is different from the most powerful stmulus for cardiac functional changes!

Back in the early and mid 60s the German's training approach had indeed been much different, with a greater emphasis on high intensity intervals. What they found was that, to a great extent they did reach high performance levels with this training programme. But, they were not seeing progressive improvement from year to year among their elite athletes. Every year they came up to the same level, fell back down in the off season, and repeated the process the next season. Then they changed the composition of the training to a higher volume, lower intensity and the long term progress began to occur.

Another reason relates to a different component of the physiological impact of high intensity intervals. Long term observation of elite German athletes has demonstrated that the body's tolerance for exposure to very high lactate concentrations and the extreme sympathetic stress associated with this type of training is quite limited. After a severe effort, immune function and other measures are disturbed for days. After a major international race, the disturbance can extend for weeks. Overtraining and tissue injury is much more likely during periods of extreme intensity. If training is interrupted due to injury or staleness, then no progress is made.

There has been a tremendous amount of press in the running world about the recent dominance demonstrated by east Africans, particularly the Kenyans. Not surprisingly, some have suggested that these runners are "genetically different" or train in "secret ways" that make them invincible in world distance running. Well the Kenyans ARE setting world records right and left and kicking the rest of the running world's preverbial butt . But do they have any physiological or training secrets? Well, to address that question, Dr. Bengt Saltin, formerly at the Karolinska Institute in Sweden, and now at the Copenhagen Muscle Research Center (Denmark), performed some interesting studies and published them in 1995. He measured maximal oxygen consumption, lactate threshold, economy, fiber type etc. in the top 12 Swedish distance runners.

Then he went to Kenya and did the same thing among some of their best runners (with the considerable help of the famous runner of the 60s, Kipchoge Keino). On average, Kenyan and Swedish runners had high and similar VO2 max values (The very best Kenyans were somewhat higher than the very best Swedes, though). However, the really noticeable differences between the dominant Kenyans and the "also ran" Swedes was in their very low lactate and ammonia accumulation at high running speeds, and their excellent running economy.

There is substantial research to indicate that there is little or no difference in the impact on maximal oxygen consumption among exercise intensities ranging from 80 to 100% of VO2 max. At intensities above 100%, the stimulus for improving maximal oxygen consumption is actually reduced, due to dramatically decreased training volume, and the inhibiting effect of lactic acidosis on cellular oxygen utilisation. During work within the 75-100% intensity range, improved exercise tolerance should be compensated for by increasing distance or time, not intensity. This increased tolerance for exercise at a given submaximal intensity is indicative of skeletal muscle adaptations.

Aerobic interval training is definitely effective, but the emphasis should be on interval durations of from 10 to 20 minutes if your event duration is greater than 4 minutes. Intervals of 4 to 8 minute duration are going to be at intensities of 85 to 100% of VO2 max. This intensity and duration is optimal for maximising/maintaining cardiovascular power. However, remember that this adaptation plateaus "early". Your incorporation of 4-8 minute intervals probably needn't ever exceed once every 8 days.

Consequently, the majority of your training time should be aimed at optimising the signal for other adaptations. Longer intervals of 10 to 20 minute duration will be at 75 to 85% depending on your abiity and training status, and are a very useful method for developing skeletal muscle endurance, "the Second Wave of Change". With both intervals the duration will generally force you into the right intensity range, if you are giving a good effort. The intermittant nature will help you to accumulate minutes of high quality work.

This means that on most of those busy days when you only have 30 minutes to train, a brief warm-up and one hard 20 minute steady state interval (temp run, AT effort, etc.) is more beneficial than resorting to a series of very short intervals. Rest intervals should not need to be very long, since lactate accumulation is not severe. For example, if you are attempting to do 5 times 5 minutes, a rest interval of at least 2 minutes but no more than 4 minutes should be used. For 20 minute intervals, rest will only be 5-6 minutes. If the intensity is appropriate, for a given interval session, you should be able to complete all the intervals at the same speed, albeit with increasing effort. Basically the long term goal is for the interval intensity to slowly become a steady state pace.

In their excellent book "Training Distance Runners", David Martin and Peter Coe talk about interval training. They suggest that you should even be able to increase the speed of the last one or two intervals. This will indicate that you have not accumulated excessive lactic acid in the training session. If you are blowing out the first one and find yourself fading on subsequent intervals or cutting your workout short, then you are clearly not performing at the right intensity.

If your event duration is in the 3-4 minute range (1000 meters for rowers), then ANAEROBIC CAPACITY will play a contributing role. Even in these short events, aerobic endurance is still the foundation of success, but your ability to tolerate very high lactic acid levels and maintain good technique (rowers, swimmers) is critical over the concluding moments of the race. In this case we employ Anaerobic Intervals Here the method and goal is very different, and this must be recognised. In these sprint intervals, 30 seconds to 2 minutes in length, 1) a severe accumulation of lactic acid is expected. Also, forget your heart rate monitors. What they read means nothing under these conditions.

Rest intervals may be up to twice as long as work intervals. Intensity will be at 105 to 120% of VO2 max pace. Lactic acid will not completely eliminated during the rest. So, each interval will start at a higher blood lactate. The goal is to sustain speed as best as possible at higher levels of lactate. Here the total work time may be as little as 6 minutes to as much as 16 minutes. The value of these workouts diminishes once you can no longer maintain adaquate technique.

The limited potential for amplification of lactate accumulation capacity and tolerance comes at a high price within the overall endurance athlete's training programme (remember the German data). These adaptations are also achieved much faster than aerobic adaptations, so sprint training need not be implemented before 4-6 weeks out from a specific competition. It doesn't take too many brutal sprint sessions to have you or your athletes broken down at the side of the road/ river/pool. For most endurance athletes, this mode of training should not account for more than 1 of every 10 workouts. More will put you at risk of becoming physically stale and psychologically brittle, and detract from the volume of training dedicated to aerobic adaptations.

Endurance Performance

Historically, there is no doubt that sport has been a center of faulty assumptions and sexism where female athletes are concerned. Social issues, and misunderstanding about female physical and medical limitations conspired to slow the development of female performance for many years, but those times are gone, at least among young athletes. Among master's athletes, we still see greatly reduced participation by the older female age groups. This participation difference will no doubt diminish over the next couple of decades. As a result, performances by the oldest females will probably improve more rapidly than those of the oldest males, as this new generation of well trained young female athletes moves into age-group competition, and are joined by more and more talented "late bloomers."

"Old" Social norms and habits are still having negative consequences on participation and performance by older (50 +) females. Modern female athletes have repeatedly demonstrated these norms are totally bogus. Currently, teenage daughters are encouraging their formally sedentary mothers and even grandmothers to take up exercise. This transfer of knowledge and norms UPSTREAM is the reverse of what we traditionally see in males. However, this is a transitional period for women in sport, so the knowledge transfer across generations is helping to speed the development of women's masters sport.

Having said all that, there are some physiological differences between the sexes that impact performance in females independent of age. Some years ago, when the marathon was first becoming a competitive event for women, the rapid improvement in female times led some to predict that female performances would soon equal those of men in the marathon. This has not happened, and it won't. The current world record for women is 2:21, compared to 2:06:50 for the men, a difference in speed of about 10%. This same 10% gap is present across the distance running performance spectrum The reason for the performance gap is not that women don't train as hard as men. There are some important physiological differences between the sexes that can't be overlooked or overcome.

The Lactate Threshold

Now we come to the second component of endurance performance, the lactate threshold. This is the exercise intensity at which lactic acid begins to accumulate in the blood stream at levels significantly above "baseline" values. This intensity sets a (slightly fuzzy) boundary between that exercise intensity which can be sustained for long periods (over one hour) versus those which lead to fatigue in minutes. We have already discussed the fact that changes in the lactate threshold are due to adaptations that occur in the exercising muscle. We call these peripheral adaptations.

The question here is, do women demonstrate a different pattern or capacity for peripheral adaptations then men? First, Female skeletal muscle is not distinguishable from male skeletal muscle. Second, within some margin of error, the fiber type distribution (percentage of slow versus fast fibers) is not different in the male and female population. Third, male and female skeletal muscle responds similarly to endurance exercise. Finally, elite female endurance athletes have similar lactate threshold values compared to men when expressed as a percentage of their VO2 max. Elite women perform at the same high percentage of their maximal oxygen consumption as their male counterparts.

Some years ago it was proposed by some that women would actually perform better at ultra-endurance type activities. This theory has been disproved both in the laboratory and in practice as a performance difference persists in the ultramarathon events. Some of you may balk and recall a recent Running Times article that suggested women had an edge in the really long events. They discussed a study in which a group of male and female runners who were matched for marathon time were raced head to head in the Comrades marathon, a 90k race. The women won by 54 minutes, suggesting a female edge in longer events. This advantage becomes bigger in an ultradistance event.

The fact remains that the performance gap between male and female record holders in the really long running races 50k to 6 days is actually more on the order of 15 to 20%, instead of the 10% difference for the standard distances. Part of this larger gap may be to lower participation, and the fact that the most talented females have not yet tested themselves over the ultradistances.

Efficiency

The third component of endurance performance is efficiency which of course has different constraints, depending on the sport. The research information comparing the efficiency of female and male athletes is both sparse and inconclusive. In running, for example females have been found to be more, less, and equally efficient compared to males men depending on the specific study. Some of this confusion comes down to how the differences in bodyweight and bodyfat were accounted for.

Now, if we look at efficiency/economy differences in other sports, things mostly boil down to body shape/

anthropometric differences. In situations like running or cycling, these may actually favor females in general, due to narrower upper bodies for a given total body mass, and potentially less wind or water drag.

Back in the 70s, a theory got started that said "Since women have more fat stores, they will be better at utilising fat during endurance performance when glycogen stores are depleted." One of the supporting pillars of the theory was that it had been noticed by one female runner/author how "fresh" many female runners looked as they crossed the finish line! Well, this shaky theory was crushed under the harsh light of science. Back in 1979, Costill and colleagues compared males and females who were equally trained during a 60 minute treadmill run. There were no differences in any measures of fat metabolism. These guys even took some muscle out of the runners' legs and tested it in a test tube.

On an absolute basis, and per kg bodyweight, women have lower sweat rates than men. However, because of their higher body surface area to volume ratio, they dissipate heat equally well. Men have an advantage in evaporative cooling, but women have an advantage in radiant cooling, so they come out even.

Strength Training and Endurance Performance

In endurance performance, we are limited by weak links in the physiological system. Making an already strong link stronger doesn't keep a chain from breaking if you still have the same weak link. Many endurance athletes are lifting weights 2 to 3 times per week and swear by it. Others never lift a weight and excel.

When a bodybuilder trains, the goal is to make each muscle fiber as big as possible. Muscle fibers have contractile protein, mitochondrial protein, and other components. Increasing the relative proportion of one component (like more contractile protein) means that you have relatively less of everything else in the same fiber (like mitochondria). From an endurance standpoint this is not a good adaptation. We even give it a name in sports physiology circles, mitochondrial dilution. The bodybuilder's muscles may actually become more easily fatigued as they get bigger, because their mitochondrial density is not increasing at the same rate. The bodybuilder accepts that because the name of the game is size, not endurance.

It is possible for the endurance athlete to gain some muscle size and maintain mitochondrial density, but it requires that the volume of endurance training be maintained. If you are a runner and you decide to get stronger in the weight room by really doing a lot of strength training 3 days a week for an hour, you will probably drop some of your running volume to fit it in. After 6 months you have gained 5-10 pounds of muscle, you look really good, and you are running 2 minutes slower for 10k! Why? Well besides having to carry around 5-10 more pounds of muscle that you can't use when you are running, you have probably lost endurance capacity in those bigger stronger quads.

Strength training helps endurance performance. It can, definitely. But we have to look at the reasons more carefully. For example, perhaps you are a runner who has had a hip injury that lingered and lingered. Over time your running style accommodated and now you run with a "seated" style and do not employ your hip extensors effectively. A weight training programme employing highly specific exercises designed to teach you to activate your hip extensors, as well as strengthen them, can make you more efficient by improving work distribution in the leg muscles, and therefore faster runner.

A lot of this change may be due to improved motor function as much as increased muscle mass. Specific strength training can help us to teach our brain to communicate with the right muscles. The same is true of the rower with the weak low back. Strengthening this area can correct the weak link and allow optimal connection between force generators and the oar.

Remember VO2 max? What is the major limitation to VO2 max? Right, the maximum capacity of the heart to pump blood and deliver oxygen to the muscles. Anytime we are doing an activity that uses a lot of muscle (running, rowing, XC skiing, mountain biking), the challenge falls on the heart to match oxygen supply with the demand. Even in the world champion, the heart is incapable of pumping as much blood as the muscles could receive. Consequently, adding muscle mass will not result in increased maximal oxygen consumption. The heart is already being asked to do all it can do. Your endurance machine is a set of highly integrated components. You have to look at how all the pieces fit together to produce the final product.

Now having said all of that, here is a thought question for you. Watch an elite marathoner run across the finish line. He or she raises toothpick size arms into the air in victory and jogs off on those skinny but brilliant legs. No excess muscle there. Just the right amount to get the job done. Now take a look at another marathon race, this time the wheelchair race for para-athletes. The winner rolls across the line with a final push of the arms, raises them in victory and you are caught staring at one impressively muscular set of pythons! For the wheelchair endurance athlete, muscle mass is an important part of the package.

The wheelchair racer is depending on a much smaller total volume of muscle to do the work of the marathon race. The total volume of muscle is small enough that the heart is no longer the limiting factor! So, in this situation, gaining muscle mass in combination with endurance training results in a more powerful endurance engine. In fact, these unique conditions may result in a greater hypertrophic response to endurance training independent of supplemental strength training in a weight-room.

Ventilation and Endurance Performance

The term ventilation is used in physiology circles exclusively in reference to gas exchange in the lungs. Now, when you hear a non-smoker trapped in a smoke-filled room gasping something about "this room needs better ventilation," she means that the room does not have very rapid air-exchange with the outside, smoke-free air. Conversely, in a room that is well-ventilated, the air always seems fresh even when lots of people are crammed together in a small enclosed space, sucking in oxygen and blowing out lots of "waste-products." You non-physiologists prefer to call this situation "a party."

Rooms depend on air-conditioning systems, or big windows and a breeze for ventilation. Our body depends on the lungs, the diaphragm and several intercostal muscles, and a sensitive feedforward/feedback controlled regulatory system to control them. The purpose of the lungs is to ventilate the blood. Blood is the transport vehicle that carries oxygen to all of our cells, and carts off the constant production of CO_2 that is produced as a by-product of both metabolism and pH buffering. The lungs are the site of pickup from and delivery to, the atmosphere.

The greater the demand for oxygen delivery and CO2 removal, the greater the air volume that must circulated in and out of the lungs each minute. All animals of any size at all have had to come up with a ventilation system to get oxygen from the atmosphere down to the most hidden of the cells via the blood. Fish have gills. Insects have a system of air tubes called trachea. We mammals own beautiful pink lungs.

Aspects of Ventilatory Function

1. Air Exchange

Ventilation is regulated in much the same manner as cardiac output. The heart increases cardiac output by increasing both stroke volume and beating frequency. The respiratory nerves control ventilation similarly. At low exercise workloads, the dominant ventilatory adjustment is an increase in tidal volume, the volume of air being moved in and out of the lungs each breath. At high workloads, an increase in breathing frequency is the primary adjustment. The two figures below visualise this. The first figure shows the overall ventilatory response during a treadmill test with progressive increases in velocity every 60 seconds, and a constant incline of 5%. The second figure breaks the ventilatory response above into breathing frequency and tidal volume. This is real, unsmoothed data collected during a test of a well trained runner.

Unlike heart function, ventilation is under considerable voluntary control (with involuntary override mechanisms!). For example, you could decrease the breathing frequency and take bigger deeper breaths to achieve the same total ventilation volume. Studies have indicated that normally the body spontaneously balances the depth of ventilation and the frequency of breathing so that ventilation is optimally efficient. You may also have noticed that at low exercise intensities, you can "play" more with your breathing, by varying its rate and depth. However, as the workload gets high, especially at workloads above the lactate (and ventilatory) threshold, the body assumes much tighter control on breathing and there is far less room for variation in breathing "strategies."

The actual act of moving air in an out of the lungs is accomplished in much the same way that a bathroom plunger works. Since the thorax is "sealed," expanding its volume causes air to rush in to the lungs to fill the relative vacuum. When we inspire air, we do so by contracting the diaphragm, pulling it down (similar to pulling up on the plunger). If you are breathing "correctly" at rest, the main movement you will notice is your stomach bulging out a bit during inspiration. This is because the diaphragm is pressing down against the abdominal cavity.

You are "belly breathing." At rest and low ventilation volumes, this is enough. However, when we need to move a lot of air in and out of the lungs, we not only increase the force of diaphragmatic contraction, we also contract muscles attached to the rib cage. This pulls the ribs up and out, further expanding the thorax and allowing more air to rush into to the lungs. All of this takes muscular work, so inspiration is an "active process." Expiration, or blowing the air back out, is basically a matter of relaxation when we are at rest.

The elasticity of the muscles and tissues is sufficient to push the air out. The process becomes more demanding as we exercise harder. During heavy exercise we exhale more forcefully and deeply in order to ensure more rapid and complete exhalation of the old air. This process also takes energy in the form of muscular work. So, the bottom line is that breathing is not free to the body. And, it gets more energetically expensive at high workloads.

2. *Gas exchange*

The lungs do some pretty cool stuff. The lung's challenge is to mix air and blood thoroughly and rapidly so that gas exchange can occur. Here comes another analogy. Let's say you have a gallon bucket (4 liters) of paint sitting with the lid open. How long will it take that bucket of paint to dry out? Days and days. But, if we spread the paint as a very thin layer over a very large wall, it will be dry in no time. By spreading the paint out we increase the total area of exposed surface between the paint and the air thousands of times and the water in the paint is quickly evaporated. At any given instant at rest, the lungs spread about 70 ml of blood (less than half of the volume of a coke can) in a "sheet" of capillaries with a total surface area of 70 square meters. That is like spreading a gallon of paint thin enough to paint a football field!

The capillaries are so narrow that the red blood cells actually have to squeeze through. This also insures that the gas exchange across the red blood cell and capillary membranes is lightning fast. Simultaneously the lungs move the inspired air down a system of 23 branches of air passages terminating with about 300 million tiny spherical alveoli that form the terminal exchange tissue in the bronchial system. These two exchange systems, the alveoli for air, and the capillaries for blood, are intertwined so microscopically close that oxygen and carbon dioxide molecules diffuse across the membranes and equilibrate almost instantaneously. Blood passes through the capillaries in about 0.8 seconds at rest and as little as 0.4 to 0.5 seconds during hard exercise. It is during this very brief exposure period that all the gas exchange between each red blood cell and the air in the lungs must take place before each return trip to the body!

Now perhaps one of you physiology student types is doing some analytical thinking that does like this: If resting cardiac output is 5 liters per minute, and maximal cardiac output were say, 25 liters/min, that would mean that 5 times as much blood passes through the lungs (and back to the heart and then to the body) and those capillaries per minute at max. Why doesn't the lung capillary transit time for each blood cell decrease from 0.8

secs at rest to 0.8/5 or a really fast 0.16 seconds during maximal exercise? Here is the answer.

Normally, the lungs only use a fraction of the total capillary volume available. Small arterioles can regulate the entry of blood into portions of the lungs. During exercise this restriction is gradually removed and the capillary volume can increase by over 3 fold to about 250 ml. This helps to minimise the decrease in capillary transit time. It does not eliminate it though. How important is that? This is another point which we will hit on again.

3. *Blood-gas transport*

Blood serves several important functions during exercise (heat removal, deacidification, glucose delivery, hormone communication to name a few). About 40 to 50% of the total volume of blood is made up of red blood cells (RBCs). For example, if your "hematocrit" is 43, then 43% of your total blood volume is RBCs. More than anything else, RBCs are just tiny, flexible sacks of hemoglobin. Each RBC contains hundreds of hemoglobin molecules, and each hemoglobin molecule has room to carry exactly 4 oxygen molecules.

This whole process is designed to function best when the atmospheric pressure is near sea level. If we get 1500 meters or more higher than that, the system begins to break down, and hemoglobin leaves the lungs without a full load of oxygen. This is why it is more difficult to breathe and exercise at altitude.

The capacity for blood to deliver oxygen can be summed up using an equation:

Hemoglobin concentration X oxygen binding capacity of hemoglobin (ml O_2/g hb) X percent saturation of hemoglobin = oxygen carried in a given volume of blood.

Hemoglobin concentration is expressed in grams of hemoglobin per deciliter of blood (g/dl). Typical values range between 12-14 for women and 14-16 for men. The binding capacity of hemoglobin for oxygen is a constant and equals 1.34 ml O_2/g hemoglobin. Finally, the percent oxygen saturation of hemoglobin when it leaves the lungs is normally about 96% (it is not 100% largely because the lung tissue has its own blood supply and this small volume of deoxygenated blood mixes in with the fresh stuff).

So, for an average person with a hemoglobin of 15, the oxygen volume contained in each liter of delivered blood will be:

$$15\text{g/dl} \times 1.34 \text{ ml } O_2\text{/g hgb} \times 0.96 \text{ saturation } (\times 10\text{dl/l}) = 193 \text{ ml } O_2\text{/ liter blood.}$$

If we substitute in 12 for the hemoglobin concentration (someone with anaemia) and 18 (a very high value occasionally seen in trained athletes at high altitude), we see that for the same cardiac output, the volume of oxygen carried by the blood would vary between 154 and 232 ml per liter, depending on the hemoglobin value. It is not hard to see how the blood oxygen carrying capacity affects the VO2 max. Remember, the muscles can only use what the heart can deliver.

If hemoglobin concentration is higher, the blood can carry more oxygen. This is an important point with relevance to altitude training, illegal EPO use, gender differences in VO2 max, anaemia etc. Second, when the blood leaves the lungs it is normally fully saturated with oxygen. This means that the lungs are very effective at ventilating the blood, even in untrained folks. This is one of the reasons why in the big scheme of things we basically disregard lung function as an area for improvement in the athlete's endurance machine. But, this issue is worth taking a closer look at.

Ventilation Issues in Endurance Performance

Sometimes you hear people say "I ran out of wind." Is that really possible? Can we reach a point in exercise when ventilation just can't keep up with demand? The answer is no, assuming you don't have acute asthma or some other severe pulmonary dysfunction. We can measure a person's maximal voluntary ventilation (MVV), the maximal volume of air they can breath in and out while at rest, and compare it with their maximal ventilation during exercise. What we see is that untrained people only use about 60 to 85% of their maximum ventilatory capacity even at maximal exercise. For example the MVV for an average male might be nearly 200 l/min.

However, during a treadmill VO2 max test, they reach a peak ventilation of only 140 l/min. Highly trained athletes use more of their capacity, perhaps over 90%, but ventilation capacity is still not a limitation on performance. Unlike the story with cardiac output, even during maximal exercise, the ventilatory capacity is not maxed out. Ventilation volumes in excess of 200 l/min have also been recorded in elite female oarswomen. Understandably, rowers get most of the big ventilation prizes because they are really big for endurance athletes, at least among humans.

Another sport that has gotten some special attention from the ventilation folks is rowing. During rowing, the body is squeezed up with the chest against the knees over 30 times a minute, limiting diaphragmatic excursion. That might create some breathing problems, but it is not the biggest issue. The real issue is the fact that rowers also use the same abdominal and intercostal muscles used for breathing to support the back during the powerful extension employed each stroke. Rowers isometrically contract all of these muscles to apply a high interthoracic pressure at the moment of the catch, when the oars take the water, to reinforce the connection between oar, back and legs. It is impossible to breathe and constrict all the abdominal and thoracic muscles at the same time.

The consequences of this competition are debated. The results of several, but not all studies suggest that elite rowers are not able to achieve the same ventilation volume at max during rowing as they achieve during cycling. The differences are not huge, but they may be significant. For example in one recent study elite rowers achieved a peak ventilation of 198 l/min during a VO2 max test cycling, but only 171 liters/min during rowing. The VO2 max values for the rowers were not different between rowing and cycling (5.03 l/min vs 5.09 l/min). This suggests that the small degree of under-ventilation at max experienced in rowing does not limit maximal oxygen consumption.

However, some physiologists interpret these results differently. It is generally accepted that elite endurance athletes achieve there highest values of VO2 max when they are performing the sport that they train for. In other words, elite runners excel most during treadmill tests. Elite cyclists max out slightly higher on cycling tests etc. In several studies national class rowers have demonstrated the same VO2 max while rowing as they did while running, or even cycling. This has not been a unanimous finding, but it appears that VO2 max for highly trained oarsman during rowing is lower than it "should be", when consideration is given to their training specificity and the very large muscle mass employed in rowing. A mechanism for this problem may be a slight ventilatory limitation imposed by the unique demands of rowing.

The muscle contraction frequency is two slow and at too high intensity to allow optimal blood flow to the working muscles, and muscle pump action by the working muscles. If this is true, then higher stroke rates might produce increased aerobic power. This is consistent with the trend in elite rowing to move toward higher stroke rates, but it is not proven.

Breathing pattern seems to be an especially important issue in rowing. Steinacker et al investigated ventilatory responses during incremental rowing exercise and observed two distinct breathing patterns. Type 1 was one complete breathing cycle per stroke cycle, with expiration occurring during the drive and inspiration during the recovery phase. Type 2 was two complete breaths per stroke, one during the drive and one during the recovery. When the intensity reached a certain point, the rowers automatically switched from type 1 to type 2. All these elite male rowers entrained their breathing to the stroke rate. Another study found the same patterns in elite female rowers. Untrained subjects tested during rowing only rarely exhibited this pattern. To make things more interesting, it appears that the breath during the stroke is "smaller" than the breath during the recovery phase.

In running or cycling max tests we usually see maximum ventilation rates of about 50 to 60. In contrast, ventilation rates as high as 88 breaths per minute have been observed during competitive rowing, accompanied by a relatively low tidal volume. All of this data suggests that the mechanics of rowing place unique demands on ventilation. Well trained rowers adapt to these demands by developing very strong ventilatory muscles and adapting a unique breathing rhythm which makes the most of the brief periods of relaxation during the stroke.

Hyperplasia

Hypertrophy refers to an increase in the size of the cell while hyperplasia refers to an increase in the number of cells or fibers. A single muscle cell is usually called a fiber. If you look at a good marathon runner's physique and compared him/her to a bodybuilder it becomes obvious that training specificity has a profound effect. We know that aerobic training results in an increase in mitochondrial volume/density, oxidative enzymes, and capillary density. Also, in some elite endurance athletes the trained muscle fibers may actually be smaller than those of a completely untrained person.

Bodybuilders and other strength-power athletes, on the other hand, have much larger muscles. That's their primary adaptation, their muscles get bigger! All the cellular machinery related to aerobic metabolism (i.e., mitochondria, oxidative enzymes, etc.) is not necessary for maximal gains in muscle force producing power, just more contractile protein. We know that this muscle mass increase is due primarily to fiber hypertrophy; that is the growth of individual fibers, but are their situations where muscles also respond by increasing fiber number?

Scientists have come up with all sorts of methods to study muscle growth in laboratory animals. You might wonder what relevance this has to humans. Keep in mind that some of the procedures which scientists perform on animals simply cannot be done on humans due to ethical and logistical reasons. So the more convincing data supporting hyperplasia emerges from animal studies. Some human studies have also suggested the occurence of muscle fiber hyperplasia.

There are two primary mechanism in which new fibers can be formed. First, large fibers can split into two or more smaller fibers (i.e., fiber splitting). Second satellite cells can be activated. Satellite cells are myogenic stem cells which are involved in skeletal muscle regeneration. When you injure, stretch, or severely exercise a muscle fiber, satellite cells are activated. Satellite cells proliferate (i.e., undergo mitosis or cell division) and give rise to new myoblastic cells (i.e., immature muscle cells). These new myoblastic cells can either fuse with an existing muscle fiber causing that fiber to get bigger (i.e., hypertrophy) or these myoblastic cells can fuse with each other to form a new fiber (i.e., hyperplasia).

8

Skills for Health

Skills-based health education is good quality education per se and good quality health education in particular. It relies on relevant and effective content and participatory or interactive teaching and learning methods. When planning skills-based health education, it is important to consider first the goals and objectives, then the content and methods. The goals of skills-based health education describe in general terms a health or related social issue to be influenced in some particular way.

The objectives describe in specific terms the behaviours or conditions that if positively influenced, will have a significant impact on the goals. Many factors influence behaviour and conditions; skills-based health education is one of them. The content of skills-based health education is a clear delineation of specific knowledge, attitudes, and skills, including life skills, that young people will be helped to acquire so they might adopt behaviours or create the conditions described in the objectives.

Once the content is delineated, methods are chosen that are most suitable to the content. For example, lectures are suitable methods for helping students acquire accurate knowledge; discussions are suitable for influencing attitudes; and role plays are suitable for developing skills. A wide range of teaching and learning methods can and should be used in enabling students to acquire knowledge, attitudes, and skills.

In skills-based health education, content refers to the specific health knowledge and attitudes toward self and others, as well as the skills necessary to influence behaviour and conditions related to a particular health issue. Skills-based health education should enable a young person to apply knowledge and develop attitudes and skills to make positive decisions and take actions to promote and protect one's health and the health of others.

Various health, education, and youth organisations and adolescence researchers have defined and categorised key skills in different ways. Despite these differences, experts and practitioners agree that the term "life skills" typically includes the skills listed in the preceding definition. To these we have added advocacy skills, because they are important in personal and collective efforts to make a strong case for behaviours and conditions that are conducive to health. The process of categorising various life skills may inadvertently suggest distinctions among them. However, many life skills are interrelated, and several of them can be taught together in a learning activity.

In efforts to achieve specific behavioural outcomes, programmes aimed at developing young people's life skills without a particular context such as a health behaviour or condition are less effective than programmes that overtly focus on applying life skills to specific health choices and behaviours. To influence behaviour effectively, skills must be applied to a particular topic, such as a prevalent health issue. Not to be overlooked, however, is the importance of building life skills to equip young people in other aspects of their development as well, such as maintaining positive interpersonal relations with teachers, students, and family members.

To contribute to skills-based health education goals and achieve the objectives of skillbased health education, teaching and learning methods must be relevant and effective. Effective skills-based health education replicates the natural processes by which children learn behaviour. These include modelling, observation, and social interactions. Interactive or participatory teaching and learning methods are an essential part of skills-based health education. Skills are learned best when students have the opportunity to observe and actively practise them.

Listening to a teacher describe skills or read or lecture about them does not necessarily enable young people to master them. Learning by doing is necessary. Teachers need to employ methods in the classroom that let young people observe the skills being practiced and then use the skills themselves. Researchers argue that if young people can practise the skills in the safety of a classroom environment, it is much more likely that they will be prepared to use them in and outside of school. The role of the teacher in delivering skills-based health education is to facilitate participatory learning (that is, the natural process of learning) in addition to conducting lectures or employing other appropriate and efficient methods for achieving the learning objectives.

Participatory learning utilises the experience, opinions, and knowledge of group members; provides a creative context for the exploration and development of possibilities and options; and affords a source of mutual comfort and security that aids the learning and decision-making process. Social learning theory provides some of the theoretical foundation for why participatory teaching techniques work. Bandura's research shows that people learn what to do and how to act by observing others. Positive behaviours are reinforced by the positive or negative consequences viewed or experienced directly by the learner. Retention of behaviours can be enhanced when people mentally rehearse or actually perform modelled behaviour patterns.

Constructivist theory provides another rationale. Vygotsky argues that social interaction and the active engagement of the child in problem-solving with peers and adults is the foundation of the developing mind. Many programmes capitalise on the power of peers to influence social norms and individual behaviours. Adults and young people tend to act in ways that they perceive to be normative or what most people their age are doing. If youngsters perceive (correctly or incorrectly) that fighting is the way most young people solve problems, then that becomes the norm or typical way most youngsters in a setting will respond.

If, on the other hand, students sense that the norm is to talk problems through and that bystanders will intervene to stop a fight rather than encourage it, most students will gravitate to that norm of behaviour. Through cooperative work with peers to promote pro-social behaviours, the normative peer structure is changed to support healthy, positive behaviours; it also may move some of the high-risk peers who are more likely to engage in damaging behaviours toward the pro-social norms.

Setting positive standards in the school environment is key; making students aware of those standards and then model them can lead more students to behave in health-promoting ways.

Studies of approaches to health education have shown that active participatory learning activities for students are the most effective method for developing knowledge, attitudes, and skills together for students to make healthy choices.

Participatory teaching methods for building skills and influencing attitudes include the following:

- class discussions
- brainstorming
- demonstration and guided practice
- role play
- small groups
- educational games and simulations
- case studies
- story telling
- debates
- practising life skills specific to a particular context with others
- audio and visual activities, e.g., arts, music, theatre, dance
- decision mapping or problem trees

Effective programmes balance these participatory and active methods with information and attitudes related to the context.

Health Education

The application of skills based health education, in particular life skills, to areas such as HIV/AIDS prevention, reproductive health, early pregnancy, violence, tobacco and substance abuse is becoming increasingly widespread. In areas such as these, individual behavior, social and peer pressure, cultural norms and abusive relationships may all contribute to the health and lifestyle problems of children and adolescents. There is now increasing evidence that in tackling these issues and health problems, a skills based approach to health education works, and is more effective than teaching knowledge alone.

There are numerous studies indicating that providing information about issues such as sex, STDs and HIV (transmission, risk factors, how to avoid infection) is necessary, but not sufficient, to lead to healthy behavioral change. Programs that provide accurate information, to counteract the myths and misinformation, frequently report improvements in knowledge and attitudes, but this is poorly correlated with behavioral change related to risk taking and desirable behavioral outcomes. Skills-based health education can be effective in the more difficult task of achieving and sustaining behavior change.

Skills based health and hygiene education programs play a vital role in combating diseases. Skills based health education can also be seen as widely applicable to a range of other areas where knowledge, attitudes and skills play a critical role as part of a comprehensive strategy for combating disease and promoting healthy life styles. This includes a wide range of diseases and conditions that affect the health of children and adolescents, including: vector borne diseases such as malaria; water and sanitation related diseases such as diarrheal diseases, trachoma and schistosomiasis; nutrition related conditions such as micronutrient deficiencies and other forms of malnutrition.

The skills based approach extends traditional methods of teaching about health, which tend to be knowledge based and didactic in approach. In contrast, skills based health education focuses upon the development of Knowledge, Attitudes, Values, and Skills needed to make and act on the most appropriate and positive health-related decisions.

HIV/AIDS is an area where the scale and impact of the problem is such that the urgency of implementing preventative measures, including skills based health education, is critical. Skills based health education programs are being increasingly adopted as means of reaching children and young people to help halt the spread of this crippling epidemic. Studies from African countries show that children between the ages of 5 and 14 have the lowest prevalence of HIV infection. Below the age of 5 they are susceptible to mother to child transmission, and after they become sexually active, the rate of infection increases rapidly—especially for girls. Children aged 5-14 need to be reached at this critical stage in their lives and offer the 'window of hope' in stopping the spread of HIV/AIDS.

Principles

A significant body of theory and research provides a rationale for the benefits and uses of skills-based health education. The theories share many common themes and have all contributed to the development of skills-based health education and life skills. Behavioural science, and the disciplines of education and child development, placed in the context of human rights principles, constitute a primary source of these foundation theories and principles.

Those who work in these disciplines have provided insights—acquired through decades of research and experience—into the way human beings, specifically children and adolescents, grow and learn; acquire knowledge, attitudes, and skills; and behave. Research and experience have also revealed the many spheres of influence that affect the way children and adolescents grow in diverse settings, from family and peer groups to school and community.

Most of the theories outlined below are drawn from Western or North American social scientists and may or may not be equally relevant to other cultures and practices. Therefore, programme designers, together with local social and behavioural scientists, paediatricians, anthropologists, educators, and others who study child and adolescent development, may want to consider the relevance of these ideas and their own cultural basis for programme design.

Child and Adolescent Development Theories

An understanding of the complex biological, social, and cognitive changes, gender awareness, and moral development that occurs from childhood through adolescence lies at the core of most theories of human development. The onset of puberty constitutes a fundamental biological change from childhood to early adolescence. An important component of social cognition in the transition from adolescence to adulthood is the process of understanding oneself, others, and relationships.

The ability to understand causal relationships develops in early adolescence, and problem-solving becomes more sophisticated. The adolescent is able to conceptualise simultaneously about many variables, think abstractly, and create rules for problem-solving. Social interactions become increasingly complex at this time. Adolescents spend more time with peers; increase their interactions with opposite-sex peers; and spend less time at home and with family members.

Moral development occurs during this period as well; adolescents begin to rationalise the different opinions and messages they receive from various sources, and begin to develop values and rules for balancing the conflicting interests of self and others. Implications for skills-based health education planning are:

- In the school setting, late childhood and early adolescence (ages 6-15) are critical moments of opportunity for building skills and positive habits. During this time, children are developing the ability to think abstractly, to understand consequences, to relate to their peers in new ways, and to solve problems as they experience more independence from parents and develop greater control over their own lives.
- The wider social context of early and middle adolescence provides varied situations in which to practise new skills and develop positive habits with peers and other individuals outside the family.
- Developing attitudes, values, skills, and competencies is recognised as critical to the development of a child's sense of self as an autonomous individual and to the overall learning process in school.
- Within this age span, the skills of young people of the same age and different ages can vary dramatically. Activities need to be developmental appropriate.

Social Learning Theory

This theory is based largely upon the work of Albert Bandura in 1977, whose research led him to conclude that children learn to behave both through formal instruction and through observation. Formal instruction includes how parents, teachers, and other authorities and role models tell children to behave; observation includes how young people see adults and peers behaving. Children's behaviour is reinforced or modified by the consequences of their actions and the responses of others to their behaviours. Implications for skills-based health education planning are:

- Skills teaching needs to replicate the natural processes by which children learn behaviour: modelling, observation, and social interaction.
- Reinforcement is important in learning and shaping behaviour. Positive reinforcement is applied for the correct demonstration of behaviours and skills; negative or corrective reinforcement is applied for behaviours or skills that need to be adjusted to build more positive actions.
- Teachers and other adults are important role models, standard setters, and sources of influence.

Problem-behaviour Theory

In 1977, Jessor & Jessor recognise that adolescent behaviour (including risk behaviour) is the product of complex interactions between people and their environment. Problem behaviour theory is concerned with the relationships among three categories of psychosocial variables. The first category, the personality system, involves values, expectations, beliefs, and attitudes toward self and society. The second category, the perceived environmental system, comprises perceptions of friends' and parents' attitudes toward behaviours and physical agents in the environment, such as substances and weapons. The third category, the behavioural system, comprises socially acceptable and unacceptable behaviours. More than one problem behaviour may converge in the same individuals, such as a combination of alcohol and tobacco or other drug use and sexually transmitted disease.

Social Influence and Social Inoculation Theory

These two theories are closely related. Social influence theory is based on the work of Bandura and on social inoculation theory by researchers such as McGuire, and was first used in smoking prevention programmes by Evans. Social influence theory recognises that children and adolescents will come under pressure to engage in risk behaviours, such as tobacco use or premature or unprotected sex.

Social influence and inoculation programmes anticipate these pressures and teach young people both about the pressures and about ways to resist them before youth are exposed. Usually these programmes are targeted at very specific risks, tying peer resistance skills to particular risk behaviours and knowledge. Social resistance training is usually a central component of social skills and life skills programmes. Implications for skills-based health education planning are:

- Peer and social pressures to engage in unhealthy behaviours can be dissipated by addressing them before the child or adolescent is exposed to the pressures, thus pointing toward early prevention rather than later intervention.
- Making young people aware of these pressures ahead of time gives them a chance to recognise in advance the kinds of situations in which they may find themselves.
- Teaching children resistance skills is more effective for reducing problem behaviours than just providing information or provoking fear of the results of the behaviour.

Congnitive Problem Solving

This competence-building model of primary prevention theorises that teaching socialcognitive problem-solving skills to children at an early age can improve interpersonal relationships and impulse control, promote self-protecting and mutually beneficial solutions among peers, and reduce or prevent negative "health-compromising" behaviours. Poor problem-solving skills are related to poor social behaviours, indicating the need to include problem-solving and other skills in skills-based health education. Implications for skills-based health education planning are:

- Teaching interpersonal problem-solving skills at early stages in the developmental process (childhood, early adolescence) develops a strong foundation for later learning.
- Focusing on skills for self-awareness and self-management, as in anger management or impulse control, as well as generating alternative solutions to interpersonal problems, can reduce or prevent problem behaviours. Focusing on the ability to conceptualise or think ahead to the consequences of different behaviours or solutions can help children make positive choices.

Theory of Reasoned Action and the Health Belief Model

The Theory of Reasoned Action and the Health Belief Model contain similar concepts. Based on the research of Fishbein and Ajzen in 1975, the Theory of Reasoned Action views an individual's intention to perform a behaviour as a combination of his attitude toward performing the behaviour and subjective normative beliefs about what others think he should do. The Health Belief Model, first developed by Rosenstock recognises that perceptions—rather than actual facts—are important to weighing up benefits and barriers affecting health behaviour, along with the perceived susceptibility and perceived severity of the health threat or consequences.

Modifying factors include demographic variables and cues to action which can come from people, policies or conducive environments. Implications for skills-based health education planning are:

- If a person perceives that the outcome from performing a behaviour is positive, she will have a positive attitude toward performing that behaviour. The opposite can be said if the behaviour is thought to be negative.
- If relevant others (such as parents, teachers, peers) see performing a behaviour as positive and the individual is motivated to meet the expectations of relevant others, then a positive individual behaviour is expected. The same is true for negative behaviour norms.

Education for health for young people has been referred to as health education, skillsbased health education, and a life skills approach. Evaluation research over the past decade has revealed more about strategies for producing the desired knowledge, attitude, skill, and behavioural outcomes that decrease risk behaviours and improve health. Three findings are important for policymakers and programme planners:

- Health education that concentrates on developing skills for making healthy choices in life, in addition to imparting health-related knowledge, attitudes, values, services, and support, is more likely to produce the desired outcome.
- Skill development is more likely to result in the desired healthy behaviour when practising the skill is tied to the content of a specific health behaviour or health decision.
- The most effective method of skill development is learning by doing—involving people in active, participatory learning experiences rather than passive ones.

Research shows that skills-based health education promotes healthy lifestyles and reduces risk behaviours. A meta-analysis of 207 school-based drug prevention programmes grouped approaches to prevention into nine categories: knowledge only; affective only; knowledge and affective; decisions, values, and attitudes; generic skills training; social influences; comprehensive life skills; "other" programmes; and health education K-12. The author found that "the most effective programmes teach comprehensive life skills".

Programmes were also grouped according to whether or not they used interactive methods. The study concluded that "the most successful of the interactive programmes are the comprehensive life skills-based education programmes that incorporate the refusal skills offered in the social influences programmes and add skills such as assertiveness, coping, communication skills, etc.". Meta-analyses by Kirby confirmed that active learning methods, along with other factors, were effective in reaching students and led to positive behavioural results.

Studies in developing countries have also established the effectiveness of interactive and participatory teaching methods for skillsbased health education. These findings together provide a clear basis for establishing a focus on this approach to health education. Skills-based health education has been shown by research to:

- reduce the chances of young people engaging in delinquent behaviour, interpersonal violence, and criminal behaviour
- delay the onset age of using alcohol, tobacco, and other drugs
- prevent peer rejection and bullying
- teach anger control
- promote positive social adjustment and reduce emotional disorders

- improve health-related behaviours and self-esteem improve academic performance

A matrix of evaluation studies in the evidence. The matrix lists selected studies that used skills-based health education and achieved changes in knowledge, attitudes, skills, or behaviour. Studies that show impact on behaviour tend to include more comprehensive interventions that include but go beyond skills-based health education.

Skills-based health education will be most effective in influencing behaviour when applied as part of a comprehensive, multi-strategy approach that delivers consistent messages over time. Strategies need to be tailored to discrete aspects and stages of behaviour. A narrow focus on skills-based health education is unlikely to sustain changed behaviour in the long term. More powerful and sustained outcomes tend to be achieved when skills-based health education is coordinated with policies, services, family and community partnerships, and mass media and other strategies.

For instance, research shows that a curriculum combined with youth community service reduces risk behaviours such as fighting, early sexual behaviour, and substance use more effectively than a curriculum alone. Indeed, the FRESH initiative emerged in response to the need for more comprehensive programming rather than singular approaches for which the expectations are often unreasonably high.

While it is important to capitalise on the success factors of effective programmes, it is also helpful to be aware of, and to try to avoid, the barriers to effective skills-based health education. Barriers of focus tend to include the following:

- infusion of health issues across a range of subjects without providing a solid foundation within one subject, where knowledge, attitudes, and skills can be linked and developed in a sequential, reinforcing strategy

- inadequate orientation and training of administrators, teachers, and other support staff
- general programmes that are less directed toward specific contexts or risk behaviours. For example, such programmes may use a model in which generic decision-making steps are presented but are not applied to a specific context, or are applied across a range of topics that are not necessarily linked.
- efforts to cover a broad array of topics, values, and skills while failing to emphasise particular facts, values, norms, and skills that students need to reduce risk or promote specific behaviour. For example, a programme may cover the physiology of reproductive health and the value of positive personal relationships but omit content on sustaining decisions to avoid unprotected sex; building skills to avoid risky situations, negotiating with a partner not to have sex, using a condom, or resisting peer pressure to use alcohol or drugs.
- presentations that are information-heavy, particularly with physiological information, with little or no attention to feelings, relationships, skills, and local situations
- too little concentrated time on the learning task

Barriers of coordination and consistency include the following:

- weak leadership, lack of genuine commitment and coordination from ministries of health and education and from school officials; for example, lack of well-defined national strategies for the promotion, support, coordination, and management of school-based programmes and insufficient staff in the ministries of education and health designated to the task of strengthening skills-based health education and life skills programmes

- insufficient infrastructure for teacher training
- lack of quality teaching materials and participatory methods
- insufficient coordination in terms of time frames and plans, leading to isolated and vertical programmes
- competition with other health topics or programmes within the school environment or inconsistent messages and learning experiences

Barriers of intensity and scale include the following:

- failure to plan for expansion or to go beyond the pilot stage
- inadequate funding
- inadequate attention to related strategies that maximise success, such as effectively implemented policies, access to related health services, and links with the community and other sectors. For example, effective school-based alcohol abuse prevention strategies may be linked to policies in the community that restrict access to alcohol to minors and links to community-school partnerships that help enforce such policies.
- inadequate mechanisms for supervising, monitoring, and evaluating programmes, including a lack of detailed documentation.

Applying proven methods of success and using available guidelines and tools, such as the WHO Information Series on School Health, listed in address many of these challenges.

PRIORITY ACTIONS

Very substantial evidence exists to support the benefits of skills-based health education. However, too few schools implement programmes of good quality, and too few programmes are implemented on a national scale.

Going to Scale

"Going to scale" means implementing interventions nationwide. It involves considering a variety of expansion models and agencies for reaching the greatest number of schools and students. Such considerations should be made from the beginning of the planning process, once the importance and feasibility of skills-based health education are understood. Expanding the reach of good-quality programmes on national and local levels then becomes a priority. Since ample evidence supports the effectiveness of skills-based health education, there is less need for further pilot projects than for nationwide coverage, which may coordinate several models, facilitators, and agencies.

Education agencies that are striving to go to scale may be able to adapt certain activities already in use, thereby expanding community-based programmes for young people. There are four major approaches for scaling up young adult programmes.

(1) Planned Expansion means a steady process of expanding the number of sites and youth served by a particular programme once it has been pilot tested.

(2) Association consists of expanding programme size and coverage through a network of organisations.

(3) Grafting means adding a new initiative to an existing programme.

(4) Explosion involves sudden implementation of a youth programme at a large scale.

The following lessons were learned from scaling up young adult reproductive health programmes:

- Programmes should prepare for scaling up by focusing on institutionalisation.
- Support such as training curricula and a cadre of trained and committed service providers is essential to institutionalisation. Changes in undergraduate- and graduate-level training in colleges and universities may be required.
- Policy shapes programme development. Policy structures can support programme efforts. However, momentum for scaling up can be gathered even without a supportive political environment, especially when the issues can gain visibility through allied groups. While certain programmes must engage the policy level more than others, and pilot projects can stimulate policy development, even government programmes may be vulnerable in a negative policy environment.
- Activists and programme planners should build on existing institutions and infrastructure when scaling up. NGOs, which are often the first to initiate young adult reproductive health programmes, can complement and reinforce government initiatives. Programmes can take advantage of existing infrastructure by forming and deepening collaborations with partner organisations. Programmes with strong ties at the local level are better able to survive change, so building a social marketing strategy is important for creating and maintaining a community constituency.
- Committed leaders are needed to support, guide, and sponsor the scaling-up process. A successful scale-up effort requires a major commitment of time and energy on the part of leaders as well as a formal governance structure.

- Make scaling up participatory, and build in flexibility. Programmes aimed at young people depend on their input for success.
- Anticipate obstacles and challenges. The environment in which a programme develops and the availability of resources may influence its shape and the effort to scale up. Programme developers and policy advocates in particular need to be sensitive to these issues. This includes developing long range financing strategies.
- Data, research, monitoring and evaluation systems are critical to scaling up effective programmes. Data and research are especially important for designing programmes, scaling them up, advocacy and securing acceptance and support for programmes.

Skills-based health education is more effective when it is taught as part of a comprehensive approach to school health than in isolation. The frameworks of FRESH and Health-Promoting Schools offer approaches for implementing skills-based health education as part of effective school health programmes.

Focusing Resources on Effective School Health (FRESH), initiated by WHO, UNESCO, UNICEF, and the World Bank in 2000, is a framework for action that proposes four components as a starting point for developing an effective school health programme as part of broader efforts to design health-promoting, child-friendly schools. If all schools were to implement these four components, there would be a significant, immediate benefit in the health of students and staff and a basis for future expansion. The aim is to focus on interventions that are feasible to put in place. The four FRESH components, listed below, should be made available together, in all schools:

- Health-related school policies. Health policies in schools can help ensure a safe and secure physical and psychosocial environment; address issues such as abuse of students, sexual harassment, and school violence; guarantee the further education of pregnant schoolgirls and young mothers; and reinforce health education for teachers and students.
- Provision of safe water and sanitation—the essential first steps toward a healthy learning environment. It is a realistic goal in most countries to ensure that all schools have access to clean water and sanitation. By providing these, schools can reinforce health and hygiene messages and act as an example both to students and to the wider community. Separate facilities for girls, particularly adolescent girls, contribute significantly to reducing dropout.
- Skills-based health education. This approach to health, hygiene, and nutrition education focuses on developing the knowledge, attitudes, values, and life skills that young people need to make and act on the most appropriate and positive health-related decisions. Individuals who possess these skills are more likely to adopt and sustain a healthy lifestyle during their school years and throughout the rest of their lives.
- School-based health and nutrition services. Health and nutrition services can be effectively delivered by or through schools provided that the services are simple, safe, and familiar and that they address issues that are prevalent and recognised as important within the community. For example, micronutrient deficiencies and worm infections may be effectively addressed with infrequent oral treatment; and short-term hunger—an important constraint on learning—can be addressed by changing the timing of meals or providing a snack. If

schools cannot provide services on school grounds they can refer to nearby services in the community.

Several strategies can support the implementation of the four FRESH components:

- Effective partnerships between teachers and health workers and between the education and health sectors
- Effective community partnerships
- Pupil awareness and participation

Skills-based health education is one important component of a Health-Promoting School. Through its Global School Health Initiative, WHO encourages the creation of Health-Promoting Schools worldwide, a concept fully embraced by UNICEF and other international agencies. Health-Promoting Schools foster health and learning with all measures at their disposal and by engaging health and education officials, teachers, students, parents, health care providers, and community leaders in efforts to improve the health of students, schoolpersonnel, families, and community members.

Health-Promoting Schools strive to blend a healthy environment, skills-based health education, and school health services with school/community projects and outreach, health promotion programmes for staff, nutrition and food safety programmes, physical education and recreation, reproductive and sexual health, and the promotion of mental health, with opportunities for counselling and social support.

Implementation of Skills-based Health Education

There are three primary ways for implementing skills-based health education within schools:

- A core health education subject—Skills-based health education can be a core (or separate) subject in the broader school curriculum.

- Carrier subject—Skills-based health education is sometimes placed in the context of related health and social issues within an existing, so-called carrier subject that is relevant to the issues, such as science, civic education, social studies, or population studies.
- Infusion across many subjects—Health topics can be included in all or many existing subjects by regular classroom teachers.

Whichever option is chosen, it is important to understand that the effort to influence behaviours and conditions associated with school-based priority health, education, and development issues is a long-term and significant commitment. Skills-based health education works best to affect behaviour where reinforcing strategies are in place. Every effort should be made to combine skills-based health education with complementary strategies such as policy development, health services, and a supportive psychosocial environment.

Given the factors vying for the attention of young people, it is unreasonable to believe that a single positive strategy might prevail over the many competing influences. Helping to ensure that teachers model health-promoting behaviours and that the school environment supports these behaviours is important. Skills-based health education should be considered but one of the four basic FRESH components of an effective school health programme, and such programmes themselves are most effective when complemented by community, national, and international strategies to support their health, education, and development goals.

Non-formal Models

In many countries, the formal curriculum time is overburdened and alternatives have been developed which do not rely on formal curriculum time, for example, non-formal or extracurricular programmes. Both the in-school and non-school population can be reached with these activities. They may operate at or near schools, or separate from schools, and tend not to rely on teachers to deliver them, for example, programmes operated by nongovernment workers, peer educators, community groups, youth organisations (e.g., Girl Guides, Boys Scouts), or faith-based organisations.

The Ministry of Education is often responsible for both formal and non-formal mechanisms for reaching children and young people so that these different mechanisms can be coordinated for maximum quality and coverage. The case study below presents an example of a successful programme that taught life skills as part of a non-formal school subject.

Behavioural Outcomes

Programmes aimed at helping young people to develop life skills without a particular context are less effective in achieving specific behavioural outcomes. It is critical that programme planners set objectives and select content on the basis of what is most relevant to influencing the behaviours and conditions that are associated with priority health issues.

The central question is what behaviours or conditions must be sustained or changed to influence the health issues. Then, what knowledge, attitudes, and skills will be the most useful to address, given the behaviours and conditions to be changed? The answers to these "whats" are then used to develop programme objectives. Setting objectives for preventing or reducing risk behaviours and risk conditions and for promoting protective behaviours and conditions is important. Such objectives are required for clearly delineating the programme content, including knowledge, attitudes, and skills that are important to achieve the behavioural and conditional objectives.

The physical, mental, emotional, and social dimensions of knowledge, attitudes, and skills need to be explored to facilitate informed decision making, the ability to practise healthy behaviours, and the creation of conditions that are conducive to health. Local factors and conditions that affect the ability of the individual to take action must also be considered; for example, using a condom properly may not be a feasible protective practise if condoms are not available.

The situation assessment information should reveal the issues most relevant to the health and development of the young people who will participate in the programme. Using this information to identify the direct and indirect factors affecting morbidity (and mortality to a lesser extent) can be particularly helpful in the process of setting priorities. Issues that emerge for school-age children and young people throughout the world are family issues; youth and interpersonal violence and conflict and seeking peace; alcohol, tobacco, and other drug use; unintentional injuries; depression and mental health; diet and physical activity; and hygiene and infectious disease, unwanted pregnancy, HIV/AIDS/STIs and malaria. Aspects of these issues vary in relevance depending on the age of the young person.

The needs and developmental abilities of young people vary with their age; thus programmes must take these factors into account. This is commonly referred to as "developmentally appropriate programming." For example, concepts in school curricula should be sequenced smoothly from primary levels to secondary levels to reinforce previous learning experiences and make links for new learning; this process is sometimes referred to as a "spiral curriculum." For sensitive issues such as HIV/AIDS, sexual and reproductive health, education should begin as interest begins to increase but before the target group has become involved in the risk behaviours.

The building blocks for dealing with such sensitive issues should be in place at the very beginning of children's education. Such building blocks include self esteem, positive values of cooperation and teamwork, the protection and promotion of health, and pro-social behaviour. However, to help young people develop positive behaviour and avoid risks, these topics must be taught in a way that is increasingly specific to actual situations in their lives.

Trained Educators

Various individuals involved in skills-based health education must be trained to ensure successful implementation of such programmes. Trained educators are more likely than those who are not specifically trained in this learning area to implement programmes as intended, that is, to teach all of the required content and to use effective, high-quality teaching and learning methods. Skills-based health education teachers must possess a mix of professional and personal qualities. Some individuals bring these qualities to the job; others must receive training to acquire them.

When properly trained, students themselves (peers), community agency workers, guidance officers or counsellors, social workers, and psychologists or other health care providers, as well as teachers, can facilitate skills-based health education. What follows is an overview of the attitudes and attributes, professional skills, and competencies teachers need to develop to teach skills-based health education, along with some suggestions for training design of these requirements.

The following descriptors identify the best programme facilitators.

- role models for healthy behaviours
- credible and respected
- skilled and competent
- able to access resources and leadership and institutional support

Teachers and other facilitators of learning involved with skills-based health education need to employ interactive teaching methods. For this reason, they need to possess or develop the following characteristics:

- Ability to play different roles—to support, focus, or direct the group as required
- Ability to act as a guide as opposed to dominating the group
- Respect for the adolescent and his or her freedom of choice and individual self-determination
- Warmth, supportiveness, and enthusiasm
- Ability to deal with sensitive issues, such as hygiene, sexual and reproductive health, HIV/AIDS prevention, dating, friendships, substance abuse, and difficult decisions bout the future. These are topics that a teacher or facilitator needs to be prepared to discuss, either by answering questions or knowing where to go for more information. This requires training in content about adolescent stages of development, body image, sexuality, and available community resources.
- Appropriate personal and professional attitudes and practices. Teachers and facilitators are often expected to work with adolescents to develop skills that they themselves may not possess, such as, assertiveness, stress management, and problem-solving.

Furthermore, teachers and facilitators may need help with their own sexual health issues, HIV/AIDS coping strategies, substance abuse problems, or violence in the home. Studies on health-promotion programmes for teachers have shown that training can result in specific health benefits to providers as well as improved attendance, morale, and quality of learning. Some parent-focused interventions have addressed this concern by helping parents (as programme providers) to develop skills in their children while also helping parents improve their own problem-solving, parenting, and stress-management skills.

- Practice what you preach. Teachers and other facilitators need extensive opportunities to practise student participatory learning methods such as open discussion, role-plays and cooperative group work. They should also model the behaviours which their training advocates.
- Accurate knowledge of, and adequate personal comfort with, the range of issues being addressed; and the ability to refer to other sources of expertise where necessary.

Many adults will need to unlearn authoritarian approaches to learning in order to become effective programme providers. Teachers and other facilitators ideally should receive quality training in both pre-service and in-service contexts. Training needs to expose teachers to, and allow them to gain experience in, participatory teaching and learning methods, with administrative support at the school level, and ongoing support from experts to foster and sustain participatory teaching and learning methods.

Training for skills-based health education should mirror the teaching and learning principles of the programmes that are to be implemented. Training should incorporate active teaching and learning methodologies that take account of what is known about adult learning styles. In reality, teachers in many countries receive neither quality pre-service training nor ongoing in-service training, and there may be little support for addressing sensitive and complex topics that require specific skills. Whether or not teachers have had the benefit of quality preparation in the past, quality training can support the development of positive attributes and substantially improve the competencies required for skills-based teaching.

The strategies utilised by skills-based teaching are familiar within traditions of learning that have existed for generations in local cultures. These traditions include learning in groups, from elders across generations, through women's networks, through peers groups, and among girls and boys together; information and culture have been passed down in these ways through history. Key elements of effective training for teachers and other facilitators include the following:

- establishing an adequate knowledge base about the issues to be addressed and networks of experts to draw on for further information
- establishing an effective, safe, and supportive training and programme environment
- inspiring broad participation and genuine interaction
- applying participatory teaching methods; for example, building competence in group process, role plays, dramatisations, debates, small group work, and open discussions
- modelling the skills addressed in the curriculum
- focusing on the whole child and adolescent, not just, for instance, on the effect of one particular health issue

- analysing adult perceptions of adolescents and adolescence, adult stereotypes and myths, and clarification of adult values around issues relevant to young people
- building skills in conjunction with providing information
- addressing sensitive issues in adolescents
- providing constructive criticism and positive reinforcement and feedback
- accessing and assessing the quality of teaching and learning resources accessing and assessing referral and support networks and community liaisons, and facilitating local participation
- fitting training to the skills level of the providers providing ample opportunity for trainees to demonstrate and practise their new skills and for ongoing coaching; including continued training and booster sessions
- allowing active participation of trainees in making decisions about programme adoption
- pairing experienced skills-based health education providers with new trainees

Skills-based Education Planning

A situation analysis is conducted to ensure that interventions are relevant to local conditions and cultures. It consists of needs and resource assessments and data collection, conducted before interventions are planned and implemented. Needs assessments involve the collection of accurate and current data that yield insight into the health issues and behaviours in a community. Resource assessments yield knowledge of the available capacities and resources in schools and communities. The following types of information might be considered:

- health status, including local public health data on morbidity and mortality
- health priorities of children and adolescents
- behaviours and health conditions that are influencing priority health issues
- knowledge, attitudes, beliefs, values, skills, and services related to priority health issues for young people and their associated behaviours and conditions
- relevant policies
- available human, financial, and material resources and existing programmes that address health and social issues

Gathering evidence from credible sources can provide valuable information about what young people know, think, feel, and do and what health conditions affect them. Many sources of information can be utilised in this process, including the following: focus groups or in-depth interviews with the actual target audience or a similar group of learners

- related literature and research
- survey results
- professional expertise
- parents, care givers, and community groups
- epidemiological data from health departments and local clinics

The points of view of different stakeholders need to be shared and considered together, and ultimately agreement has to be reached. Where agreement proves elusive, it is the needs of the learners that ultimately must be central to decisions about what to include.

Role of Stakeholders

Schools may involve members of the school and community in planning goals and objectives for interventions. Such involvement can help ensure that the interventions will address the needs of learners and will be maintained over time. School teams may include headmasters, teachers, students, school-based service providers such as nurses or counsellors, parents, and support staff.

Members of school teams should represent a variety of backgrounds and viewpoints, be committed to the idea of health promotion, be interested in skills-based health education, work well in a team, and be able and willing to make a commitment of time. The team members work together to maintain and promote the health of all people who are working and learning at school, and to plan skills-based health education. Community advisors can complement the school team and provide ongoing advice and support from the community.

Partners from the community sector may includes local government officials, religious leaders, media and business representatives, community residents and youth agency members, health and social service providers, and representatives of non-governmental agencies. Together, school teams and community advisors assess needs and develop programme goals and objectives, and may work together in implementing and evaluating the interventions.

With the results of the situation analysis in hand, especially the identified needs and available resources, the school teams of students, teachers, and families, with support from other community advisors, can play an active role in defining the goals and objectives of the programme. A goal describes in broad terms what it is hoped the intervention will achieve in the long term. A goal is a fairly grand statement, targeting a change in health status, such as reductions in teenage suicides or unwanted teen pregnancies. Many strategies are required to achieve outcomes at this level.

Outcome objectives target risk behaviours or conditions related to the goal. For example, if the goal is reduced teenage suicide or unwanted teen pregnancy, target behaviours or conditions might include delaying the initiation of sexual intercourse and increasing the number of teachers who serve as trusted adults to whom students can go when feeling depressed. Sub-Objectives (process objectives) define in specific, measurable, and attainable terms what is to be accomplished to help achieve the outcome objectives.

For skillsbased health education, this means describing the activities and interventions that are to be implemented over a given period of time to influence knowledge, attitudes, skills, and other factors associated with the outcome objectives and, ultimately, the goal. For example, sub-objectives could include increasing knowledge about which factors constitute depression, or developing skills for negotiating alternatives to sex.

Advocacy

A first step in putting a programme into action is gathering support and resources. To gain support, it may be necessary to advocate for the programme. Policymakers need good reasons to increase support for any health or education effort. They must be able to justify their decisions. Advocacy is the art of influencing others to support an idea, principle, or programme.

An advocate for skills-based health education must convince school policy and decisionmakers and communities that school-based efforts in support of it are appropriate and doable and that these efforts can help reach generally supported goals for young people. The goal is to convince decisionmakers to take actions that invest in and strengthen school health programmes. Arguments about the importance and effectiveness of skillsbased health education can be used as part of this advocacy effort.

Convincing people may be easier when the following two questions have been answered first: What factors cause one person to say yes to another person? and What techniques produce this result? While we cannot force people to think or act in a certain way, our ideas and knowledge can shape the environment of their thinking.

9

Sports Dieting

The basic idea behind detox diets is to temporarily give up certain kinds of foods that are thought to contain toxins. The idea is to purify and purge the body of all the "bad" stuff. Although detox diets vary, most of them involve some version of a fast: that is, giving up food for a couple of days and then gradually reintroducing certain foods into the diet.

Many of these diets also encourage you to undergo colonic irrigation, otherwise known as giving yourself enemas to "clean out" your colon. (An enema flushes out the rectum and colon using water.) Still others recommend that you take herbal supplements to help the "purification" process. There are tons of detox diets out there.

Typically they involve 1 or 2 days on a completely liquid diet and another 4 or 5 days adding brown rice, fruit, and steamed vegetables to the diet. After a week of eating only these foods, you gradually reintroduce other foods—except for red meat, wheat, sugar, eggs, and all prepackaged or junk foods—into your diet. Lots of claims are made about what a detox diet can do, from preventing and curing disease to giving people more energy to making them more focused and clearheaded. Of course, eating a diet lower in fat and higher in fiber can help many people feel more healthy, but proponents of detox diets claim that this is because of the elimination of toxins. However, there's no scientific proof that these diets help rid the body of toxins faster or that the elimination of toxins will make you a healthier, more energetic person.

If detox diets appeal to you, there are a couple of things to keep in mind. For starters, detox diets are intended for short-term purposes only. And these diets are usually recommended not as a way to lose weight, but to help "clean out the system." Because normal teenagers need lots of nutritional goodies, like enough calories and protein to support rapid growth and development, diets that involve fasting and severe restriction of food are not a good idea. For teens who are involved in sports and physical activities that require ample food, fasting does not provide enough fuel to support these activities. For these reasons, detox diets can be especially risky for teenagers.

It is not recommended that people with diabetes, low blood sugar, or eating disorders go on detox diets. You should also know that this type of diet can be addicting. That's because there's a certain feeling that comes from going without food or having an enema—almost like the high other people get from nicotine or alcohol. This can become a dangerous addiction that leads to health problems, including serious eating disorders and even death.

In addition, many of the supplements used during detox diets are actually laxatives, which are designed to make people go to the bathroom more often. Laxative supplements are never a good idea because they can cause dehydration, mineral imbalances, and problems with the digestive system.

Finally, people who fast for several days may drop pounds, but most of it will be water and some of it may be muscle. Fasting for longer periods can also slow down a person's metabolism, making it harder to keep the weight off or to lose weight later.

We're not telling you that eating lots of veggies and fiber and drinking lots of water is a bad idea. But you do need to make sure you're getting all of the nutrients you need from other foods, including protein from lean meats, eggs, beans, or peas and calcium from low-fat or fat-free milk or yogurt. You definitely shouldn't start a detox diet or stop eating from any major food group without talking to your doctor or a registered dietitian.

The human body is designed to purify itself. Your liver and kidneys will do the job they're supposed to do if you eat a healthy diet that includes fiber, fruits, veggies, and plenty of water. If you're feeling tired or run down, or if you're concerned that you're overweight, talk with a doctor who can help you determine the cause and recommend ways to address the problem.

Body Mass Index (BMI)

One of the biggest questions guys and girls have as they grow and develop is whether they're the right weight. One place to start is by learning about body mass index, or BMI, a calculation that estimates how much body fat a person has based on his or her weight and height. Check out our BMI calculator to find out what your BMI is. Although you can calculate BMI on your own, it's a good idea to ask a doctor or health professional to help you figure out what it means.

Diet-Plan Diagnosis

Want to drop a few pounds before that big date on Friday? Feeling the need to lose weight to boost your athletic performance? Many people look for fast or easy ways to slim down at some point in their lives. And there are hundreds of diet plans out there to lure you. But before you choose between the all-juice diet and the no-carb diet, read on to find out exactly what these diets do—and don't do—for you.

Commercial weight-loss plans typically fall into two categories: Those that drastically reduce a person's calorie intake or restrict the dieter to certain foods and those that require a person to take dietary supplements. Dietary supplements are usually pills, but they sometimes include special food bars or drinks.

Most of the popular diets on the market today rely on a person's natural tendency to want to lose weight quickly. They play into a desire for fast results, which is what happened to Jamie, 16, who followed a 5-day juice diet. Although Jamie lost the weight she wanted, a week later the scale showed she was back to her original weight.

It's quite common for people to quickly gain back all the weight they lose after a few days on a highly restrictive diet. Here's a doctor's answer on why: "The first thing to be aware of with quick weight-loss diets is that our bodies simply aren't designed to drop pounds quickly," says Steven Dowshen, MD, an expert in hormones and the endocrine system. In fact, doctors say that it's nearly impossible for a healthy, normally active teen or adult to lose more than about 3 pounds per week of actual fat from their bodies, even on a starvation diet.

Losing water weight is also the key to the quick weight-loss claims of some of the diet pills on the market. Many of these pills contain laxatives or diuretics—ingredients that force a person's body to eliminate more water. Other diet pills rely on ingredients that claim to speed up a person's metabolism (the process by which the body turns food into energy and stores unused calories as fat); suppress appetite; or block the absorption of fat, sugars, or carbohydrates.

Do these types of supplements actually do what they say they will? Unfortunately, there's usually no reliable scientific research to back up the claims provided by the product's manufacturer. In addition, there are many unknowns about the substances used in diet supplements, so dietitians and doctors consider them risky. What research studies do show is that most of the people who try one of these "crash" diets regain all the weight they lost within a few weeks or months.

Radically cutting back on calories can make you tired, jittery, and moody. These symptoms usually go away when you resume healthy eating habits, but over the long term, a highly restrictive diet may cause other health problems. You may lose some of your hair, your fingernails may become brittle, dark circles may appear under your eyes, and your muscles may shrink and weaken. Sometimes staying on a highly restrictive diet for a long period of time can cause lasting damage to your body, especially to the heart and kidneys. Following extreme diets over the long term or a pattern of extreme dieting followed by binge eating are both signs that a person may have an eating disorder.

Drastically reducing your food intake depletes the body's access to the vitamins, minerals, and fiber that it needs to stay healthy. If a diet requires you to cut out all dairy products, for example, you are also losing valuable calcium. Over a prolonged period, a lack of calcium puts a person at increased risk for osteoporosis (pronounced: ahs-tee-oh-puh-ro-sis), a condition in which bones become brittle and more susceptible to injury as a person ages. Some diets—like those that omit all red meat—may leave the dieter lacking iron, which can lead to anemia, especially in teen girls. And trying to replace the foods you're cutting out with vitamin pills is a bad idea. Foods like fruits and vegetables contain more than just vitamins and minerals—they are some of the best sources of fiber. Fiber can help to prevent disease.

Restricting food intake over a long period during a person's teenage years can stunt growth. Following restrictive diets over a long period can also delay some of the changes associated with puberty, such as breast development in females and muscle bulk in males. Another side effect of restrictive diets in teenage girls is irregular menstrual periods—or even not getting a period at all.

Another effect of very low-calorie diets is a decrease in resting energy expenditure, or the amount of calories a person burns at rest. One reason for this "slower metabolism" is that people on restrictive diets often lose muscle mass, and muscle burns more calories than fat—even while a person is resting. This makes continuing to lose weight even more difficult and regaining weight easier.

What about the long-term effects of taking diet pills? Common ingredients in diet pills include caffeine, alcohol, 5-hydroxytryptophan (5-HTP), chromium (or chromium picolinate), phentermine, and vanadium. These ingredients may carry health risks for certain people. Ephedrine (also known as ephedra or ma huang), an ingredient in many diet and sports supplements during the late 1990s and early 2000s, was linked to heart problems and may have played a role in the death of at least one professional athlete. The U.S. Food and Drug Administration decided the health risks associated with ephedra were too great, and it banned the substance in December 2003.

If you have any health conditions or are taking medication, always check with your doctor before taking weight-loss supplements because the ingredients in some supplements may interact with specific drugs. For example, 5-HTP may cause adverse reactions in people who take certain medications for depression.

Even ingredients that seem like a normal part of your diet can carry risks when used in weight-loss pills or other stimulants: For example, the average caffeine-based weight-loss pill contains as much caffeine as 6 cups of coffee. Imagine how wired you'd be if you took two or three of these pills each day! The side effects associated with these products include rapid heart rate, increased blood pressure, dizziness, sleeplessness, seizures, and even addiction. Furthermore, it's important to know that most diet supplements have not been tested on teen users. Not only does this mean that the dosages prescribed may not be accurate, it could mean that taking certain supplements might carry unknown risks for teens.

Regardless of concerns about the effectiveness and safety of restrictive diets, keeping the pounds off long term should be the major goal for anyone who wants to lose weight—and that can be more challenging than losing them in the first place. Weight loss is most likely to be successful and lasting when a person changes his or her habits to reduce the overall number of calories he or she eats while at the same time increasing the number of calories burned through exercise. Exercise not only burns calories, it also builds muscle. The more muscle you have, the more efficient your body becomes at burning calories, even when you aren't exercising. You don't have to become a gym rat, though: Walking the family dog, cycling to school, and doing other things that increase your daily level of activity can all make a difference.

Research confirms that one reason people get less exercise these days is because of an increase in "screen time"—in other words, the amount of time spent watching TV, looking at the computer, or playing video games. The American Academy of Pediatrics recommends limiting all screen time to 1 hour per day. If you're hanging with your friends at the mall instead of chatting to them on the computer, for example, you're getting more exercise.

A survey on health and nutrition conducted by the Centers for Disease Control and Prevention shows that serving sizes for both kids and adults have increased over the past 10 years, and that this is a contributor to obesity. If you super-size your fries or always go for extra hot fudge on your sundae, you are probably taking in more calories than your body can use. Another key dietary factor in weight gain today is the increased consumption of flavoured beverages, such as sodas, sweetened juice drinks, and sports drinks. Some people keep a food diary to track what they eat and drink. Writing everything you eat in a daily diary might help you identify those hidden foods that contribute to unwanted weight gain—like the candy bar you usually munch between third and fourth period.

The best way to build a weight-loss programme that's right for you is to talk to your doctor or a registered dietitian. During your appointment, your doctor or dietitian may ask you what types of foods you eat, how much weight you want to lose, and the reasons why you want to lose weight. He or she will also help you figure out approximately where your weight should be based on your height and other factors and suggest a sound weight-loss plan that meets your individual needs. The eating plan must include enough calories per day to keep your body working and developing properly. And if you're cutting calories to lose weight, your body will still need to get the same amount of nutrients to stay healthy.

Staying active is an important part of keeping off the weight you've lost. If you achieved your weight-loss goal by eating a variety of foods in smaller portions and exercising regularly, chances are better that you will stick with a healthier lifestyle and keep the pounds off in the long run.

Dietary Supplements

Dietary supplements are products that include vitamins, minerals, amino acids, herbs, or botanicals (plants)—or any concentration, extract, or combination of these—as part of their ingredients. You can purchase dietary supplements in pill, gel capsule, liquid, or powder forms.

In many cases, no one really knows. The U.S. Food and Drug Administration (FDA), which normally checks out the safety of foods and medicines before they come on the market, does not check on the safety of dietary supplements before they're sold. The FDA has to wait until it receives reports of problems caused by supplements before it can investigate and ban a dietary supplement. This is what happened with the herb ephedra (also called ma huang or herbal fen-phen) in 2003 when the FDA pulled the supplement from the U.S. market after it was linked to the death of a well-known baseball player.

Some athletes take dietary supplements believing that these improve their performances. However, claims for these improvements are often exaggerated or not based on scientific evidence. And some supplements may be hazardous to teens. Anabolic steroids, manmade hormones similar to the male hormone testosterone, are unsafe and illegal. That's because the large quantities of these steroids that are found in the supplements can have devastating side effects on the body, including heart damage, kidney damage, and bone problems. Studies also show that steroids may be addictive, and that even small doses can interfere with growth in teens.

Because sports supplements like creatine are unregulated, there is no standard dose. So users have no way of knowing what levels, if any, are safe, especially for teens who are still growing. The same goes for androstenedione, the supplement that gained attention because professional baseball player Mark McGwire used it. Research suggests that this hormone supplement may lead to health problems such as acne, gynecomastia (breast enlargement in guys), and heart problems.

Some people think that taking amino acid powders is helpful for increasing their muscle mass, but these powders don't actually have any special muscle-building effects. Amino acids are the building blocks of protein. Although it's scientifically true that they're required to build muscle (along with enough exercise), the human body can easily get all the amino acids it needs from the protein in food. So, if you work out properly and eat a balanced diet with enough protein, taking amino acid supplements won't actually do anything for you—except maybe empty your wallet.

Energy bars are also often used as a dietary supplement. These high-calorie, fortified treats should be used with caution, though. They may serve a purpose for athletes who burn lots of calories in high-intensity activities, like competitive cycling. But for most people they can add unwanted calories to the diet, and they're not particularly filling as a meal replacement.

If you'd like to lose a few pounds, you might be tempted to try some of the many herbal weight-loss products available today. But none of these herbal remedies work—and some can have serious side effects.

Herbs like chickweed, ginseng, kelp, and bee pollen, often included in diet aids, do nothing to promote weight loss—and some can be harmful or deadly in large doses. The only safe and effective way to take off excess pounds remains healthy eating and exercise. If you are concerned about your weight, talk to a doctor or dietitian. He or she can help you get to a healthy weight.

The best way to get your daily dose of vitamins and minerals is from food. Although there's usually nothing wrong with a teen taking a basic multivitamin, if you're eating well, you probably don't need one. If you do choose to take a multivitamin, stick with a basic supplement and avoid brands that contain higher doses than 100% of the RDA for any vitamin or mineral. Some vitamins can build up in the human system and cause problems when taken in excess amounts.

Talk to your doctor about additional vitamin and mineral supplements. If you can't eat dairy products for example, you might need a calcium supplement. Vegetarians might want to take vitamin B12 (a vitamin that is found mainly in food that comes from animals and may be missing in a vegetarian diet). Teens whose doctors have put them on weight-loss diets of less than 1,200 calories a day or teens with food allergies should also discuss vitamin and mineral needs with their doctors.

Check with your doctor before you take any dietary supplement, including vitamins and minerals. If your doctor starts you on a supplement, watch for warning signals that could indicate problems: stomach discomfort, pain, headache, rashes, or even vague symptoms like tiredness, dizziness, or lethargy.

Because it's not always clear what goes into some supplements, people with food allergies should be particularly wary. Some supplements contain ingredients from shellfish and other potential allergens, and you just don't know how you'll react to them. When it comes to supplements, be a skeptical consumer. We all love to look for the quick fix. But if it looks too easy, it probably is.

Safety of Weight Lose

Weight loss is a tricky topic. Lots of people are unhappy with their present weight, but most aren't sure how to change it—and many would be better off staying where they are. You may want to look like the models or actors in magazines and on TV, but those goals might not be healthy or realistic for you. Besides, no magical diet or pill will make you look like someone else.

Being healthy is really about being at a weight that is right for you. The best way to find out if you are at a healthy weight or if you need to lose or gain weight is to talk to a doctor or dietitian. He or she can compare your weight with healthy norms to help you set realistic goals. If it turns out that you can benefit from weight loss then you can follow a few of the simple suggestions listed below to get started.

Weight management is about long-term success. People who lose weight quickly by crash dieting or other extreme measures usually gain back all (and often more) of the pounds they lost because they haven't permanently changed their habits. Therefore, the best weight management strategies are those that you can maintain for a lifetime. That's a long time, so we'll try to keep these suggestions as easy as possible!

Make it a family affair. Ask your mom or dad to lend help and support and to make dietary or lifestyle changes that might benefit the whole family, if possible. Teens who have the support of their families tend to have better results with their weight management programmes. But remember, you should all work together in a friendly and helpful way—making weight loss into a competition is a recipe for disaster!

Watch your drinks. It's amazing how many extra calories can be lurking in the sodas, juices, and other drinks that you take in every day. Simply cutting out a couple of cans of soda or switching to diet soda can save you 360 calories or more each day. Drink lots of water or other sugar-free drinks to quench your thirst and stay away from sugary juices and sodas. Switching from whole to nonfat or low-fat milk is also a good idea.

Start small. Small changes are a lot easier to stick with than drastic ones. Try reducing the size of the portions you eat and giving up regular soda for a week. Once you have that down, start gradually introducing healthier foods and exercise into your life.

Stop eating when you're full. Lots of people eat when they're bored, lonely, or stressed, or keep eating long after they're full out of habit. Try to pay attention as you eat and stop when you're full. Slowing down can help because it takes about 20 minutes for your brain to recognise how much is in your stomach. Sometimes taking a break before going for seconds can keep you from eating another serving.

Avoid eating when you feel upset or bored—try to find something else to do instead (a walk around the block or a trip to the gym are good alternatives). Many people find it's helpful to keep a diary of what they eat and when. Reviewing the diary later can help them identify the emotions they have when they overeat or whether they have unhealthy habits. A registered dietitian can give you pointers on how to do this.

Eat less more often. Many people find that eating a couple of small snacks throughout the day helps them to make healthy choices at meals. Stick a couple of healthy snacks (carrot sticks, a low-fat granola bar, pretzels, or a piece of fruit) in your backpack so that you can have one or two snacks during the day. Adding healthy snacks to your three squares and eating smaller portions when you sit down to dinner can help you to cut calories without feeling deprived.

Five a day keep the pounds away. Ditch the junk food and dig out the fruits and veggies! Five servings of fruits and veggies aren't just a good idea to help you lose weight—they'll help keep your heart and the rest of your body healthy. Other suggestions for eating well: replace white bread with whole wheat, trade your sugary sodas for lots of water and a few cups of low-fat milk, and make sure you eat a healthy breakfast. Having low-sugar, whole grain cereal and low-fat milk and a piece of fruit is a much better idea than inhaling a donut as you run to the bus stop or eating no breakfast at all! A registered dietitian can give you lots of other snack and menu ideas.

Avoid fad diets. It's never a good idea to trade meals for shakes or to give up a food group in the hope that you'll lose weight—we all need a variety of foods to stay healthy. Stay away from fad diets because you're still growing and need to make sure you get proper nutrients. Avoid diet pills (even the over-the-counter or herbal variety). They can be dangerous to your health; besides, there's no evidence that they help keep weight off over the long term.

Don't banish certain foods. Don't tell yourself you'll never again eat your absolutely favourite peanut butter chocolate ice cream or a bag of chips from the vending machine at school. Making these foods forbidden is sure to make you want them even more. Also, don't go fat free: You need to have some fat in your diet to stay healthy, so giving up all fatty foods all the time isn't a good idea. The key to long-term success is making healthy choices most of the time. If you want a piece of cake at a party, go for it! But munch on the carrots rather than the chips to balance it out.

Get moving. You may find that you don't need to cut calories as much as you need to get off your behind. Don't get stuck in the rut of thinking you have to play a team sport or take an aerobics class to get exercise. Try a variety of activities from hiking to cycling to rowing until you find ones you like.

Build muscle. Muscle burns more calories than fat. So adding strength training to your exercise routine can help you reach your weight loss goals as well as give you a toned bod. A good, well-balanced fitness routine includes aerobic workouts, strength training, and flexibility exercises.

Forgive yourself. So you were going to have one cracker with spray cheese on it and the next thing you know the can's pumping air and the box is empty? Drink some water, brush your teeth, and move on. Everyone who's ever tried to lose weight has found it challenging. When you slip up, the best idea is to get right back on track and don't look back.

People today eat way more than they used to—and way more than they need to. This means that they're constantly taking in more calories than their bodies can burn. Unfortunately, lots of us don't realize that we're eating too much because we've become so used to seeing (and eating!) large portions.

Portion sizes began to increase in the 1980s and have been ballooning ever since. Take bagels, for example: 20 years ago, the average bagel had a 3-inch diameter and 140 calories. Today, bagels have a 6-inch diameter and 350 calories. One bagel that size actually contains half a person's recommended number of grain servings *for an entire day*!

The price of such overabundance is high. It's common knowledge that people who consistently overeat are likely to become overweight. But they also risk getting a number of medical problems, including high blood pressure, high cholesterol, type 2 diabetes, bone and joint problems, breathing and sleeping problems, and even depression. Later in life, people who overeat are at greater risk for heart disease, heart failure, and stroke.

It's easy to understand why the food industry tends to serve way more food than is necessary: Customers love to feel like they're getting the best value for their money! But the value meal is no deal when it triples our calories and sets the stage for health problems.

So what can you do to take back control? A good place to start is knowing about two things that can help you eat smart: serving sizes and recommended amounts of different foods.

Portion-Control Tips

Being aware of realistic portion sizes and visualising portions or using the "divided plate" concept will help you avoid overeating. But sometimes these visual cues can be hard—especially when foods are difficult to measure, like a sandwich, or they're foods like chips and cookies that we tend to eat right out of the bag.

Most important, make it a habit to let your stomach rather than your eyes tell you when you're done with a meal. The key to maintaining a healthy weight is to listen to your body's natural signals about when it's hungry and when it's full. Sometimes these signals can be confused by constant overeating or constant dieting, which is why it pays to watch portion sizes and make smart food choices.

Motivation and the Power

Have you ever set a goal for yourself, like getting fit, making honour roll, or being picked for a team? Like lots of people, maybe you started out doing great, but then lost some of that drive and had trouble getting motivated again. Everyone struggles with staying motivated and reaching their goals. Just look at how many people go on diets, lose weight, and then gain it back again! The reality is that refocusing, changing, or making a new start on something, no matter how small, is a big deal. But it's not impossible. With the right approach, you can definitely do it.

So how do you stay motivated and on track with your goal? It all comes down to good planning, realistic expectations, and a stick-to-it attitude. Here's what you need to do. First, know your goal. Start by writing down your major goal. Your major goal is the ultimate thing you'd like to see happen.

Make it specific. It's easier to plan for and master a specific goal than a vague one. Let's say your goal is to get fit. That's pretty vague. Make it specific by defining what you want to achieve (such as muscle tone and definition or endurance), why you want to get fit, and by when. This helps you make a plan to reach your goal.

Make it realistic. People often abandon their goals because their expectations are unreasonable. Maybe they expect to get ripped abs in weeks rather than months, or to quit smoking easily after years of lighting up.

Let's say you want to run a marathon. If you try to run the entire distance of 26.2 miles tomorrow without any training, you're unlikely to succeed. It takes the average person 4 months of training to run that far! But the bigger risk is that you'll get so bummed out that you'll give up your marathon dreams—and running—altogether.

Part of staying motivated is being realistic about what you can achieve within the timeframe you've planned. Competing on the Olympic ski team is a workable goal if you are 15 and already a star skier. But if you're 18 and only just taking your first lesson, time isn't exactly on your side.

Write it down. Put your specific goal in writing. Then write it down again. And again. Research shows that writing down a goal is part of the mental process of committing to it. Write your goal down every day to keep you focused and remind you how much you want it.

Break it down. Making any change takes self-discipline. You need to pay constant attention so you don't get sidetracked. One way to make this easier is to break a big goal into small steps. For example, let's say you want to run a marathon. If it's February and the marathon is in August, that's a realistic timeframe to prepare. Start by planning to run 2 miles and work up gradually to the distance you need.

Then set specific daily tasks, like eating five servings of fruit and veggies and running a certain amount a day. Put these on a calendar or planner so you can check them off. Ask a coach to help you set doable mini-goals for additional mile amounts and for tasks to improve your performance, such as exercises to build strength and stamina so you'll stay motivated to run farther.

Reaching frequent, smaller goals is something to celebrate. It gives you the confidence, courage, and motivation to keep running—or doing whatever it is you're aiming to do. Check in with your goal. Now that you've broken your goal down into a series of mini-goals and daily tasks, check in every day. It helps to write down your small goals in the same way you wrote down your big goal. That way you can track what you need to do, check off tasks as you complete them, and enjoy knowing that you're moving toward your big goal.

Positive self-talk also boosts your attitude and motivation. Tell yourself, "I deserve to make the honour roll because I've really been working hard" or "I feel great when I swim—I'm doing well on my exercise plan!"

Share with a friend. Another boost is having supportive people around you. Find a running buddy, a quit smoking buddy, or someone else with a similar goal so you can support each other. Having a goal buddy can make all the difference in times when you don't feel motivated—like getting up for that early-morning run.

If you're not getting support from someone when you really need it, you may need to take a break from that friendship and surround yourself with people who want to help you succeed. For instance, if you've been going to your friend's house to study together every Thursday after school, but now your pal is turning on the TV, IMing friends online, or gabbing on the phone and ignoring your pleas to get down to work, it's time to find another study buddy. You can't stay focused on your goal if your friend doesn't share that goal—or, even worse, is trying to hold you back. Seek out others who are on the same path you are and work with them instead.

Obesity

Being obese and being overweight are not exactly the same thing. An obese person has a large amount of extra body fat, not just a few extra pounds. People who are obese are very overweight and at risk for serious health problems. To determine if someone is obese, doctors and other health care professionals often use a measurement called body mass index (BMI). First, a doctor measures a person's height and weight. Then the doctor uses these numbers to calculate another number, the BMI.

Once the doctor has calculated a child's or teen's BMI, he or she will plot this number on a specific chart to see how it compares to other people of the same age and gender. A person with a BMI above the 95th percentile (meaning the BMI is greater than that of 95% of people of the same age and gender) is generally considered overweight. A person with a BMI between the 85th and 95th percentiles typically is considered at risk for overweight. Obesity is the term used for extreme overweight. There are some exceptions to this formula, though. For instance, someone who is very muscular (like a bodybuilder) may have a high BMI without being obese because the excess weight is from extra muscle, not fat.

Causes of Obesity

People gain weight when the body takes in more calories than it burns off. Those extra calories are stored as fat. The amount of weight gain that leads to obesity doesn't happen in a few weeks or months. Because being obese is more than just being a few pounds overweight, people who are obese have usually been getting more calories than they need for years.

Genes—small parts of the DNA that people inherit from their parents and that determine traits like hair or eye colour—can play an important role in this weight gain. Some of your genes tell your body how to metabolise food and how to use extra calories or stored fat. Some people burn calories faster or slower than others do because of their genes.

Obesity can run in families, but just how much is due to genes is hard to determine. Many families eat the same foods, have the same habits (like snacking in front of the TV), and tend to think alike when it comes to weight issues (like urging children to eat a lot at dinner so they can grow "big and strong"). All of these situations can contribute to weight gain, so it can be difficult to figure out if a person is born with a tendency to be obese or overweight or learns eating and exercise habits that lead to weight gain. In most cases, weight problems arise from a combination of habits and genetic factors. Certain illnesses, like thyroid gland problems or unusual genetic disorders, are uncommon causes for people gaining weight.

Sometimes emotions can fuel obesity as well. People tend to eat more when they are upset, anxious, sad, stressed out, or even bored. Then after they eat too much, they may feel bad about it and eat more to deal with those bad feelings, creating a tough cycle to break. One of the most important factors in weight gain is a sedentary lifestyle. People are much less active today than they used to be, with televisions, computers, and video games filling their spare time. Cars dominate our lives, and fewer people walk or ride bikes to get somewhere. As lives become busier, there is less time to cook healthy meals, so more and more people eat at restaurants, grab takeout food, or buy quick foods at the grocery store or food market to heat up at home. All of these can contain lots more fat and calories than meals prepared from fresh foods at home.

The number of people who are obese is rising. About 1.2 billion people in the world are overweight and at least 300 million of them are obese, even though obesity is one of the 10 most preventable health risks, according to the World Health Organisation. In the United States, more than 97 million adults—that's more than half—are overweight and almost one in five adults is obese. Among teenagers and kids 6 years and older, more than 15% are overweight—that's more than three times the number of young people who were overweight in the 1970s. At least 300,000 deaths every year in the United States can be linked to obesity. In the United States, women are slightly more at risk for becoming obese than men. Race and ethnicity also can be factors—in adolescents, obesity is more common among Mexican Americans and African Americans.

Obesity is bad news for both body and mind. Not only does it make a person feel tired and uncomfortable, it can wear down joints and put extra stress on other parts of the body. When a person is carrying extra weight, it's harder to keep up with friends, play sports, or just walk between classes at school. It is also associated with breathing problems such as asthma and sleep apnea and problems with hips and knee joints that may require surgery.

There can be more serious consequences as well. Obesity in young people can cause illnesses that once were thought to be problems only for adults, such as hypertension (high blood pressure), high cholesterol levels, liver disease, and type 2 diabetes, a disease in which the body has trouble converting food to energy, resulting in high blood sugar levels. As they get older, people who are obese are more likely to develop heart disease, congestive heart failure, bladder problems, and, in women, problems with the reproductive system. Obesity also can lead to stroke, greater risk for certain cancers such as breast or colon cancer, and even death.

In addition to other potential problems, people who are obese are more likely to be depressed. That can start a vicious cycle: When people are overweight, they may feel sad or even angry and eat to make themselves feel better. Then they feel worse for eating again. And when someone's feeling depressed, that person is less likely to go out and exercise.

The best way to avoid these health problems is to maintain a healthy weight. And the keys to healthy weight are regular exercise and good eating habits. To stay active, try to exercise 30 to 60 minutes every day. Your exercise doesn't have to be hard core, either. Walking, swimming, and stretching are all good ways to burn calories and help you stay fit. Try these activities to get moving:

- Go outside for a walk.
- Take the stairs instead of the elevator.
- Walk or bike to places (such as school or a friend's house) instead of driving.
- If you have to drive somewhere, park farther away than you need to and walk the extra distance.
- Tackle those household chores, such as vacuuming, washing the car, or cleaning the bathroom—they all burn calories.
- Alternate activities so you don't get bored: Try running, biking, skating—the possibilities are endless.
- Limit your time watching TV or playing video games; even reading a book burns more energy.
- Go dancing—it can burn more than 300 calories an hour!

Before you start trying to lose weight, talk to a doctor, a parent, or a registered dietitian. With their help, you can come up with a safe plan, based on eating well and exercising. Remember that teenagers need to keep eating regularly. Don't starve yourself because you won't get the nutrients you need to grow and develop normally.

You may also want to keep a food and activity journal. Keep track of what you eat, when you exercise, and how you feel. Changes can take time, but seeing your progress in writing will help you stick to your plan. You might also want to consider attending a support group; check your local hospital or the health section of a newspaper for groups that meet near you. Above all, surround yourself with friends and family who will be there for you and help you tackle these important changes in your life.

It seems like every time you turn around, someone is talking about dieting. Every tabloid at the supermarket has details on the hottest celebrity fad diets. Whenever you turn on the TV, there's another infomercial raving about a liquid diet plan or diet supplement. During gym class your best friend always complains about her "big" hips and how she's going on a diet to get rid of them.

This constant focus on weight and dieting may leave you wondering whether you need to go on a diet yourself. The truth is that not all teens who diet actually need to lose weight. Many times, friends, family, and society influence the way we see our bodies. Pressures like these can prompt some teens to take drastic dieting measures, leading to malnutrition and eating disorders such as anorexia and bulimia. And because teens are still growing, drastic dieting can be especially harmful to their developing bodies. Other teens may mistakenly think that in order to be in top form for their chosen sport, they need to be as thin as possible.

These pressures are one of the reasons why the best person to see when you have a question about dieting is your doctor. Your doctor can help you determine what is a healthy weight for your body size and shape. He or she can help you decide whether you need to be on a diet at all. And if necessary, your doctor can refer you to a dietitian or nutrition specialist.

10

Sports Technologies

Almost any sport could benefit from equipment enhancements as well as novel measurement and analysis of athletes' performance. From popular sports such as golf, baseball, and basketball to extreme sports such as snowboarding, motocross racing, and rock climbing, athletes can all gain from a better understanding of their muscle movements, orientation, and heart rate response.

Sport is an extremely exciting field in which to apply our craft. Results over the last decade of research on applying ubiquitous computing technologies to enhance sports are indeed encouraging. Researchers have learned a great deal about sensors and how to embed them in everyday objects. Accelerometers, gyroscopes, microphones, and cameras all lend themselves nicely to a range of sports applications. Computer vision algorithms are enabling researchers to analyse not only a single player's motions but also the patterns of a group of players simultaneously.

Pervasive computing researchers are studying three areas of sports technologies: athletic performance, leisure and entertainment, and how technology could affect the rules of the game. Improving sports performance and learning The history of sports performance studies is littered with success stories. Instruments have been built into golf clubs to offer golfers a computer analysis of their swing, and runners use heart rate monitors to track their training progress. Researchers continue to innovate, creating new ways to understand human performance in sports. For example, Joan Vickers has been examining neuromotor psychology by studying the gaze of athletes while they perform specific sport skills using helmet-mounted eyetrackers.

The research question here isn't to instrument everything on the human body but rather to understand what the most appropriate sensors are and how they should be used. Being "appropriate" here means enhancing players so that they want to use sensors in their training, enabling unobtrusive instrumentation so that coaches can analyse the best data available, and cooperating with judges so that they make good, socially acceptable calls on the field.

Sports are also closely tied to the availability of leisure time and the desire for entertainment. Using technology in sports entertainment offers two possibilities. The first is in participatory games. For example, game arcades have already incorporated various technologies into soccer balls, golf clubs, baseball bats, motorcycles, and boxing gloves to make sports games more entertaining. Companies such as Laser Quest are creating innovative new games with laser tag equipment, such as the team mission game of protecting the queen bee. Laser tag games can be every bit as exhausting as professional sports.

As another example, fitness clubs have started to incorporate video games in their exercise equipment. For example, in the mid-1990s, Life Fitness connected its Lifecycle to a Super Nintendo. The faster you pedaled, the faster your counterpart on the video game screen went. This kind of equipment encourages users to exercise harder The second possibility is to use technology to enhance spectators' enjoyment. Major tennis tournaments now measure the speed of serves, for example, to satisfy spectators' curiosity about what it might be like to receive such serves.

On the other hand, TV viewers rejected the use of highlighted trails of hockey pucks during live broadcasts of Hockey games. The pucks were instrumented with 20 infrared emitters, and sensors around the rink picked up the infrared signals to track them. Fans hated the trails, so TV broadcasters eventually pulled the trails out of their live coverage of the games. How to design technology for spectator enjoyment has been less than clear.

The key appears to be balancing tradition, distraction, and satisfaction of spectator curiosity. Spectators enjoy total immersion in watching live sports, so the technologies introduce must assist in this immersion rather than disrupt it. Interaction with sports authorities A technology's acceptance not only involves spectators but also the sports' governing bodies. The US Golf Association heavily regulates the modification of golf balls, clubs, and other equipment.

The so-called "dimple wars" in the 1970s ignited quite a controversy about such equipment; people even feared that "old" golf courses would become obsolete because balls were traveling much further than before due to new ball design. As another example from the past, bicycle design modifications have been severely restricted, with several newer, fast recumbent-type designs rejected for international competition. Other controversial technologies include the Cyclops tennis line-calling system. In most cases, sports' governing bodies are reluctant to adopt new equipment technologies and standards. Indeed, in many cases, the rules themselves must be changed to accommodate new technology. Occasionally, however, governing bodies can themselves be the catalyst for change.

In a rule change in May, for example, the World Taekwondo Federation reduced the number of scoring judges required around the competition ring from four to two when the competition includes the new force-sensing electronic chest protectors. Interestingly, these new chest protectors aren't even on the market yet, so the governing organisation is one step ahead of the technologists.

Sports Agility

Agility is the ability to change the body's direction efficiently, and this requires a combination of balance, coordination, speed, and strength. Aside from improving sports performance, why would an individual need to maintain or improve agility? Dodging requires agility, such as jumping out of the way of an oncoming car or avoiding an unexpected hole. If you ever need to run down a crowded street to catch a bus or escape an assailant, agility will help you avoid knocking yourself out on a utility pole or tripping over a dog leash.

Agility is the ability to change the direction of the body in an efficient and effective manner and to achieve this you require a combination of:

- Balance
  - The ability to maintain equilibrium when stationary or moving (i.e. not to fall over) through the co-ordinated actions of our sensory functions (eyes, ears and the proprioceptive organs in our joints)
  - Static Balance—ability to retain the centre of mass above the base of support in a stationary position

  - Dynamic Balance—ability to maintain balance under changing conditions of body movement
- Speed
  - the ability to move all or part of the body quickly
- Strength
  - the ability of a muscle or muscle group to overcome a resistance
- Co-ordination
  - the ability to control the movement of the body in co-operation with the body's sensory functions e.g. catching a ball (ball, hand and eye co-ordination)

How to Improve Agility

We can improve our agility by improving the component parts of agility and practicing the movements in training.

In various fields of sports competition, the body is constantly asked to perform movements from unfamiliar joint angles. The main objective for agility ladder programmes is to promote a wide range of different foot and movement patterns. These skilled movements become second nature and the body is able to respond quickly to various angles that are required in sporting events. We can improve our agility by practicing the movements in training and an agility ladder is an essential tool in a complete agility programme. The standard ladder is 10 yards long with 18 inch squares but you can construct your own ladder using sticks or tape.

When beginning an agility ladder programme introduce 2 to 4 movements. Once you master these patterns then introduce new patterns. Keep in mind that this is a general recommendation as the introduction of movements depends on your athlete's ability to master the movements.

Exercises 1 & 2

Detailed below are some ladder drills you could use with your athletes.

- Run through the ladder placing one foot in the middle of each square
- Emphasize arm swing, powerful high knee drive with the toes dorsiflexed and quick ground contact

- Run through the ladder touching both feet in each square.
- Emphasize arm swing, powerful high knee drive with the toes dorsiflexed and quick ground contact.

Exercise 3

- Begin by standing sideways to the ladder
- Moving in a lateral fashion to your right, step into the first square with the right foot
- Step in with the left foot
- Step back out with the right foot
- Step back out with the left foot
- Repeat the sequence from 2 to 5 all the way along the ladder

Exercise 4

- Perform the drill in a sideways position to the ladder
- Moving to the right, place the right foot into the first square
- Next, step across the ladder with the left foot
- Remove the right foot from the ladder placing it next

to your left foot

- Now, step forward into the second square with the left foot
- Next, step across the ladder with the right foot
- Remove the left foot from the ladder placing it next to your right foot
- Repeat the sequence from 2 to 7 all the way along the ladder

Exercise 5

- Start straddling one side of the ladder—right foot in the first square and your left foot outside of the ladder
- Do a jump to your right so your right foot stays in the ladder square and your left foot lands in the next ladder square
- Do a jump to your left so your left foot stays in the ladder square and your right foot lands outside the ladder
- Do a jump to your left so your left foot stays in the ladder square and your right foot lands in the next ladder square
- Do a jump to your right so your right foot stays in the ladder square and your left foot lands outside the ladder
- Repeat the sequence from 2 to 5 all the way along the ladder

Exercise 6

- Begin standing sideways to the ladder
- Step into the first square with the right foot
- Next, step over the ladder to the other side with the left foot

- Step with the right foot laterally to the next square
- Next, step over the ladder to the other side with the left foot
- Step with the right foot laterally to the next square
- Repeat the sequence from 3 to 6 all the way along the ladder

Exercise 7

As Exercise 6 but moving laterally with the left foot.

How to measure Agility

There are a number of tests to measure an athlete's agility. They include:

- *Hexagonal Obstacle Agility Test* – suitable for sports with multidirectional movement
- *Illinois agility run test* -- suitable for sports with multidirectional movement
- *Lateral Change of Direction test* – suitable for sports with multidirectional movement
- *Quick Feet test* – suitable for sports with multidirectional movement
- *'T' Drill test* – suitable for sports with multidirectional movement
- *Stork Stand Test* (balance test)

Speed through a ladder can indicate much about an athlete's quickness. A time of less than 2.8 seconds for males and 3.4 seconds for females for running the length of a 20 rung ladder, one foot in each rung at a time, is considered as excellent for college athletes.

Hexagonal Obstacle Test

Testing and measurement are the means of collecting information upon which subsequent performance evaluations and decisions are made but in the analysis we need to bear in mind the factors that may influence the results. The objective of the Hexagonal Obstacle test is to monitor the athlete's agility.

Required Resources

To undertake this test you will require:

- 66 cm sided hexagon marked out on the floor
- Stop watch
- Assistant

The Hexagonal Obstacle Test is conducted as follows:

- The athlete stands in the middle of the hexagon, facing line A
- At all times throughout the test the athlete is to face line A
- On the command GO the watch is started and the athlete jumps with both feet over line B and back to the middle, then over line C and back to the middle, then line D and so on
- When the athlete jumps over line A and back to the middle this counts as one circuit
- The athlete is to complete three circuits
- On completion of three circuits the watch is stopped and the time recorded
- The athlete rests and then repeats the test
- On completion of the second test determine the average of the two recorded times.

If you jump the wrong line or land on a line then the test is to be restarted.

Analysis

Analysis of the result is by comparing it with the results of previous tests. It is expected that, with appropriate training between each test, the analysis would indicate an improvement in the athlete's agility.

Performance Assessment

For an evaluation of the athlete's performance select the gender, enter the average time from the two tests and then select the 'Calculate' button.

Lateral Change of Direction Test

Testing and measurement are the means of collecting information upon which subsequent performance evaluations and decisions are made but in the analysis we need to bear in mind the factors that may influence the results. To monitor the development of the athlete's speed with directional change.

Required resources

To undertake this test you will require

- Flat surface—track
- Three cones
- Stop watch
- Assistant

How to conduct the test

The three cones are set five metres apart on a straight line.

- The athlete starts at the middle cone
- The Coach gives the signal to start and points in a specific direction, right or left
- The athlete moves to and touches the first cone, returns past the middle cone (start) to the far cone

and touches that one and then returns to the middle cone, touching that one.

The coach starts the stopwatch on giving the 'Go' command and stops the watch when the athlete touches the middle cone. The better of the two trails in each starting direction, right and left, are recorded and the best score in each direction is used for scoring.

Analysis

Analysis of the result is by comparing it with the results of previous tests. It is expected that, with appropriate training between each test, the analysis would indicate an improvement.

Quick Feet Test

Testing and measurement are the means of collecting information upon which subsequent performance evaluations and decisions are made but in the analysis we need to bear in mind the factors that may influence the results. The quick feet test provides information on the presence of fast-twitch muscle fibre in the muscles involved in sprinting and indicates your potential to execute quick movements. Hereditary factors such as limb length, muscle attachments, and proportion of fast-twitch fibres do place a limit on one's maximum potential, but we can improve our speed and quickness with proper training.

Required resources

To undertake this test you will require

- Flat surface
- 20 two-foot long sticks or a 20-rung rope ladder
- Stop watch
- Assistant

How to conduct

Place 20 two-foot long sticks 18 inches apart or a 20-rung stride rope ladder on grass or athletics track. Athletes should pump their arms vigorously in a sprint-arm motion and use very little knee lift while running down the ladder without touching the sticks/rungs. The coach starts the stopwatch when the athlete's foot first touches the ground between the first and second stick/rung and stops the watch when contact is first made with the ground beyond the last stick/rung. Record the better of two trials.

Analysis

Analysis of the result is by comparing it with the results of previous tests. It is expected that, with appropriate training between each test, the analysis would indicate an improvement in the athlete's foot speed.

Target group

This test is suitable for active athletes but not for individuals where the test would be contraindicated.

Reliability

Reliability would depend upon, how strict the test is conducted and the individual's level of motivation to perform the test.

Validity

There are published tables to relate results to a potential level of fitness and the correlation is high.

Speed and Agility

Developing speed and agility in sport is specific to the game or sport an athlete plays. In team or court-based sports, it differs from the technique of a 100m sprinter, in that the track athlete can run flat-out, with maximum stride length and stride rate in a straight line. For example, the speed and agility requirements in a court-based sport are very different to those of a field-based team sport. In badminton, because of the very small court, an athlete will take a maximum of one or two steps in a particular direction to cover the court, involving a high frequency of diagonal, lateral and forward and backward movements.

A netball, hockey, or rugby player, on the other hand, would rarely travel more than thirty metres, so the most important qualities are very different—acceleration and the ability to change direction rapidly, are key in team sports. To improve speed and agility, strength and conditioning coaches would include specific workouts targeting that physical quality into the weekly programme of an elite team sport athlete, in addition to the endurance or strength training they were doing.

To produce an enhancement in performance at elite level, requirements of what the player or sport specifically needs are carefully considered, before drills which develop the skills are designed, mostly concentrating on acceleration and change of direction. In rugby or hockey, a player would accelerate into position, either to find space, or to make a challenge, but those movements are often angled runs, changes of direction whilst running, or running in a curve, so any exercises or drills designed to improve that ability, would, necessarily be sport-specific.

In sport, agility is characterised by fast feet, body coordination during change of direction and sports skill performance, and reaction time/ ability. It is an amalgam of balance, speed, strength, flexibility and coordination. Although a performer's agility relies heavily on the acquisition of optimum sports technique, it can also be enhanced by specific conditioning. A variety of performance-enhancing agility drills, systems and items of equipment are available to the sportsmen of today and their coaches. The 'science' of agility (and speed and power) training has made rapid strides recently, especially in terms of its accessibility to the mainstream sporting world.

Bibliography

Ehrman, J K, Gordon, P M, Nisich, P S and Keteyian, S J., *Clinical Exercise Physiology*, Champaign, Illinois: Human Kinetics, 2003.

Eston, R and Reilly, T., *Exercise Physiology Laboratory Manual: Tests, procedures and data:* Volume II. London: E & F N Spon, 2001.

Foss, R and Keteyian S J., "Physiological Basis for Sport and Exercise", New York: McGraw-Hill, 1998.

Hoffman, J., *Physiological Aspects of Sport Training and Performance,* Champaign, Illinois: Human Kinetics, 2002.

Jones, A and Poole, D., "Oxygen Uptake Kinetics in Health and Disease", London: Routledge, 2004.

Kamen, G., *Foundations of Exercise Science,* Baltimore: Lippincott, Williams and Watkins, 2001.

Kolkhorst, F W and Buono, M J., "Virtual Exercise Physiology Laboratory", Philadelphia: Lippincott, Williams and Watkins, 2004.

Malina, R M, Bouchard, C and Bar-Or, O, "Growth, Maturation and Physical Activity", Champaign, Illinois: Human Kinetics, 2004.

Maud, P J and Foster, C, "Physiological Assessment of Human Performance". *Champaign, Illinois: Human Kinetics,* 1995.

Maughan, R and Gleeson, M "The Biochemical Basis of Sports Performance", New York: Oxford University Press, 2004.

______________ and Burke, L M., "Sports Nutrition". *Handbook of Sports Medicine and Science.* Oxford: Blackwell Publishers, 2002.

McArdle, W D, Katch, F I and Katch, V L, "Exercise Physiology: Energy, Nutrition and Human Performance". Baltimore: Lippincott, Williams and Watkins, 2001.

Powers, S K and Howley, E T., *Exercise Physiology: Theory and Application to Fitness and Performance,* New York: McGraw-Hill, 2004.

Robergs, R A and Roberts, S O., "Exercise Physiology", *Exercise, Performance and Clinical Applications,* St. Louis: Mowby Year Book Inc., 1997.

________________ and Keteyian, S J., "Fundamental Principles of Exercise Physiology: For Fitness, Performance and Health", New York: McGraw-Hill, 2003.

Roche, A F, Heymsfield, S B and Lohman, T G., "Human Body Composition", Champaign, Illinois: Human Kinetics, 1996.

Sharkey, B J., *New Dimensions in Aerobic Fitness,* Champaign, Illinois: Human Kinetics, 1991

Swain, D P and Leutholtz, B C., *Exercise Prescription: A Case Study Approach to the ACSM Guidelines,* Champaign, Illinois: Human Kinetics, 2001.

Watkins, J., *Structure and Function of the Muscloskeletal System,* Champaign, Illinois: Human Kinetics, 1999.

Weltman, A,"The Blood Lactate Response to Exercise", *Monograph 4.* Champaign: Illinois, Human Kinetics, 1995.

Index

Actual sports movement 195
Age-related change 189
Anaerobic capacity 188
Anaerobic enzymes 189
Anaerobic Fitness 8
Analytical thinking 219

Basic Need Satisfaction Scale 114
Behavioural intentions 111
Body Mass Index (BMI) 263
Brutal sprint sessions 209

Calf stretch 4
Cardiovascular capacity 7
Chi-square analysis 126
Coach-dominated activity 167
Common volleyball strategy 165
Control-Receiving Drills 15

David Martin 208
Decision-making process 97
Down syndrome 3
Dribbling 18

Endurance Performance 210
Exercise behaviour 93
Exercise intensities 217
Exercise psychology 93

Food Drug Administration (FDA) 269

Glycolitic enzyme activity 189
Goalkeeping 32

Human motivation 93
Hyperplasia 225
5-hydroxytryptophan (5-HTP) 266

Intermittant Exercise 202
Internal consistency 102
Interval training 204

Mark McGwire 270
Maximal oxygen consumption 199
Maximal Voluntary Ventilation (MVV), 222
Mitochondrial density 196
Multivariate Analyses of Variance (MANOVAs) 119
Muscle fiber hyperplasia 225
Myogenic stem cells 225

Neck Backward Bending 3
Neuromuscular junctions 190

Perceived Autonomy Support (PAS) 98
Peripheral cardiovascular adaptations 199
Player-dominated game 167
Plyometric training 5

Rhythm drills 6

Satellite cells 226

Sedentary individuals 192
Self-determination Theory (SDT) 94, 107
Self-determined motivation 121
Skeletal muscles 190
Standardised Root-Mean-square Residual (SRMR) 117
Steven Dowshen 264
Strength Training 9
Stretching 1

Tackling technique 30
Trunk Backward Bending 3

Variance Proportions Factors (VPF) 101
Ventilatory Function 217

Weight training programme 214
Weight-loss programme 268
World Health Organisation 281